CHESTER SILVER 1837-1962

CHESTER SILVER
1837 - 1962

with special reference to

THE CHESTER DUTY BOOKS
1784 - 1840

by

MAURICE H. RIDGWAY, F.S.A.

GEE & SON (DENBIGH) LTD.

ISBN 0 7074 0285 9

(*Cover illustration* — Bowl by Iverna Cubbin, Chester, 1922)

Printed and Published by
GEE & SON (DENBIGH) LTD.
CHAPEL STREET, DENBIGH LL16 3SW

To

my

Grandchildren

I thank my God upon every remembrance of you
(Philippians i, 3)

Contents

		Page
PREFACE	... ...	9
ACKNOWLEDGEMENTS	... ...	11
BOOKS REFERRED TO	... ...	13
ILLUSTRATIONS	... ...	15–16
THE GOLDSMITHS COMPANY OF CHESTER FROM 1837	... ...	17
Admissions to the Company since 1837	... ...	34
Wardens of the Chester Goldsmiths Company	... ...	36
Catalogue of Plate held by the Company	... ...	37
Recreation	... ...	42
Records held by the Company	... ...	43
The Company Banner	... ...	44
Portraits of Members	... ...	45
The Company of Goldsmiths after 1962	... ...	45
The Coat of Arms	... ...	46
The Mark of Origin	... ...	46
THE RELATIONSHIP BETWEEN THE COMPANY AND THE ASSAY OFFICE		49
THE CHESTER ASSAY OFFICE	... ...	52
Assay Masters at Chester	... ...	59
Assay plates and books	... ...	60
Registrations at Chester	... ...	62
The Income and Expenditure of the Assay Office at Chester in the 19th Century	... ...	63

The Plate Duty Books 1784-1840 64

A summary of the weights and duty recorded in the Plate Duty Books 67

Silversmiths mentioned in the Plate Duty Books with dates when their names appear 1784-1840 72

Record of the work registered in the Chester Plate Duty Books 1784-1840 75

Unfamiliar words used in the Plate Duty Books 103

Weights of silver and gold assayed at Chester 105

Some silversmiths who used the Chester Assay Office 114

The assaying of gold at Chester 146

BUTTON, CLASP AND BUTTON MAKERS 149

CADDY SPOONS 150

COFFIN PLATES 153

FLAT WARE 155

THIMBLES 156

THE WATCHCASE MAKERS 157
ILLUSTRATIONS 1-49

MEMOIR OF THE LAST DAYS OF THE CHESTER ASSAY OFFICE ... 159
  By Alderman Grahame Jones

CHESTER ASSAY MARKS 1797-1962 169

INDEX OF PERSONS AND FIRMS 175
ILLUSTRATIONS 50-62

APPENDIX 1 179

APPENDIX 2 192

Preface

My first volume *Chester Goldsmiths from early times to 1726*, originated in my work with Sir Leonard Stone who had been appointed Chairman of the Committee called to report on the Assay Marks governing the various assay offices in the country. This became known as the Stone Committee. Sharing a common interest in silver he asked me to do some of the field work necessary on Chester silver for the final report to Parliament. I was not aware at the time that this would involve not only the closure of the Chester Assay Office but also the closure of the Chester Goldsmiths' Company. With the willing cooperation of the then Bishop of Chester, the Right Reverend Gerald Ellison who agreed to speak on the matter in the House of Lords, the future of the Chester Goldsmiths' Company was assured and it remains one of the ancient Companies of the City. Although the right to assay silver had ceased since 1962, the Company is now allowed to mark any silver made in the City of origin. My second volume, *Chester Silver 1727 to 1837*, became a natural follow up as is the appearance of the present volume. In the meanwhile the rediscovery by Philip Priestley of the three volumes of the Chester Plate Duty Books from 1784 to 1840 in the Birmingham Reference Library has added much new information, which is now included. No attempt has been made to include in this work his magnificent survey of the work of Watchcase makers, and the reader is therefore asked to refer to his *Watchcase makers of England 1720-1920*.

Rhydycroesau   MAURICE H. RIDGWAY

Oswestry

Books Referred To

Jackson's Silver and Gold Marks. Ed. Ian Pickford. Antique Collectors Club. Third Edition revised 1989.

Chester Goldsmiths from Early Times to 1726. Maurice H. Ridgway. Sherratt. Altrincham. 1968. (abbreviated G.C.)

Chester Silver 1727-1837. Maurice H. Ridgway. Phillimore and Co. Ltd. 1985. (abbreviated C.S.)

British Coin weights. Paul and Bente Withers. Galata Print Limited. Llanfyllin, Powys. 1993.

A Dictionary of Newcastle Goldsmiths. Margaret Gill. 1976.

The Collector's Dictionary of Silver and Gold. Michael Clayton. Country Life. 1971.

Caddy Spoons. John Norie. Published by John Murray.

Watchcase Makers of England. Philip Priestley. N.A.W.C.C. bulletin supplement. 1994.

Dictionary of Gold and Silversmiths from the London Assay Office Registers. 1838-1914. John Culme, 2 Volumes. Antique Collectors Club. 1987.

History of Old Sheffield Plate, etc. Frederick Bradbury. Reprint. 1968.

History of the Sheffield Smelting Company Ltd. 1760-1960. Ronald E. Wilson. Ernest Benn Ltd. London. 1960.

Chester Silver. A loan exhibition. Sotheby's and The Grosvenor Museum, Chester, 1984.

Touching Gold and Silver. Exhibition at Goldsmiths' Hall, London. 1978.

The Silversmiths of Birmingham and their marks 1750-1980. Ed: Kenneth Crisp Jones. NAG Press, London. 1981.

The Birmingham Assay Office 1773-1993. Jennifer Tann. 1993.

The Finial. Organ of the Silver Spoon Club. Sticker, Cornwall.

Acknowledgements

Anyone engaged upon a work of this nature is bound to be indebted to a great many friends and fellow collectors, who bring to his notice examples of gold and silver, thus making his research as complete as possible. It is therefore with considerable pleasure that I can now record them.

Brian Beasley, Peter Boughton, Sandy and Helen Campbell, Simon and Cathlyn Davidson, G. P. Dyer, Martin Gubbins, Susan Hare, Mike and Alison Hayle, Grahame Jones, Peter Jones, Vic Jones, Anthony Kaye, Marilyn Lewis, Joyce Lowe, Peter and Janet Lowe, Nicholas Moore, John Norie, David Orfeur, Catherine Phillips, Ian Pickford, Philip Priestley, Colin M. Simpson, Paul and Bente Withers. Also the Goldsmiths' Company of Chester and the Assay Offices at London, Birmingham, Sheffield, the Reference Library at Birmingham, the Cheshire Record Office and the City Record Office.

Over the years others have died.

Judith Banister, Michael Clayton, Rt. Rev. Gerald Ellison, John Lowe, Gerald Sanders, Sir Leonard Stone, A. Vincent Ward, all of whom were long and faithful friends.

I am also extremely grateful to the great auction houses of Christie's, Sotheby's and Phillip's for their generous help at many times and for the use of photographs, and to Lord Leverhulme, the Marquess of Cholmondley and the Goldsmiths' Company of London for their encouragement and financial assistance.

List of Illustrations

1. George Lowe (1) 1768-1841.
2. George Lowe (2) 1793-1876.
3. The 1841 copper plate. (Birmingham Assay Office)
4. The 1860 copper plate. (Birmingham Assay Office)
5. Examples of marks in the second book of makers' marks.
6. Examples of marks in the second book of makers' marks.
7. Water jug by George Lowe (2) 1830-31.
8. Ornate wine ewer by William Smith, Liverpool, 1879-80.
9. Casket by William Smith, Liverpool, 1875-76.
10. Salt by William Smith, Liverpool, 1877-78.
11. Marks on No. 10.
12. Mustard pot by John Lowe, 1842-43.
13. Four boat shaped salts by John Lowe, 1878-79.
14. Mark of John Sutter on a teaspoon, 1837-38.
15. Mark of John and Thomas Lowe on a mustard spoon, 1840-41.
16. Mark of John Lowe on a teaspoon, 1855-56.
17. Mark of Henry Tarlton on a watchcase, 1855-56.
18. Grapefruit spoon by D.F, 1948-49.
19. Box by J. Millward Banks, Birmingham, 1911-12.
20. Blade by J. Millward Banks, Birmingham, 1911-12.
21. Toast rack by Walker and Hall, Sheffield, 1907-08.
22. Mug by John Miller, Newcastle on Tyne, 1825-26.
23. Three graded jugs by Lowe & Sons, 1947-48.
24, 25, 26. Tea pot, sugar basin and creamer by J. Lowe, 1881-82.
27. Marks on 24, 25, 26, J. Lowe, 1881-82.
28. Mershom pipe by John Helsby, Liverpool, 1843-44 (Sotheby, Belgravia).
29. Cylindrical toilet box by John and Thomas Helsby, 1843-44.
30. The marks of Isaac Simmons, Manchester with Chester assay marks, 1842-43.
31. The mark of Isaac Simmons, Manchester with Sheffield assay, 1846-47.
32. Pepper by Saunders & Shepherd, London, 1903-04. (Glasgow Museums)
33. Vesta Case by Alex Ritchie, Iona, 1911-12. (Sotheby, Belgravia)
34. Antique mug by Nathan & Hayes, Birmingham, 1906-07.
35. Spoon finial by F. J. Ross, Winchester, 1933-34.

36. The gold marks of 18 ct., Chester.
37. String box by James Deakin & Son, Ltd., Sheffield, 1900-01.
38. Marks on the String box, 1900-01.
39. Three miniatures (1 to r) Saunders & Shepherd, J. M. Banks and Saunders and Shepherd.
40. Bowl by Iverna Cubbin, Chester, 1922-23. (Williamson Art Gallery, Birkenhead)
41. Mark of George F. Lowe, Chester (1871-1934).
42. Mark of A. Vincent Ward on a small salt spoon, 1955/56.
43. Bebington Borough Mace, Wirral by A. Edward Jones (Dunstan Works), 1937/38.
44. Warden's stave, Bunbury Parish Church, Cheshire by John C. Webb, St. Alban's, 1961/62.
45. Grahame Jones at the Assay Office, 1962. (Cheshire Life)
46. Francis Maurice Lowe and A. Vincent Ward, marking the last piece of silver assayed at Chester, 24 August 1962.
47. Marks used in the last few months of the Chester Assay Office, including those of Margaret Joyce Lowe and her brother John ffoulkes Lowe.
48. The Francis M. Lowe blade showing the Sheffield marks for 1992 and the Chester City of origin mark and those of the maker, Greg Mora of Chester.
49. The four punches used for the City of origin mark.

*   *   *   *

50. a. & b.   Spoon by John Lingley, c. 1580.
51. Castor by Benjamin Brancker, Liverpool, c. 1735. (Shelagh Collingwood)
52. a. & b.   Covered bowl having the mark of John Bingley. (S. J. Phillips)
53. Chocolate stand by William Richardson, 1721-22. (Shelagh Collingwood)
54. a. & b.   The Conway Bailiff's oar by Richard Richardson (1), 1725-26. (Phillips, Chester)
55. The maker's mark of John Scasebrick on a Portuguese moidor weight, 1772. (P. & B. Withers)
56, 57.   Pair of Candlesticks by James Duke, Chester, 1771-72. (Grosvenor Museum, Chester)
58. Tea caddy by Richard Richardson (2), 1764-65.
59. Pair of cylindrical beakers by Richard Richardson (2). (Bourdon Smith)
60, 61.   Fruit knife by Richard Richardson (2) or (4). (Shelagh Collingwood)
62. Mote spoon by Richard Richardson (2) or (4) (?). (Shelagh Collingwood)

The Goldsmiths Company of Chester from 1837

By the time William IV died (1837) the age of the Richardsons who had dominated the 18th century at Chester had passed. Much of their fortune had been accumulated not only from their flourishing business but by careful investment in the mines in North Wales and Scotland. There was an increasing interest in the mining of lead, from its use as an essential ingredient on the battlefields of Europe and America as well as satisfying the domestic requirements at home. The Richardsons were quick to seize any such opportunity, and although lead was their chief concern they extended their interests to the mining of copper and later coal.

The last of the Richardson goldsmiths was Richard Richardson (4), and although his chief interest lay elsewhere, his connection with the Company at Chester was valued and his workmen continued to produce interesting silver. He was appointed Assay Master between 1785 and 1791 when he resigned so that George Walker could take his place. He then moved from Shotwick to Capenhurst in Wirral, where he pulled down the old half timber hall and built a new one nearby. In 1810 he married Dorothea Bower(s) of Chesterfield by whom he had five children none of whom became goldsmiths. After his death in 1822 his eldest son, Richard, became Lord of the Manor of Capenhurst, and having studied Law at the Inner Temple took Holy Orders, built a church at Capenhurst and became perpetual curate there in 1845. He died in 1885. There were to be no further Richardson goldsmiths in the Company until Richard Richardson, a direct descendant of Richard Richardson (1), (who had moved from Worcester to Chester at the end of the 17th century) an Innholder from Zimbabwe was elected to the Company in 1980 along with his son, also Richard, thus renewing the link.

With the death of Richard Richardson (4) in 1822 the families of Walker and Lowe became the dominant goldsmiths at Chester. George Walker had served his apprenticeship under Richard Richardson (2) and was some years older than George Lowe, having obtained his freedom on 25 July 1767 and was admitted to the Company in July 1770. He worked alongside Joseph Duke and was made Warden with him in 1773. In 1791 he became Assay Master. He died in 1809 and was followed in the office of Assay Master by his son, John Walker. Another son, George Walker, served his apprenticeship under him. Their premises were in Eastgate Street and the registers at St. Peter's

Church refer to several of their children baptised there. George Walker was admitted to the Company in 1794 when his father was Assay Master and became Warden in 1811 continuing as such until 1839 when Thomas Lowe succeeded him in conjunction with George Lowe.

George Lowe (1) was the son of a miller, and established his work at Chester after serving his apprenticeship in London. He had been born at Trafford on 4 May 1768 and may have served his apprenticeship under the Batemans in London where he registered his first mark a GL within a rectangular frame. No silver has been found with his London registered mark. When he moved to Chester he married in 1792 Mary Cawley of Alpraham, Cheshire. He occupied premises at the Cross, Chester in a building which formed part of the Pentice. His stay here was limited for the building was pulled down to widen the road and in 1804 he moved to a house in Bridge Street Row which he bought for £900. He is known to have had other interests as he owned a salt works at Winsford, Cheshire. His marriage to Mary Cawley produced a large number of children, of whom George, Robert, John and Thomas were goldsmiths. The link with the Cawleys associated them with the New Connection in John Street, but he still maintained a close link with Bunbury Parish Church where he had been married and where he and his wife were to be buried, Mary in 22 June 1819 and George in 1842 having died just after Christmas 1841. His son, George Lowe (2) had moved from Chester and settled in Gloucester whilst his brother, Robert Lowe, moved to Preston; John and Thomas remained at Chester. George married Jane Colley Hunt from Hockley near Birmingham. He registered his mark at Chester, G.L within conjoined circles though the Plate Duty Books seem to show that it was also used at the time of George (1). At the time of the introduction of the second copper plate, George Lowe registered his mark GL within a rectangular frame. Before George Lowe (1) died in 1841 there was a disastrous break with George Walker (1), his son John and other members of the Walker family. Thomas Walker having served his apprenticeship was admitted in 1834 and became assistant Assay Master. Arthur Davies Walker became a brother the following year by virtue of being the eldest son of a brother, and Charles Burton Walker was admitted to the Company although he was a bookseller and could have done little to encourage the work of a goldsmith in the City. Both George Walker (1), and his sons John and Thomas had done some excellent work for the Company, but were all dismissed from the Company following a financial disgrace, and their work is not known after 1835.

The Lowe family continued to contribute to the Company for over a century. By 1837, George Lowe (1), George Lowe (2), John Lowe (1), Thomas Lowe and Robert Lowe had all been admitted. Joseph Lowe, William Hyatt, Edward Jones and James Evans completed the Company at this time.

18

Very shortly after 1837 the Minute Book of the Company records the Walker disgrace although it does not go into details. The following minute of 1 April 1840 describes the conclusion of the matter.

'At a special meeting of the Goldsmiths' Company of the City of Chester held at the house of Mr George Lowe agreeable to notice signed by the two Wardens in consequence of a true Bill having been found at the present City Sessions against their Assayer and Assistant Assayer Mr John Walker and Mr Arthur Davies Walker for frauds supposed to have been committed by them against Her Majesty's Commissioners of Stamps, Present Mr George Lowe, Mr Josh Duke, Mr John Lowe, Mr Thomas Lowe, Mr W. Hyatt, Mr Edward Jones, Mr Jas Evans.

We the undersigned being the whole of the said Company of Goldsmiths now resident or inhabiting within the City of Chester (except the said John Walker and Arthur Davies Walker) Do hereby revoke annul and make void the several appointments of them the said John Walker and Arthur Davies Walker to be from henceforth an Assayer and Assistant Assayer and do direct that immediate application be made to the said John Walker and Arthur Davies Walker to deliver up all books, papers, stamps, dies, punches, scales, weights and other implements belonging to the said Company and in their or either of their possession to the said George Lowe and on their or either of their refusal so to do to take such lawful steps for obtaining possession thereof as the said Company may be advised to take.

The said George Lowe having tendered his resignation as one of the Wardens for the present year and the same having been accepted we do hereby appoint Mr William Hyatt as Warden in the room of the said George Lowe.

And we do hereby appoint the said George Lowe as Assay Master during our pleasure in the room of the said John Walker and the said George Lowe be sworn in accordingly.

And we do hereby appoint Mr Joseph Duke as assistant Assay Master during our pleasure in the room and stead of the said Arthur Davies Walker and that the said Joseph Duke be sworn in accordingly.

And we do hereby appoint Mr Edward Jones Clerk or accountant to the said Company. And we do hereby direct that proper premises be taken by the said Company as their future Assay Office.

And we do hereby further direct that in future a box be provided for all the stamps and punches with three locks and keys and one key to be kept by each Warden and one by the Assay Master.

Thomas Lowe	Wardens
William Hyatt	
John Lowe	
James Evans	
Edward Jones	
George Lowe	Assay Master
Joseph Duke	Assistant Assay Master

The offenders were dismissed from the Company, and the changes made at that time were of the nature of an expedient that was necessary to institute safeguards to preserve the good name of the Company and of the Chester Assay.

The first action in this matter was directed upon the members themselves, for there seemed to be some doubt as to whether some members of the Company had legally qualified as members. This applied first to George Lowe (2). He had for some time been working in Gloucester as a goldsmith. He was therefore asked to present his indentures which he did on 16 July 1840 and had to wait seven years before he was admitted as a brother on 16 August 1847. He had returned home from Gloucester to help look after his elderly father and he built a fine country home at 'Mayfield', Bunbury. The qualifications of others were also examined. John and Arthur Davies Walker had already been dismissed, and the rest of the Walker family were now subject to an enquiry. On 22 February 1841 the Company assembled 'do revoke, annul, and make void the said admission of Mr. John Walker Junr as a member of the Company'. The reasons given were that although he had been admitted he had not served an apprenticeship to a brother of the Company and had not been a freeman at the time of his admission having refused to qualify as a member of the same Company, and having been admitted on the Sabbath day.' This statement seems to refer to a minute of 5 July 1834 which stated that he had been admitted a brother 'according to ancient use and custom as the elder son of a brother and having been bound by indenture to a brother of the Company for seven years'. The admission seems to have been done at the commencement of the seven years not at the end of it. The same action now applied to other members of the family. Arthur Davies Walker, already dismissed as assistant Assay Master was now dismissed as a member 'not having had his admission entered upon a stamp as by Law required'. Charles Burton Walker 'he not being a freeman at the time of his admission and not being brought up to the trade of a Goldsmith but to that of a Bookseller, and 'not having his admission entered on a stamp as by Law required' was likewise expelled. Henry Walker for 'not having served an appenticeship to a brother of the Company as by law required and not having been sworn in he refusing to qualify' was also rejected. After this eventful meeting 22 February 1841 the Walkers were no longer involved in the Company affairs.

There had been sporadic attempts to close provincial offices over several centuries, and the Walker incident did little to help. Coupled with this the Company were already having trouble with the Liverpool watchcase makers who submitted their goods to Chester for assay and were attempting to break away and form their own Assay Office.

For over a century the Watchmakers (usually watchcase makers) had been linked with the Goldsmiths' Company and some were admitted to the Company if qualified, though most were not so linked, but still registered their marks on the Company copper plates. The first of these plates dating from the 1700/1 Act, and the second from 1841 contain many marks which belong only to Watchcase makers from Liverpool, Manchester, Newcastle on Tyne and later Birmingham. It is often difficult to distinguish them in the absence of many of the Company books. A note found in the Company records and dated 21 June 1815 states . . .

> Chester Assay Office has no particular District. Goods may be sent to be marked in Chester from any part of the Kingdom not within the Birmingham and Sheffield district and is appointed by Act of Parliament of 12 & 13 Wm111 c.iv.

The claim that Chester was independent of all other assay offices was voiced as early as the 16th century, and renewed at the time when William the Third forced the Chester office to close along with other known and established assay offices throughout the country in 1696. This corresponded with the introduction of the Britannia standard for silver at a time of coinage reform. The closure was to be only temporary as it was found not to work, and it became necessary to reopen the Assay Office at Chester ('where formerly there had been a mint'). The Goldsmiths' Company was invited to manage this along with others who had formerly worked in the Mint at Chester. Chester became again an authorised Assay Office by the 1701 Act. It was however to be conducted under new rules. These rules regulated the type of marks to be used by goldsmiths, the use of a new copper plate to record them, the introduction of the Britannia marks, a new series of date letters and the use of a new City mark. This system was to operate until 24 August 1962 when the Assay Office closed.

When Birmingham and Sheffield applied successfully in 1773 for Assay Offices, Chester's independence was again threatened, but continued to function even though Matthew Boulton of Birmingham had used Chester for assay purposes for some time in preference to London seemingly on personal grounds, based upon a belief that his Midland's accent had been ridiculed by London in the early years. He now strengthened his case by complaining that the goods he had sent to Chester had been damaged. The impact on Chester seems to have been slight, and throughout the discussion there is no reference to it to be found in the Minute book of the Company, which is surprising. The Company survived these threats and was able to continue with the support of several local goldsmiths including those from Liverpool and Manchester. With the formation of these two new assay offices came a ban on those goldsmiths living outside a radius of thirty miles from the centres of Birmingham and Sheffield from using the Chester office. This was lifted in 1854 which resulted in a great increase in the number of firms using Chester.

George Lowe (1) the Prime Warden had resigned in April 1840 and was for a short time appointed assay master to replace John Walker. When he died in December 1841, Thomas Lowe, his son, became assay master with Joseph Duke, assistant assay master. With these changes came new life to the company. A new copper plate was introduced in 1841, the old one having lasted from 1701 was completely covered with marks including those of numerous watchcase makers. The new copper plate was divided into twenty five squares each labelled with the letter of the alphabet (except z), leaving the top free to have the date letters registered and other marks to complete the assay required.

A small red volume containing a list of plate and an inventory of some of the Company's spare time activities was also begun. This was added to and amended until the twentieth century. The Company also asked for a qualified assayer. One Joseph Green who came from London took over from Joseph Duke. He was an employee of the Company not a brother and remained until about 1874 when following a long period of ill health he was given a superannuated pension.

The Company was not without problems. The watchase makers who used the Chester Assay Office, particularly those living in and around Liverpool, were constantly in trouble over their wares. Steps had to be taken to deal with them as it was considered that they were attempting to defraud the public. On 11 January 1843 the Company gave notice that . . .

'Some workmen having repeatedly sent to Hall gold and silver watchcases the component parts whereof have been found to differ in goodness and having in some instances resorted to fraudulent schemes of sending parts of a better quality to convey others which are inferior in standard, and the wardens having perceived that some gold case makers after receiving work from the Assay Office, have turned out parts that are good and substituted rims and other parts of a base quality, they think it necessary to give notice that the rims, wires, edges bottoms and every part must be of the goodness of 22 or 18 carats fine in gold cases and 11 oz 2 dwts fine in silver cases that if one part only in gold or silver cases be found deficient in goodness not only that article but every one in the parcel will be defaced and the wardens in discharge of the duty they owe to the public and the fair trader are determined to prosecute all such persons as may be detected in their nefarious practice of changing any parts of their works they have delivered from the Hall . . . etc.'

In 1845 there is a copy of a letter from Chester (9 April) written to Mr Ralph Samuel of Liverpool which states . . .

'I do hereby give notice that silver work by you on or about the 4th day of this instant sent to the Chester Hall for the purpose of being assayed has after three several assays duly made thereon been found to be of coarser alloy than the standard allowed by law, and is in consequence thereof liable

22

to be and will accordingly be cut broken and defaced and in addition thereto you are liable to certain pecuniary and other penalties.'

The plea to have a separate Liverpool Assay Office either instead of or supplementary to Chester had its champion in a Mr John Stuart. His case was defeated on the grounds that he had only recently started the manufacture of watches and cases, whereas Mr Ralph Samuel employed a hundred men and boys and looked forward to an expanding industry. This might have added strength to the argument, but Mr Samuel, having given due thought to the matter, discovered that there were considerable advantages in having a Chester mark as it had established such a high reputation among overseas customers. The mark had become a status symbol and was referred to as the 'Liverpool' mark.

Throughout 1845 and until March 1846 there was considerable activity involving the Board of Trade. There had been many attempts to close the Chester Assay Office. The Company was faced with litigation in this matter and being doubtful whether their funds would meet the cost of the trial of 'The Queen v the Company of Goldsmiths of Chester' they resolved 19 February 1846 that 10% of each officers salary should be withheld until the expenses of the trial and all other expenses and arrears of the Company had been paid. At the same meeting it was resolved that more commodious premises in Goss Street be obtained for the use of the Assay Office. They continued to rent the building for £10 a year until 1853 when it was purchased by them for £393. The Assay Office remained there until it was sold in 1962. It was later demolished.

A report made by the Inspector General of stamps and taxes referred to Chester in 1851. It states that there were only four Chester based goldsmiths, two of whom were appointed, as Prime Warden (Mr John Lowe) and assistant Warden (Mr John Garner). The Assay Master was Mr Thomas Lowe, brother of Mr John Lowe (but 'not of the trade') and an assistant, Mr Green. The Prime Warden and the assistant each received £5 a year and the assistant received 3/6 per day for attendance. The Assay Master received £300 a year less 20% to cover expenses incurred over the recent prosecution of the former Assay Master. He also received the produce of the diet and the scrapings of gold. The assistant assay master received £2 a week and the clerk (Mr Edward Jones) £20 a year. These salaries were paid out of the charges made for marking silver. The assay days were Thursdays and Fridays, though more days were available should the demand increase. The diet box had produced in the last half year 2 oz 6 dwt 18 of gold and 8 oz of silver. The revenue from assaying was based upon the following terms 1s 6d for a gold watch case, 4d for a silver watchcase, 3d for gold pendants and 1d for a silver one. Other articles were at the rate of 1d an ounce for silver and 3d for gold. Private assays were 6d for silver and 1s for gold. At this time the majority of silversmiths sending in for assay at Chester came from

Liverpool, twelve being mentioned, there were four from Chester and one from Manchester, Mr. George Ward.

Recognising that both Liverpool and Chester could be the losers in any battle, both parties acted together. The opposition of Mr R. Samuel to any closure of the Chester Assay Office became a forceful argument in retaining the status quo. Goldsmiths' Hall, London were still trying to establish that both Liverpool silversmiths and the Chester Assay Office were at fault, and that if proved should lead to the closure of the Chester office. In correspondence at Goldsmiths' Hall is the following letter from the Hall to Mr James Wilson MP, dated 21 June 1855.

'I have had more difficulty in procuring wares recently marked at Chester where very little gold or silver is marked excepting watchcases and these are not kept in shops but are sent chiefly from Liverpool by manufacturers there and immediately after they are marked are despatched to the watch movement makers at Coventry and elsewhere. I sent a person to Coventry and he succeeded in buying some gold watches the cases of which have been marked exactly. They bear the mark of this year. I sent for reports of Assays of four cases manufactured by Ralph Samuel of Liverpool all of which are worse than standard, some of them viz No. 21456 being upward of one carat worse than the 18 carat grade for which it is marked.'

This kind of evidence did not reflect favourably upon either the Chester Assay Office or upon Mr Ralph Samuel.

On 11 June 1855 a special meeting of the Chester Company was convened to oppose the Bill introduced by Mr Wilson and the Chancellor of the Exchequer for the purpose of abolishing the Assay Office at Chester. This Bill was designed to close not only Chester but also York, Exeter and Newcastle-on-Tyne Assay Offices. Only the Assay Offices at London, Birmingham and Sheffield were to remain.

The City now enlisted the support of Lord Robert Grosvenor. Mr John Lowe went to London to oppose the Act and present the Chester case. With the help of a Mr Roberts (who sent a bill to Mr Thomas Lowe with 19 pages of itemised expenses for £172.6.2) the situation was clearly put in April 1856 and the discussion and evidence was set out before a select Committee on gold and silver wares appointed by the House of Commons. The minutes and proceedings of the Committee were printed and made available in May 1856, and it is from this report that the following information is gleaned.

The Committee was anxious to discover the truth behind accusations that some wares were being incorrectly assayed, and that false punches were in use on gold wares at Liverpool. There had been a recent Act of 1854, which had lowered the permitted standard for gold from 18 cts to 9 cts and Mr Ralph Samuel and Mr John Lowe gave valuable evidence to the

Committee as to how this was leading to a good deal of dishonesty in the trade.

Mr Samuel informed the Committee that he was a manufacturer of both gold and silver watchcases only, and had been so occupied for the past twenty five years. His output was considerable, six hundred gold and six hundred silver cases a month. He had in fact virtually monopolised the Liverpool trade for many years. Almost all his work was sent to Chester for assay and the Chester mark was looked upon as the hall mark of Liverpool quality. The Chester mark signified to the trade that the watch was of 'Liverpool character', and thus had a world wide reputation, especially in North and South America and in certain manufacturing districts in England. This world reputation for such 'Liverpool' cases, having watch movements of equal reputation, made Mr Samuel claim that even if the latter were housed in London assayed cases, they would not have the same market value except in Scotland where for some reason London watches were deemed preferable. Since the law had recently made it possible for silversmiths outside the previous thirty mile limit of operation to use the Assay Office at Chester, he had had orders from some distance, quoting Mr Kelvey of Gainsborough who felt compelled to have his watches assayed with the so called 'Liverpool' mark.

There had been a suggestion, doubtless fostered by the London, Sheffield and Birmingham goldsmiths that ideally Provincial Offices like Chester should be closed down so that assaying might be centred at these Offices. The Liverpool silversmiths joined with the Chester Goldsmiths to oppose any such suggestion and signed a petition to prevent this. When Mr Samuel was reminded that about 1840 he and many others had signed a petition to esablish an assay office at Liverpool, independent of Chester, he replied that since then they, and especially he, had changed their opinion and wished to support the claim of Chester being retained as their trade there had doubled during the past ten years.

A great many uncased watches or movements were being sent to America where they were encased in gold cases, many of which were fraudulently using forged London and Chester marks and punching an 18ct mark upon 9 ct gold. The bulk of the English trade with the United States was in uncased movements but a considerable trade was done in silver watches. Because of the high price of labour in the States it was more profitable for them to concentrate on gold case making. Contrary to the expectations of those who had brought about the 1854 Act, which had lowered the standard of gold, it had not helped the Liverpool gold case makers to compete favourable with those in America. The Americans who had visited Liverpool were willing to place large orders for lower standard gold cases providing that an 18 ct mark could be placed upon them. This Mr Samuel refused to do. His statement is a curious one, for it was the legal requirement for the

Chester Assay Office alone to put on the 18 ct and 9 ct marks upon a gold watchcase. It is to his credit that he refused to become party to the fraud. That the Americans were capable of perpetrating the fraud themselves seems clear for they sent fraudulent watches to Australia, where successful diggers welcomed them as luxury items. Havanna, Buenos Ayres, Montevideo, Rio, Pernambuco and Brasil were additional important markets for such watches. The Committee was told that previous to the 'panic in Melbourne', Mr Samuel had enormous trade with Australia sending parcels of 300, 400 and 500 watches at a time. At one time he himself had shipped £8000 worth of watches and jewellery and he claimed to be the largest manufacturer in the world, making 200 gold and 400 silver watchcases a week. Had the Liverpool watchcase makers been prepared to do as the Americans had asked, the 1000 or 2000 watch movements which were going to America weekly, would go out with watchcases, but Mr Samuel refused to supply unmarked cases for the American market. The outcome of these discussions confirmed the importance of the Chester Assay Office, and did not recommend that Liverpool should either take its place, or establish a separate Assay Office. The Liverpool watchcase makers were perfectly satisfied with the result even though some fifteen years earlier they had petitioned for an office to be established there. There were some at Liverpool who acted as though Liverpool had in fact such an Office. As evidence of this a Mr Alfred Lutschaunig produced a book in 1872, which was a manual of hall marks and a reference for gold and silversmiths included tables for the proper mixing of alloys of gold and silver to make them of standard fineness. A second edition of 1878 is known, in which he mentioned 'The Manager of the Liverpool Assay Office'! The Liverpool Trade directory of 1872 appears to establish this office at 50b Lord Street, Liverpool. Lutschaunig and Co were gold and silver refiners and analytical chemists; they also list Melville Chambers, 39 Cable Street as an address for the 'Assay Office'. In spite of their claims, they could not have had any legal or official status and were probably bullion dealers carrying on a commercial assay of gold and silver.

One of the satisfactory results of the report was that it gave a new independence. The increased income of the Company brought about by the revenue from assays, prompted them to review the salaries of their officials. Duty which had been paid on watchcases had ceased in 1794 but the cost of assaying continued.

In August 1856 at the time of the elections the salary of John Lowe, who had done so much in the recent discussions, was raised to £50 a year, that of Mr Green to £80 'for scraping and as a warden'. Daniel Davies (auditor and assistant) and Thomas Woolley, weigher, had their salaries raised to £20 each year on condition that they audited the weighing and account books every half year. Members of the Council were to have 30/- a year for an excursion and the apprentices 7/6 for a similar treat. Another revision of salaries took place 16 August 1862 which again reflected an increase in work. John Lowe had his salary increased from £60 to £100 a year, Thomas Woolley from £50 to £80, James Lowe from 30/- to 40/- a week, E. Tatler 21/- to 26/- a week, G. Lowe, weigher, £20 to £25 a year, J. F. Lowe, auditor £20 to £25 a year. John Lowe did not survive long to enjoy the increased salary for he died 11 September 1864. The Goldsmiths 'as a mark of high estimation in which he was held by members of the Company' defrayed his funeral expenses and made an allowance of £5 to each member, and £2.10.0 to each apprentice to provide a suit for mourning on the occasion. He had managed to combine civic and church duties with those of an active goldsmith, becoming City Sheriff in 1841, Prime Warden 1854/55 and again in 1864/65. The spiritual needs of the Company and the apprentices were looked after when he appointed the Reverend G. L. Whitehead as Chaplain to the Company with a yearly stipend of £25.

John's son, John (2) Foulkes Lowe was elected Warden on the death of his father and George Bennett Lowe became auditor in his place. John (1) Lowe's brother, Thomas, with whom he had worked in partnership and had shared his mark was now a very old man and going blind. He could only sign his name with a cross on 22 September 1864 and on 27 September at a special meeting convened at the Hall, Goss Street, after twenty two years as Assay Master he resigned. The Company considered his retirement and he was granted an allowance of £200 a year, and $\frac{2}{3}$ of his former salary. His place as Assay Master was taken by James Foulkes Lowe 'an able and skilful man and experienced in assaying gold and silver'. Thomas Lowe died in February 1866. The Company again defrayed his funeral expenses as they did for Edward Jones the Clerk in 1867.

Shortly before John Lowe's death in 1864 the Company had planned to acquire land and property which could be used for housing members should the need arise. For this a licence was necessary and on 18 March 1862 such a licence was applied for.

'To apply to the Crown for licence to hold land already purchased, and to be purchased of the value of £3345'.

The Company sought Council's opinion on the matter. It seems that the Company was incorporated by the 12/13 William 3 Ch.4 but to have no power to hold land in mortmain, but that under 7 and 8 William 3 Ch.37 power is vested in the Crown to grant licences to Corporations and other bodies to purchase and hold lands in mortmain. Council advised the Company to apply to the Crown for a licence to do so. Council's opinion was that of Henry Rowcliffe of Lincoln's Inn and was expressed on 5 March 1862.

The Company had already purchased property in Goss Street where they conducted the Assay Office, and when Queen Victoria granted the licence in the 25th year of her reign the licence included this property and referred to

> 'certain other Properties in Chester and in Flintshire to the value of £2295, have lately agreed to purchase 2 Freehold houses, shippon and stable in the City of Chester £1050' and agreed to hold them mortmain.

The Attorney General granted the licence on a payment of £110 on 22 May 1862. Land at Pentre, Flintshire, property at Whitefriars, and two houses in Princess Street were also held by the Company as well as three in Back Brook Street. By December of that year (1862) the premises in Princess Street had been sold to the Town Council for £500, and the following May the Company added two more acres to the field at Pentre for a sum 'not exceeding £140'. In 1866 the property in Whitefriars was sold for about £1200 and the following year the Company drew up a number of resolutions connected with the insurance of individual members of the Company.

On 29 December 1887 Richard Edward Tatler and Andrew Nixon Godwin made a declaration under the Merchandise Marks Act 1887.

On 3 August 1889 the annual meeting, which involved the change of date letter, the confirmation of the appointment of the Wardens, and other matters changed the date of the annual meeting to 1 July. From then on there was a slight change in the formation of the City and Sterling marks; these changes began on 7 October 1889 when new punches for assaying silver were instituted.

There was a regular revision of the amounts paid to the officers and workmen at the Assay Office. When trade seemed to be better they received more, as happened in 1884 when they increased the salary of the Assay Master to £140, when less it was reduced as in 1886 along with other salaries by a third. In 1895 owing to a new prosperity the salaries were again listed.

James Foulkes Lowe	£50
Thomas Woolley	£26
John Woolley	£26
G. W. Williams	£26
W. N. Godwin	£13
G. L. Whitehouse	£10
John F. Lowe	£26
R. E. Tatler	£26
A. N. Godwin	£26
W. F. Lowe	£26
G. B. Lowe	£10
Mrs John Woolley	£4

They all sign the book except Mrs Woolley. She was not a member of the Company, for no woman had ever been elected to the Company during its long history. A custom which is still (1996) observed.

In the early years of the 20th century the Company was forced to reduce the salaries, which must have caused considerable hardship to those concerned when it was reduced to $\frac{2}{3}$ of normal salary. One of the results of the Great War was the action taken by the General Workers Union on 8 January 1920 when everyone in the Assay Office joined in a strong protest and demanded an increase in wages and improved conditions. Regrettably they made their demands at a time when there was a shortage of work. Someone had leaked the amounts received in past years for assaying silver and gold and had based their demands upon these figures which were in any case strictly confidential. The outcome of this protest hardly benefitted the staff. In January 1920 the staff was reduced by four boys and two girls who were given fourteen days notice and in April 1921 four of the younger men were sacked. The others were given a rise of ten shillings per week. Sefton Williams who had joined the Company in 1913 after serving his apprenticeship under his father for seven years, had joined the Assay Office staff but had been called up. When he returned he was advised by the Company that it would be to his advantage if he remained in the Army rather than claim a place at the Office again, even though they had made up his pay to the amount that he would have received had he remained. The lean period followed for some time and the Company was forced in 1924 to sell £500 War stock towards clearing an overdraft at the Bank of £676. They had been financially secure during the War and had invested £4000 in War stock and Australian Investments at 4%, but the lean years which had followed had depleted this considerably.

Birmingham sought to take advantage of the financial problems of the Chester Assay Office and tried to persuade Chester to drop their Agency in Birmingham. In 1923 Chester made it quite clear that they would not agree to this, even though their agent was far from satisfactory. Instead in 1930, Harold S. Smets, a dealer in gem stones, of 107 Vyse Street, Birmingham was officially appointed as parcels agent to the Chester Office at Birmingham. After this large quantities of silver came from Birmingham to be assayed at Chester. The advent of this trade from Birmingham, though frowned upon by that city, was a most welcome reward to Chester for their patience during the earlier years of depression.

In 1919 the City was called upon to honour the great contribution made in the War by the Rt. Honourable David Lloyd George and the City Council voted that he should be granted the Freedom of the City. This required him to be a member of a City Company and the Company of Goldsmiths was chosen for this honour. There were difficulties in that an apprenticeship of seven years to become a member was required, and further the Rt. Hon.

David Lloyd George was not the son of a Chester Goldsmith! It was therefore decided to make him an Honorary Goldsmith, a position which had never been granted before and would break with Company tradition. It was resolved therefore to mark the occasion by obtaining a fine Chester cake basket which had been made by Richard Richardson (2) 1765/66 (*Chester Silver*, p. 153) for presentation to the Prime Minister. The basket was suitably inscribed with the Arms of the Company. Unfortunately Lloyd George never came to receive it, nor was he ever admitted. In 1929 the minute book records . . .

> The cake basket bought and inscribed for Mr Lloyd George had not been collected in ten years.

It still remains in the Company, somewhat ruined by an irrelevant inscription.

In 1931 the Company along with the Assay Offices in London, Birmingham and Sheffield was asked to comment upon the introduction of a 14 ct standard for gold. This suggestion was brought about by pressure from overseas. The Assay Offices agreed but it involved the abolition of the 12 and 15 ct standard which had been in use. This new standard came into use 1 July 1932 at their annual meeting.

Two years later in 1934 there came a suggestion that a special mark ought to be issued to mark the Silver Jubilee of King George and Queen Mary. There were objections to the use of the Sovereign head alone as it might get confused with the long abandoned duty mark which ceased in 1 May 1890. The design showing the mark of both King George and Queen Mary was accepted. It was only to be used on silver and would cease to be used at the end of the calendar year 1935. The Company was willing to celebrate the Jubilee by buying a Chester made tankard weighing 14 oz 20 dwt costing £4.13.2, carrying the Jubilee mark, and extending their laboratory at a cost of £383. Somewhat by contrast they gave only a guinea to the Prince of Wales Jubilee Fund which was launched at the Town Hall.

1935 saw also the acceptance of the assaying of Platinum. For this, a new mark had to be introduced.

No new members had been admitted to the Company since Hugh Foulkes Lowe in 1931. He had served his seven years apprenticeship by May but had to await his entry into the Company as his Freedom had not been granted at the Town Hall. This was done at the annual meeting on 1 July 1931. There was to be a break until 1937 when on 17 November, Francis (known as Frank) Maurice Lowe, the son of James Foulkes Lowe and John Edward Vincent Ward, son of Thomas William Ward were admitted. They had both worked in the Assay Office.

The Chester date letter changed from N to O on 1 July 1939 and on 14 July the Company recorded the birth days of the members serving in the Assay Office. The reasons why this was done is puzzling, but it may have been due to the uncertainty of the times.

Frank Ernest Clark	27 September 1874
Hugh Cawley Lowe	26 January 1881
James Foulkes Lowe	18 February 1882
Arthur Vincent Ward	22 January 1885
Thomas William Ward	19 February 1892
Arthur Godwin	22 August 1900
Frank Cyril Clark	25 July 1901
Hugh Foulkes Lowe	24 April 1910
Francis Maurice Lowe	26 October 1916

The Second World War began at the beginning of September 1939 and on 5 September the Company accepted a 20% reduction for Company members and ordered a 10% cut in staff members. As expected the call up for armed service affected the younger men. As in the 1914-1918 War, the Company declared that taking into consideration payments given for army service they should agree to make up the salaries to the amount they would have received had they still been at the Assay Office.

The War years had a devastating effect upon many enterprises not directly connected with the war. Gold when permitted could only be used at 9 ct and there was a limited amount of assaying. The yearly meeting continued on 1 July and the Assay Master and the two Wardens continued to be appointed though they did not change, they still took the oath required by law and changed the date annually. They also tried to enforce the law as it concerned the Company, though the one example noted seems to have been an isolated example, and it is difficult to understand why the case should have concerned Chester so much. The firm of Joseph Horton and Son of 5/6 Church Street, Wrexham, Pawnbrokers and Jewellers, had been caught selling a wedding ring which had not been assayed. The Wardens had every intention of taking them to Court, but a polite letter from the firm and an apology, produced a happy ending to the incident and no action was taken. It is amazing to think that this took place in 1943 at the height of hostilities.

Little happened at the Assay Office or to the Company during the War years. James Foulkes Lowe and H. C. Lowe kept the Company together, but in 1946 James Foulkes Lowe died. The Company as an expression of their sorrow sent his widow £25. A Vincent Ward was made Warden in his place and Hugh Cawley Lowe appointed Prime Warden. Frank Ernest Clark remained as Assay Master. He retained this office until he retired 8 December 1954. Shortly before in November 1953, Hugh Cawley Lowe, the Prime Warden died and Thomas Ward joined A. V. Ward as Wardens.

They saw a steady increase in the amount of work passing to the Chester

Office. 'Hall' marking had for a long time been associated only with the London Assay Office derived from Goldsmiths' Hall, but towards the end of the 19th century the Company had referred to the Chester Assay Office as 'The Hall' which was in Goss Street.

In 1954, F. C. Clark resigned as Assay Master, and A. V. Ward took his place, and T. W. Godwin and T. W. Ward became Wardens. It was in A. V. Ward time that the office handled great quantities of silver. Birmingham manufacturers and many from elsewhere found Chester could handle silver more expeditiously than any of its rivals. The Assay Master, Mr Ward, told of baskets of silver being sent to the General Railway Station where it was collected and dealt with immediately, the staff working until late in the night to have it returned the following day.

In spite of the increase of work and the efficiency in handling the silver the Government was determined to review the situation and a Committee was formed in 1955. It was not until 1957 that the Company meeting on 20 August agreed that Sir Leonard Stone, who had been appointed Chairman of the Hallmarking Committee should be given access to the Company records with a view to paying compensation and payments to those members of the Company and staff 'in the event of its closure' and that now 'he will be able to carry on your negotiations'. This must have come as a shock to many, but others saw it as a profitable way to retire gracefully from the Assay Office, even though it meant the closure of the Office, and because of the unusual link between the Assaying and the Company, (which dated back to the 16th century) the possible demise of the Company of Goldsmiths' of Chester. The relationship between the two bodies had never been satisfactorily explained since the 1700/01 Act but they had worked well together over the years especially when civic pride was involved. Times had changed in recent years and they had seen the closure of other provincial assay offices, York in 1857, Newcastle in 1883, and Exeter in 1884, all of which had been forced to close due to the limited amount of work they received and the revenue from which did not cover their expenses. Chester however had continued to thrive.

It seemed clear that the primary work of Sir Leonard Stone's Committee was to clear up the often ambiguous and contradictary words found in the various 18th and 19th century Acts, which became increasingly confused when applied to Scotland.

There was also a 'snob' value attached to some provisional city marks. Liverpool discovered that the Chester mark on her watchcases had an added retail value even to the extent that it was sometimes called 'the Liverpool Mark'. At the turn of the century articles made in the 'Celtic' manner were sent to Edinburgh, and Chester for assay though made in Yorkshire, Lancashire and other places far removed from the point of assay.

When eventually the Report of the departmental Committee on Hall

Marking was presented to Parliament by the President of the Board of Trade, the Rt. Hon. Sir David Eccles in March 1959, Chester was singled out in Appendix C for special mention and plans were drawn up for the dissolution of the Company as well as the closure of the Assay Office, providing ways in which the pensions and compensations of the staff could be met.

Neither the Chester Company, nor the Assay Office are listed as witnesses who gave evidence at the Committee, though it seems clear that the Assay Master and others would have been satisfied with their pension and were in favour of the proposal even though it involved such a drastic rejection of their past history.

When the Report had been submitted in March 1959 to the House, John ffoulkes Lowe announced, as the minutes of the Company record, that on 6 April 1959 he would conduct a campaign to retain the Chester Assay Office and also the Company of Goldsmiths. He was almost alone in this challenge. He was not a member of the Assay Staff and thus had no vested interest. It seemed to be a repeat of the events of a hundred years earlier when his grandfather John Lowe had won a similar battle, and retained both.

The Company had asked Mr Hugh Jones of David Hughes, Solicitors to act for them in future negotiations, but John ffoulkes Lowe acted alone, and did not attend the meeting on 20 August 1957. The slow procedure of Parliament then continued. In the House of Lords the Bishop of Chester, Dr Gerald Ellison made a well informed speech supporting an amendment which had been put to the Committee, that preserved the existence of the Company when the Act passed into law. As the Assay was now removed from Chester the Company was given no power to Assay silver as they had had before the 1700/01 Act.

24 August 1962 marked the closure of the Assay Office. The documents which were considered to belong to the Company, including the early Minute books were retained by the Company, but the copper plates and records of those who recorded their marks, and the Plate Duty Books were transferred to the Assay Office at Birmingham.

One of the younger men who had to seek other employment at Goldsmiths' Hall, London, was Grahame Jones. His account of those last days is found on page 159.

As soon as the fate of the Assay Office was known there was an added interest in the mark. The date letter had changed from L to M on 1 July 1962 and in those few months before August 24 a remarkable collection of silver and gold imported from London was assayed at Chester, especially by John ffoulkes Lowe and his sister, Margaret Joyce Lowe using their own new mark JL above JL within a square. The Lowe family had ceased to employ silversmiths since the war.

33

There were others who took advantage of this short period. Francis Maurice Lowe imported three sets of flat ware from the Sheffield Smelting Co. and made three sets of cutlery for members of his family of the old English design each consisting of 6 table forks, 6 dessert forks, 6 tea spoons, 6 dessert spoons, 6 table spoons and 2 serving spoons. As he had no mark he borrowed that of the Assay Master A. V. Ward. To him also goes the honour of submitting the last piece hallmarked at Chester also marked AVW and now in the Ridgway Gallery of the Grosvenor Museum, Chester. His son, Peter J. Lowe also turned his hand to make a circular hand raised tray $5\frac{7}{8}$ inches diameter, his father having helped him in the work. Having no mark of his own he borrowed that of his cousin Grahame Jones (G.J.) who was soon to leave for the London Hall.

Admissions to the Company since 1837

GEORGE WALKER (1) (see p. 17)

GEORGE LOWE (1) (see p. 18)

ARTHUR DAVIES WALKER (see p. 19)

CHARLES BURTON WALKER (see p. 19)

HENRY WALKER (see p. 20)

WILLIAM HYATT. Apprenticed to 'a brother' seven years. April 1840 Warden, confirmed 5 August 1840. William Hyatt, Warden 1841 confirmed 30 December 1841. William Hyatt 1843 (not after 5 August 1843). Became a weigher in room of an auditor. Apparently went to Worcester. In 1859 was granted £2 'at Worcester' and 30/- the following year.

THOMAS LOWE (see p. 18)

EDWARD JONES. Apprenticed to George, John and Thomas Lowe. Admitted to the Company 5 August 1839. Appointed 'Clerk or accountant' 1841 to 1861. Allowed 'one of five houses' owned by Company 1861. Died 1867.

JAMES EVANS. Admitted to the Company 5 August 1839 having served his apprenticeship to the Lowes. Audtior 1841 to 1845. Resigned 27 February 1845 to become Warden and Weigher in place of W. Hyatt 5 August 1845, in April 1846 left the city (for Preston) and was replaced by John Garner as Warden. In 1859 was granted £2 and the following year 30/-.

GEORGE LOWE (2). Having lived in Gloucester was admitted and formerly made a member of the Company 16 July 1840 (see p. 90).

RICHARD HALL. Seven years by Indenture to George Lowe, admitted 2 July 1841. Made Warden 5 August 1843. Resigned February 1845.

JOHN GARNER. Apprenticed to Lowes. Admitted 5 August 1842. Warden 15 April 1846 to 1861, the year he died.

(Rev.) GEORGE LOWE WHITEHOUSE. Admitted 5 August 1845. Chaplain. 5 August 1851. Paid £25 a year 1867.

GEORGE LOWE (3). Son of George Lowe (2). 16 July 1840 presented indenture. Admitted 1847. Weigher 20 February 1861.

THOMAS WOOLLEY. Apprenticed to John Lowe. Admitted after seven years 1 January 1852. Resigned as Weigher 20 February 1861 to become Warden. Drawer 31 August 1874. Became Weigher 18 December 1876.

DANIEL DAVIES. Apprenticed to J. Lowe. Admitted 8 September 1858. Auditor 5 August 1854. Resigned as Audtior and became Drawer in place of J. Garner at £1/1/- a week.

RICHARD EDWARD TATLER. Apprenticed to J. Lowe. Admitted 11 May 1861. Drawer 27 October 1864.

JAMES FOULKES LOWE. Son of John Lowe under whom he served his apprenticeship. Admitted 10 February 1862. 1861 Assistant Drawer. Assay Master in place of Thomas Lowe 27 October 1864. (see p.   ).

JOHN WOOLLEY. Apprentice to his brother Thomas Woolley. Admitted 8 September 1862. Drawer 27 October 1864. In 1866 drew 35/- a week.

GEORGE BENNETT LOWE. Apprentice to J. Lowe. Admitted 5 August 1864. Auditor 22 September 1864 at £25 a year. Weigher 1864 to 1876 (when he died).

WILLIAM FOULKES LOWE. Admitted after seven years 8 August 1871 to John Lowe and George Lowe. Assistant Assay Master 12 December 1876 at £25 a year.

ANDREW NIXON GODWIN. Apprentice to Thomas Woolley. Admitted 8 August 1871. Hireman 1874. Clerk 12 December 1876.

HENRY RILEY HORTON. Apprentice to J. F. Lowe. Admitted 4 August 1877.

GEORGE HENRY WILLIAMS. Apprentice to J. F. Lowe. Admitted 5 February 1878.

FREDERICK WILLIAM WARD. Apprentice to Thomas Woolley. Admitted 5 August 1879.

FREDERICK DUKE WOOLLEY. Apprentice to Thomas Woolley. Admitted 29 September 1887.

WILLIAM NETHERSIDE GODWIN. Apprentice to Andrew Nixon Godwin. Admitted 22 December 1893.

JOHN CECIL LOWE. Apprentice to John F. Lowe. Admitted 1 July 1895.

FRANK ERNEST CLARK. Apprentice to Thomas Woolley. Admitted 1 July 1896.

HUGH CAWLEY LOWE. Admitted 1 July 1902.

GEORGE FREDERIC LOWE. Apprentice to J. Foulkes Lowe. Admitted 1 July 1904. (see p. 131)

JAMES FOULKES LOWE. Apprentice to James Foulkes Lowe. Admitted 4 August 1904. (see p. 125)

GEORGE WILLIAMS. Admitted January 1906.

ARTHUR VINCENT WARD. Apprentice to his grandfather Thomas Woolley. Admitted 2 July 1906. (see p. 143).

HAROLD LOWE. Apprentice to W. F. Lowe. Admitted 1 July 1910.

SEFTON RICHARD WILLIAMS. Son of George H. Williams. Admitted 1 July 1913.

THOMAS VINCENT WARD. Brother of Arthur Vincent Ward. Admitted 28 January 1915.

ARTHUR GODWIN. Son of William N. Godwin. Admitted 3 November 1921.

FREDERICK CYRIL CLARK. Son of Frank E. Clark. Admitted 13 September 1922.

HUGH FOULKES LOWE. Son of Hugh Cawley Lowe. Admitted 1 July 1931.

FRANCIS MAURICE LOWE. Son of James F. Lowe. Admitted 17 November 1937.

JOHN EDWARD VINCENT WARD. Son of Thomas William Ward. Admitted 17 November 1937.

JOHN ffOULKES LOWE. Son of George F. Lowe. Admitted 13 December 1954.

GRAHAME JONES. Apprentice to Francis Lowe. Admitted 26 February 1960.

Later admissions to the Company:

PETER JAMES LOWE. Son of Francis Maurice Lowe. Admitted 14 May 1964. (see p. 45)

Wardens of the Chester Goldsmiths' Company

	Prime Warden	*Senior Warden*
5 July 1837	George Walker	George Lowe (1)
5 July 1838	George Walker	George Lowe (1)
5 July 1839	George Lowe (1)	Thomas Lowe
5 August 1840	Thomas Lowe	William Hyatt
5 August 1841	Thomas Lowe	William Hyatt
30 December	John Lowe	William Hyatt
5 August 1842	John Lowe	William Hyatt
5 August 1843	John Lowe	Richard Hall
5 August 1844	John Lowe	Richard Hall
27 February 1845	John Lowe	James Evans

| 5 August 1845 | John Lowe | James Evans |
| 15 April 1846 | John Lowe | John Garner |

(remained in office until John Garner died)

20 February 1861	John Lowe	Thomas Woolley
5 August 1861	John Lowe	Thomas Woolley
22 September 1861	John Foulkes Lowe	Thomas Woolley
5 August 1862	John Foulkes Lowe	Thomas Woolley

(on 3 August 1889 the date to change to 1 July. John Foulkes Lowe and Thomas Woolley remained in office until 1 July 1907)

| 1 July 1907 | John Foulkes Lowe | Richard Edward Tatler |

(remained in office until 1911)

| 1 July 1911 | George Henry Williams | George Frederic Lowe |

(remained in office until 1914)

| 1 July 1914 | George Henry Williams | William Netherside Godwin |
| 1 July 1915 | George Henry Williams | William Netherside Godwin |

(remained in office until 1926)

| 1 July 1926 | William Netherside Godwin | Frank Ernest Clark |

(remained in office until 1928)

| 12 June 1928 | Frank Ernest Clark | Hugh Cawley Lowe |

(remained in office until the death of William Foulkes Lowe, Assay Master)

| 19 November 1931 | Hugh Cawley Lowe | James Foulkes Lowe |

(remained in office until February 1946)

| 20 February 1946 | Hugh Cawley Lowe | Arthur Vincent Ward |

(remained in office until December 1953)

| December 1953 | Arthur Vincent Ward | Thomas W. Ward |
| December 1954 | Thomas W. Ward | Arthur Godwin |

(remained in office until the closure of the Assay Office 24 August 1962)

Catalogue of Plate held by the Company

A small red Morocco bound book which measures $5\frac{1}{2}$ by $3\frac{1}{2}$ inches was designed to contain a catalogue of the plate held by the Company. It was amended several times as plate was added or items lost. It was used by the Company until the time of A. V. Ward the last assay master, who may have been responsible for the pencilled note at the end of the catalogue which reads . . .

> Previous entries are cancelled. The articles were disposed of during World War 1.

This comment is only partly correct. In the Minute Book under 22 January 1915 is . . .

> that the silver plate belonging to the Company be sold at the first favourable opportunity excepting only those which bear the Hall marks of this office,

37

The minute was carried unanimously. Nothing further is known of the silver until a minute of 25 January 1929 when it was mentioned that the sum of two pounds owing to the Company by Mr G. Williams for silver bought from the Company in 1927 had not been paid. The Company decided to deduct the two pounds from his retirement cheque.

The book appears to date from about 1840 and contains the following entries.

Page 1   TANKARDS
Silver
1 Tankard with top
1 Tankard with top
1 Tankard without top

CUPS
Silver
1 pint cup
1 pint cup

Page 2   CUPS
1 half pint cup
1 cup 2 handles
(later) 1 Quart cup

WAITERS
Silver
1 twelve inch
1 eight inch with foot
1 six inch square
1 six inch round
1 $3\frac{1}{2}$ inch round

Page 3   SALTS
Silver
4 Oval Salts
2 Gilt Salts

JUGS
Silver
1 Claret Jug
1 Cream Jug

BOATS
Silver
2 Butter Boats

Page 4	LADDLES
	Silver
	8 Sauce Laddles
	3 Soup Laddles (originally written as 1)
	1 Punch Laddle
	1 Sugar Laddle
	MUFFINEERS
	Silver
	1 Small Muffineer
	1 Large Muffineer
Page 5	EPERNGNE
	1 Eperngne
	1 Large Dish Glass
	3 Small Glass Dishes (changed to 2)
	3 Branches
	LABELS
	Silver
	10 Wine Labels
Page 6	SKEWERS
	Silver
	2 Skewers
	FUNNEL
	Silver
	1 Wine Funnel
	1 Wine Funnel
	1 Vegetable Fork
Page 7	JUGS
	Silver 2nd
	3 Silver Cream Jugs (1 crossed out)
	3 Silver Cream Jugs
	CUPS
	1 Pint Cup (crossed out)
	1 Claret Jug with Wicker Handle
Page 8	BLANK

Page 9	SPOONS
	Silver
	5 Gravy Spoons
	3 Marrow Spoons
	37 Table Spoons
	23 Dessert Spoons (23 amended to 35)
	4 Salt Spoons (amended to 3)
Page 10	SPOONS
	4 Salt Spoons Ornamented (amended to 3)
	35 (in later hand) Teaspoons
	4 Dessert Spoons (crossed out)
Page 11	FORKS
	Silver
	6 Dessert Pearl Handle Forks
	27 Table Forks (amended to 25)
	3 Table Forks (3 crossed out)
	31 Dessert Forks (31 crossed out amended to 11)
	49 Dessert Forks
	6 Table Forks (6 crossed out)
	46 Table Forks
Page 12	FORKS
	1 pr Game Carver
	FORK
	Silver
	12 Dessert Forks (12 crossed out)
	49 Dessert (crossed out)
Page 13	KNIVES
	Silver
	1 Fish Knife
	2 Butter Knives
	6 Dessert Pearl Handle Knives
Page 14	KNIVES
	23 Table Knives (amended to 24)
	24 Dessert Knives
	CARVERS
	1 pr Game Carver
	6 Dessert Pearl Handle Forks

40

Page 15	*Silver*
	1 Cream Jug (crossed out)
	1 Wine Taster
	1 pr Sugar Tongs

Page 16   BLANK

Page 17   CUPS
Silver
1 Two Handled Cup
1 Half Pint Hooped Can
2 Small do
(later additional item) 1 Two Handled Cup

Page 18   *Silver*
Sugar Basin Teapot Cream Jug
1 Mustard Pot
2 Salts Lined

Page 19   (Note stuck in to say . . .)

'Previous entries all cancelled. The articles were disposed of during World War 1.'

Every page crossed out about the same time.

*   *   *   *

What silver was sold has not been stated. The difference between the statement in the 1915 minutes and that in 1927 still leaves the matter in doubt. In 1976 the pieces which remain with the Company are recorded in either *Chester Goldsmiths* or *Chester Silver,* the exceptions being a Jubilee tankard (1935/6) and a small Irish ash tray (diameter $3\frac{3}{8}$ inches).

The nineteen pieces of silver in the keeping of the Company are . . .

2 Table Spoons by Nathaniel Bullen 1703/04 (*Chester Goldsmiths,* p. 130).

2 Rat Tail Dessert Spoons. Thomas Robinson 1716/17 (*C.G.,* p. 179).

Tumbler Cup. Richard Richardson (1) 1721/22 (*C.G.,* p. 169).

Basting Spoon. Rat Tail. William Richardson 1723/24 (*C.G.,* p. 173).

Tumbler Cup. Benjamin Pemberton 1726/27. (*Chester Silver 1727-1827,* p. 125).

Marrow Scoop. William Richardson 1733/34. (*C.S.,* p. 186).

Pap Boat. E.H. engraved on base, Richard Richardson (2) 1739/40. (*C.S.,* p. 164).

Pap Boat. Assayed on inside. Richard Richardson (2) 1743/44. (*C.S.,* p. 140).

Tumbler Cup. Richard Richardson (2) 1755/56. (*C.S.*, p. 167).
Cake Basket. Richard Richardson (2) 1765/66. (*C.S.* p. 153).
Two Handled Porringer. George Walker 1771/72. (*C.S.*, p. 171/172).
2 Serving Spoons. Old English with single drop. Top marked with crests of the Company and City. Richard Richardson (4) 1785/86. (*C.S.*, p. 184).
Small Irish Ash Tray with beaded edge, diameter $3\frac{3}{8}$ inches.
Mustard Pot with blue liner. Maker I.W. within oval. Chester 1823/24. (*C.S.*, p. 213).
Tankard Jubilee Mark. Chester 1935/36.
Silver Dish made by Grahame Jones with the 1962 mark.

Silver

The Company silver is currently on long term deposit at the Ridgway Gallery, Grosvenor Museum, Chester. (see p. 37)

Documents

All minutes books and papers belonging to the Company are on long term deposit in the archives at the Town Hall, Chester.

Recreation

The Company had for long associated itself with the life and pleasurable activities of the City. They had taken part in the City Mystery plays but these had ceased in the 16th century. Contributions towards the Races had also been a feature of the Company but these too had been abandoned perhaps due to the spread of Methodism. Many of the members of the Company had been linked to the visits of John Wesley. The Walker families and the first Lowes were known to have entertained these preachers, and later the Lowes were closely connected with the new chapels, though still retaining their loyalty to their local parish churches. To fill the gap they concentrated upon certain leisure activities planned to satisfy the desires of the apprentices as well as the members. Among the papers rescued from the Assay Office when it closed was a small red morocco leather bound book entitled *Chester Goldsmiths Company, Catalogue of Plate* (see p. 37). It also contains at the end of the book a list of articles which the Company held for 'amusements', and it reveals the nature of the amusements they practiced. The book was probably started by John Lowe in 1841 at the time when the new copper plate was introduced. The list given is as follows.

AMUSEMENTS
1 Kite

RIFLE PRACTICE
1 Target Stand

ROUNDERS
2 Paddles
Balls
With Peg Sticks

ARCHERY
2 Bows
Arrows
1 Target

CRICKET
2 Superior Bats
2 Common Bats
1 Set Wickets
Bails

CRICKET
2 Balls
Football

Records held by the Company

Information supplied by Marilyn Lewis, Chester City Archivist.

A mid sixteenth century book containing the names of those admitted to the Company, the oath of Master, Steward and Assay Master and the minutes of the Company. The minutes continue to 1725 but there are no entries for 1703-1722.

Minute book including orders, election of officers, admissions, etc., 1703-1803.

Minute book 1808-1882.

Minute book including admissions 1882-1964 and admissions 1839-1964.

Account book, 1663-1803.

Letters patent being a licence to the Goldsmiths Company of Chester to hold property in mortmain. Great seal (in original box). 13 June 1862.

Miscellaneous Company papers, comprising eleven documents 1702-1845 including a statement concerning rights of those who have served seven years apprenticeship to set up a trade in the city. 1702.

A declaration by Francis Langton of Liverpool, silversmith and jeweller concerning his crime of making several pairs of silver buckles without having had them hallmarked. 1776.

A statement that goods may be sent for marking in Chester from any part of the Kingdom not within the Birmingham or Sheffield district 1831.

A volume containing certain Acts of 1739-1902.

Chester Assay Office statistics of gold and silver wares 1901-1955.

A list of Chester Assay Masters 1785 to the 20th century.

A miscellaneous collection of papers relating to the Richardson family beginning with extracts from G. Wharton, *Hemerologium: or a Register Astronomical, Meteorological, Chronological for the ears of the World 5605 Christ 1656,* printed by John Grismond, London. This includes Manuscript notes relating to processes used by goldsmiths, and members of the Richardson family. 1661-1794.

Also nine 17th century papers, relating to the Richardson family and Percy Pigott's apprenticeship to Alexander Pulford.

Copies of 102 papers in the custody of Mr Richard Richardson (Tod's Hotel, West Nicholson, Zimbabwe) who was admitted to the freedom of Chester in April 1985 he being a direct descendant of Richard Richardson (1).

In private possession

A book containing a list of plate held by the Company from about 1841, and a list of goods used for recreation.

The Company Banner

Most of the Chester Companies had banners and several of them are preserved in the Grosvenor Museum. The Chester Goldsmiths Company had one and the Chester Archaeological Society asked that it be shown at their meeting on 16 November 1891. The Assay Master (Mr James Ffoulkes Lowe) brought it to the meeting and a note in the Journal says . . .

'he brought his banner painted by Randle Holme'

A note later in the Journal contradicts the name of the painter who was one of the three Randle Holme painters and heralds in the 17th century claiming that it was much later than his time. The older members of the Company at the time of the closure of the Assay Office remember they had seen it but said that it was so dilapidated that they destroyed it.

NOTE. *Chester Archaeological Journal.* NS xviii. p. 158.

'The oldest of the Goldsmiths colours bears the name of George Walker who was Assay Master 1808 and continued so until 1814. The other colour of the Company bears the date 1850'.

(This is inaccurate as George Walker (1) died in 1809.)

Portraits of Company Members

There were several portraits of Assay Masters and Wardens which hung in the Assay walls in Goss Street. They were painted in oils on canvas. Towards the end of the life of the Assay Office, one member who was a keen amateur painter used the canvases for his own work, and regrettably none remain. There is an oil painting of John (1) Lowe which hangs in the shop of Lowe and Sons, Bridge Street Row, Chester, and there are several photographs which have been preserved of earlier members of the Lowe family.

The Company of Goldsmiths after 1962

The Act of 1962 required the closure of the Assay Office but the Company was saved and it reverted to the status it had held before the Act that had established it. The positions of Assay Master were abolished and the offices of Alderman and Steward introduced.

Membership

Until the Assay Office closed, membership was restricted to those who had been apprenticed to a working member of the Company and had served their full term apprenticeship, the necessary indentures being deposited at the Town Hall for safe keeping. Following the closure of the Office it was agreed to extend membership to:

1. Freeman of the City of Chester who had obtained their Freedom through servitude or birthright (i.e. being descended from former members of the Company.).
2. Honorary Freeman.

The Company have also admitted two honorary members who have had strong links with the Company for a considerable time.

The admission of Honorary Members to the Company had been established when it was agreed to admit the then Prime Minister, Mr Lloyd George into the Company. However, due to the Great War he did not take up the offer.

At the time of writing (1996) there are twelve members (including two Honorary Members).

The members of the Goldsmiths' Company of Chester in 1996 are Grahame Jones, Alderman; Peter J. Lowe, Steward; Roger J. Lowe; George F. Lowe; Andrew J. F. Lowe; Anthony J. F. Lowe; R. Geoffrey Richardson; Jeremy P. Williams; Arnold G. Ward; Hugh W. Lowe.

Honorary members are Maurice H. Ridgway and Joyce Lowe.

Gallery, Grosvenor Museum, Chester.

Coat of Arms

The Company appear to have adopted the arms of the London Goldsmiths with a slight variation. This was the Coat of Arms incorporated into the Assay Office building in Goss Street, Chester. When the building was demolished the cartouche was preserved and is currently on display at the Grosvenor Museum, Chester. In 1977, however, the Company at their meeting decided to re-adopt the Coat of Arms as described by Randle Holme in his book *Academy of Armourie* published in 1698.

The Chester Goldsmiths Company Mark of Origin

Following the idea of Canon Maurice Ridgway, the Company sought permission from the Committee of Assay Offices of Great Britain to stamp on Chester made gold, silver and platinum a special mark to denote the place of origin. Authority was granted and the Company agreed to adopt the mark of a single wheatsheaf on a square shield with cut corners. The conditions (inter alia) were agreed as follows:

1. That the stamp be placed at a suitable distance from the hallmark.
2. That the geographical boundaries for qualification be defined as those existing in 1962.
3. That a member of the Company be appointed to be responsilbe for the safety and use of the punches and to maintain a register of the items stamped.

    Alderman Grahame Jones has been appointed to be responsible for the Mark of Origin.

Table showing the amount of wares that have been marked with the City of Origin Mark, Chester

Year	9 ct	14 ct	18 ct	22 ct	Platinum	Silver
1988	4	—	56	—	—	8
1989	30	—	83	1	5	1
1990	45	—	56	8	4	—
1991	125	—	273	3	8	42
1992	53	—	180	5	3	3
1993	96	—	74	9	6	9
1994	36	—	45	2	6	1
1995	32	1	145	6	10	2
Total	421	1	910	34	42	66

Total number of wares marked (to 1 November 1995) 1,474

Greg Mora, of O. C. Jewellery, Manufactory and Design, Abbey Green, Chester

Walton, of Lowe and Sons, Bridge Street Row, Chester.

Eric Irwin, Northgate Street, Chester.

Notable Pieces with the City of Origin Mark, Chester

THE FRANCIS LOWE MEMORIAL BLADE

Francis known as Frank or Buddy to his family and friends was born in 1916 and was indentured to serve a term of seven years apprenticeship as a Goldsmith and Assayer at the Chester Assay Office. He was admitted to the Worshipful Company of Goldsmiths and became a Freeman of the City of Chester by Indenture on 30 October 1937. In 1939 he was enlisted for the Second World War and when hostilities ended he returned to the Assay Office and his workmanship was of the highest order. When the threat of closure was threatened he fought to keep the Assay open, this he failed to do and it closed 24 August 1962 by Act of Parliament. Shortly afterwards he joined the sales team at Boodle and Dunthorne at their Eastagte Street shop and remained there until he retired becoming an Alderman of the Goldsmiths' Company. He died suddenly 5 February 1991 aged 74 years.

He had a great love of the river from youth, founding with others the Motor Boat Club. He had an abundant knowledge of the river based upon his own experience.

It was a very happy thought that the Chester Goldsmiths Company at the suggestion of Alderman Grahame Jones should wish to give a blade in his memory to be awarded annually to the outstanding lady or gentleman members of the Chester based Dee rowing clubs. Melted into the ingot were old sterling silver trophies which had been won by the Lowe family. The ingot was then wrought by hand into a replica of a rowing blade by a Chester Goldsmith, but was sent to the Sheffield Assay Office for marking. The Goldsmiths Company then struck the Mark of Origin (a single wheatsheaf, on the blade).

The rowing trophies which were melted down were

1876	J. F. Lowe (Cox)
1904	R. Lowe (3), J. Lowe (Stroke)
1966	R. Lowe (Bow)

The winners of the Francis Lowe Oar receive a replica of the blade to keep for themselves.

(Contributed by Grahame Jones
Worshipful Company of Goldsmiths)

THE SPIRIT OF CHESTER BOWL

The bowl and stand was presented by Lowe and Sons, Chester to commemorate the opening of the Ridgway (silver) Gallery at the Grosvenor Museum, Chester in 1992, by H.R.H. The Prince of Wales. The diameter of the bowl is 8 inches. Total height 1.95 inches. Weight of bowl 11.5 ounces and of the stand 2.25 ounces.

The bowl has a wide flat rim with convex bowl. The centre of the bowl is engraved with a six pointed star, based on the face of the clock on the Eastgate. The rim is engraved with six half timbered gables in two alternating designs representing the black and white buildings for which Chester is renowned. Engraved in Gothic Script round the inner rim is an inscription recalling the nature of the presentation and on the reverse rim, 'Designed by Rachel Walton'. There are five marks on the rim, the Sponsor's mark (L & S within a shield) for Lowe and Sons, Sheffield Assay Office mark, Lion passant, Date letter and City of Origin mark. There are two marks on the stand, Lion passant and the Date letter.

Rachel Walton is the daughter of Edward Walton the Jewellers of Chester and the present owner of Lowe and Sons. Rachel Walton in 1986-90 took a B.A.(Hon.) degree at Middlesex Polytechnic. After working as manager of Reema Pachachi's Fashion Jewellery in Fulham in 1991, she has been a fashion designer and precious stone sorter with Fred E. Ullman in Hatton Garden, London.

Information from Peter Boughton,
Grosvenor Museum.

The Relationship Between the Company and the Assaying of Silver and Gold in Chester

From perhaps the 15th century the assaying of silver at Chester had been carried on through the Goldsmiths Guild, one of the many City Companies at Chester. They claimed the right to do so by a Statute made in the third year of King Henry the Fourth and the supervision of their duties was conducted by the Master and Wardens who were to see that . . .

> '. . . all plate and other worke that can beare a touch of gold or silver to be assayed by the said Wardens or their Deputyes, and that all plate or other work which upon tryall shall be found sterling or Standard shall be touched and Marked by the Wardens or their Deputy if it be found defective to be broken in pieces'.

This is taken from the long statement drawn up on 1 February 1686/7 which goes on to state that the marks to be used on the assayed silver were to be the coat and crest of the City of Chester on two separate punshons with a letter for the year. These were called the Wardens marks. The statement was signed by Peter Edwardes, Master, Ralph Walley and Peter Edwardes, Wardens, and five other Goldsmiths of the City. Previous to this statement the Master had been called Alderman, and the single title of Steward, usually given to a junior Goldsmith was now given to the two Wardens. The oaths of the Assay Master and of the Wardens are then given in full. Within a short time, on 25 March 1697 no Goldsmith in the country was permitted to work in silver less in fineness than 11 oz 10 dwts in every pound Troy. This statute meant that all Assay Offices, except London, were suspended. It was a severe blow to the provisional offices at York, Exeter, Bristol, Norwich and Chester. Eventually, a further Statute had to be passed in 1700/1 which re-established an Assay Office at Chester and at places where 'mints were lately erected for recoining the silver money of the Kingdom', these were York, Exeter, Bristol, Norwich and Chester and slightly later Newcastle. The mint at Chester in William IIIs reign had opened in October 1696 and lasted until June 1698. Coins only 1696 and 1697. The Chester Goldsmiths exercised their ancient privilege of assay alongside the new moneyers at the Chester Castle Mint. The Company continued to meet during this period, accept new members and apparently made plate. When

49

the new Act came into force, the Company accepted the new rules of the Act, by using the new Chester mark, a new series of date letters and new marks for the Chester Goldsmiths. They abandoned their earlier copper plate (now missing or lost) and instituted a new copper plate upon which Goldsmiths and Silversmiths from many areas recorded their marks, including those of watchcase makers. This copper plate smothered in marks, was to last until 1840 and is now on loan to the Grosvenor Museum.

In this way the Chester Goldsmiths were able to provide a continuity with the Plate Assay Act of 1700 although the relationship was anything but clear. Sir Leonard Stone in the Report of the Departmental Committee on Hallmarking, presented to Parlitament in March 1959, drew attention to this in an appendix where it states that until 1700 the Goldsmiths at Chester never had any other status than that of a Craft Fraternity, and that the Company set up by the statute of 1700 did not inherit any property from the Craft Fraternity except minute books and documents, these being the only inheritance of the new Company. In spite of these observations the legal ownership of the minute books and other documents of the Chester Craft Fraternity of Goldsmiths and since 1701 of the Company of Goldsmiths is open to considerable doubt. The members assumed membership of the new Statutory Incorporation. This laid the foundation of a subsequent bitter quarrel.

When eventually the report of the Stone Committee came before the House of Lords on 4 April 1962, only that part which affected Chester and the closure of the Assay Office there, was presented for a third reading, as a Private Bill, which included the dissolution of the Chester Company of Goldsmiths. It was the Bishop of Chester who drew attention to this and as a result saved the Company by means of an amendment.

In the recently published definitive work *British coin weights* by Paul and Bente Withers, published by Galata Print Ltd. (1994) it is noted that an extremely important duty of the Assay Master was to punch his mark on coin weights. It was not known whether this had applied in Chester until recently, for it did not apply to all Assay Offices. When verified, weights were stamped by the Assay Master (as at Chester), or by an anchor at Birmingham, and a lion in Sheffield. Chester we now know had the initials of the Assay Master and the lion passant marks put there by the Assay Master towards the end of the 18th century with his own mark (at Chester in 1774 for John Scasebrick). At this period coins from overseas were in use in this country and had to be weighed, there was also the risk of counterfeit coinage being used which had to be tested against an authorised standard weight. There are interesting references to this in *Adam's Weekly Courant*.

Tuesday, August 31, 1773.

'Chester. August 31. We hear from the Assay Master of this City that he daily expects from his Majesty's Director of the Mint, Standards, to enable him to adjust the Money Weights and Scales'.

In *Adam's Weekly Courant October 12, 1773* there is an advertisement placed by John Thomas, Pewterer, Brazier, and Scale Maker near the Cross in Chester saying . . .

'. . . that the weights have not been entrusted to the care of a second Person, but have been most exactly adjusted by himself, and to distinguish them from those sold by others are all stamped with the initial letters of his Name . . .'

John Thomas had no authority to take the place of the official Assay Master at Chester and this was pointed out in a further extract from *Adam's Weekly Courant 8 February 1774.*

'John Scasebrick, Assay Master, in this City having complaints that the money weights by him sold, or adjusted are not heavy enough, begs leave to inform the public, that he strictly followed the example of the Bank of England, and the most eminent Banker in London, and can produce the best Authority for making the Guinea Weight 5 Pennyweights 3 grains, the half and Quarter in proportion. And all other Weights of 5 Pennyweights 3 grains and a half, rather more, of which sort there have been numbers sold by a Tradesman in this City, are an imposition on the Public.
N.B. Money Weights and Scales of the true Standard by the said John Scasebrick at his Room on the city Walls, opposite Sir Robert Cunliffe.'

and again on 30 August 1774 in the *Adam's Weekly Courant* . . .

'John Scasebrick, Assay Master takes this method to acquaint the Public, that he has just returned from London, and brought down a large quantity of Act of Parliament Money Weights of 5 dwts 8 grs and 5 dwts 6 grs, with halves and quarters, which are all accurately adjusted by a Standard Set of Weights he had from His Majesty's Assay Master at the Mint.
    The above weights are sold at his Rooms at Mrs Jordan's, the Top of Clayton Lane, or at Mrs Harvey's Shop, the Bottom of Northgate St.
N.B. All weights adjusted and sold by me, will be marked with the Lion and the letters J.S. which Weights I will uphold to be the true Standard.'

Only four examples of the Mark of John Scasebrick are known. It does not appear on the copper plate as he did not make silver, but the marks are found on coin weights accompanied by the mark of the lion passant. (See P. & B. R. Withers, *British Coin weights,* p. 337 and illustration 55 of this volume).

The Chester Assay Office

Chester had for long played an important part in the marking of silver, and later of gold. In the early years this had been controlled by the Chester Guild or Company alone and its wares were made by goldsmiths who were connected with the Company, which also took an important part in the life of the City. With the 1700/1 Act the Company, deprived, with other provincial centres by the 1696 from assaying, was invited to assay silver and gold once more on the grounds that a mint had been established there. The Act opened the doors to anyone who registered their mark at Chester to qualify for this privilege. New marks had to be registered and a new City mark was to be used, as well as a new set of annual date letters. This presented the Company and Assay Master with many new problems, especially in the control of the marking of silver, and the subsequent search for those who were trying to pass off sub standard silver. There was now no longer any need for them to be linked as brothers in the Company and on the earliest surviving copper plate of 1701 marks appear of persons who came from Shrewsbury, Knutsford, Warrington, and elsewhere. Within a few years many more came to register their marks and had their silver marked at Chester but who had nothing to do with the City and its corporate life. There were still others in the early 18th century who continued to avoid the assay rules. Among them the Liverpool based goldsmith Benjamin Brancker and Robert Shields, though the former is reported to have been accepted as a member of the Company, although his mark is not recorded on the copper plate nor are any specimens of his work known with the Chester mark. Towards the end of the 18th century the Liverpool silversmiths including Robert Jones, Joseph Walley, Thomas Helsby and Nicholas Cunliffe and a number of watchcase makers registered their marks at Chester and made use of the Assay Office there.

The copper plate was not renewed until 1841 and an enormous number of silversmiths, watchcase makers, ring and buckle makers, button and medal makers registered their marks.

By the beginning of the 19th century there were few Chester based goldsmiths and fewer still who were members of the Company. This was partly due to the fact that membership qualifications demanded patrimony or an apprenticeship to a member for seven years, where strict terms of behaviour had to be observed. Women were not admitted to the Company which ruling disqualified Mary Huntingdon who submitted silver of various kinds from 1815 and who lived and worked in Chester. Sheffield and Birmingham had in 1773 managed to get permission to assay plate but by its rules were prevented from admitting anyone beyond (at first) a radius of twenty five miles, a restriction which was lifted in 1854. Chester and London had no such restriction so when it was lifted from Sheffield and Birmingham work came to Chester. London makers especially the toy makers and lesser silversmiths used Chester, as they found it more convenient and quicker. The Liverpool watchcase makers also provided much extra trade.

The nature of their work after the period of the Plate Duty books can only be judged from surviving examples. The Plate Duty books survive only from 1784/5 to 1840, three volumes only and the third volume ends rather abruptly. During those years the names of silversmiths submitting silver to Chester with an indication usually of their place of origin, the type of silver being sent, the weight, the Duty payable are fully recorded. These all received the extra punch showing that duty had been paid on both gold and silver. The watchcase makers were no longer included after 1798 and their names no longer appear, unless they submitted small gold or silver boxes which they made as a sideline.

After 1840 it is necessary to turn to the remaining registration books now kept at Birmingham.

In the first two of these volumes of registrations which cover 1863 to 1876 and 1877 to 1885 there are 427 registrations made by individuals or firms. 267 from Birmingham, 75 from London, 45 from Coventry, 27 from Liverpool, 17 from Manchester, 4 from Bristol, 3 each from Hull and Derby, 2 each from Newcastle on Tyne, Belfast and Chester. One each from Bradford, Dublin, Halifax, Rugby, Bury, Leeds, Glasgow, and Leamington Spa. The third volume runs from 1894 (April 28) to 1905 (July 29). Here the registrations come from a much wider field. Stirling, Taunton, Rhosllannerchrugog, Londonderry, Dublin, Belfast, Bombay, Geneva and Melbourne (Australia) in fact almost every part of the United Kingdom and many other parts of the world. A fourth volume runs from 1905 to 1921.

The conflict and rivalry which was apparent during the 19th century was partly due to the relationship between industrially manufactured silver and Sheffield plate which catered for the demands of a middle class, and the individual designs of craftsmen whose work was more costly to produce. The influence of tastes spurred by foreign designs prompted the silversmiths to plagiarize them. This had been the policy of the industrialist Matthew Boulton at Birmingham working in the mid 18th century. He frequently and blatantly copied other designs both from England and abroad rather than develop his own. This was followed in London by Rundell, Bridge and Rundell, who employed five hundred workmen producing quite

53

remarkable silver. Pugin and Flaxman were responsible for many of the designs. But there was a whole range of silversmiths whose names are unrecorded who were responsible for their finished silver. Some of their original designers and craftsmen were eventually able to launch out on their own, a notable example being Paul Storr.

For these persons the London Hall was close at hand and most of their work was assayed there. Birmingham had its own Assay after 1773 and also felt the influence of Pugin and Hardman who were both Birmingham men. It was to them that the great Catholic revival both Anglican and Roman turned to equip their new churches. The influence of the French Roman Catholic escapees and the Catholic Emancipation Act in 1835 enabled the Catholic Church to build the Cathedral of St Chad at Birmingham in 1841. A. W. N. Pugin became champion of the gothic revival which showed itself in the numerous churches built under the influence of the Oxford Movement. He had become a Roman Catholic in 1835 and was in close partnership with John Hardman another Roman Catholic. Together they produced some outstanding gothic revival silver for their congregations, ciboria, flagons and even the Canterbury processional Cross.

John Hardman and Son continued to use many of the original designs, and added to their number those of George E. Street, John H. Powell and William Burgess all of which carry the Hardman mark, designers being overlooked in the interests of the manufacturers. Elkingtons also concentrated upon the massive production for the 1851 Exhibition.

Whilst all this activity was taking place at London, Birmingham and Sheffield, Chester received none of their goods after 1773 when Matthew Boulton was compelled to leave Chester for his own Assay at Birmingham. There seems to be strong evidence to support the idea that both James Duke, Richard Richardson (4) and John Walker of Chester and possibly Robert Jones of Liverpool sometimes used London or Sheffield makers and had their works assayed at Chester. The quality and extent of the work from the London and Birmingham firms were their own advertisement. The richer middle classes and the new churches of the north west which had benefited from the Industrial Revolution turned to Birmingham and London and those who registered at Chester, after 1854, received only small items.

Although Sheffield played an important part in assaying silver their concentration upon Sheffield plate and other plated wares, made them no rival to the Birmingham and London manufacturers. Their work was concentrated upon the firm of James Dixon and Sons and later on Walker and Hall (who registered their mark at Chester, 4 January 1907).

The Chester Plate Duty Books show that between 1784 and 1840 there were 121 different registrations at Chester, of whom only 13 were Chester makers compared with at least 43 from Liverpool and 13 from Manchester. The appearance of William Pugh a Birmingham gold worker from 1810 to

1814 seems odd. Between these dates he produced nine gold boxes some of them described as 'snuff boxes'. Sir Charles Jackson mentions him at Birmingham where he also registered his mark. At this period William Pugh was not supposed to send silver to Chester. Robert Bowers, the Lowes, the Walkers and the last of the Richardsons represent the working goldsmiths from the Chester Company and J. Falconer, Mary Huntingdon and the Twemlow family represent the non Company goldsmiths and watch-case makers.

As noted elsewhere George Lowe (1) had served his apprenticeship in London where he seems to have been an apprentice to the Bateman family. He registered his mark first in London in 1791 as a smallworker. The quantity of letters in the Lowe archives seem to indicate this, and he kept in touch with the Batemans after he returned to Chester. The Chester City punch bowls were made by them and there is a tea urn in the City collection which carries the mark of Peter, Ann and William Bateman with the London assay mark for 1801, which has been overstruck by George Lowe. The infuser attached to the urn has the mark of Paul Storr who had first registered his mark at London in 1807. In the Lowe Day Book is an entry for . . .

a tea kitchen weighing 89 ounces 15 dwts for £24.13.8 from Messrs Bateman.

Later in 1830/31 a small bachelor tea pot (see *Chester Silver* p. 109 illustrated 43) was made by George Lowe and the decoration of naturalistic flowers and leaves on the lid finial seems to show that a London connection was still maintained.

The extensive watchcase industry in and around Liverpool, which spread into Yorkshire and Derbyshire, kept the Chester Assay Office busy and this continued when the duty on them was withdrawn in 1798. Ring making in gold and making of buckles, clasps, buttons and other small items in silver were not exempted by this rule and this too brought considerable trade to the Assay Office. The duty continued to be paid and marked with a special punch on items other than watchcases until 1890.

The import of foreign silver caused the government to draw up a statute in 1867 which provided the mark of an F within an oval along with the importers punch and the City mark to be struck on such silver after its standard had been approved. The mark was to be placed there by the Assay Office nearest to the port of entry. In this case both Chester and London provided a suitable office. Liverpool and Chester were neighbours, which accounts for the large number of Chester marked pieces of imported silver.

For a short time Liverpool became an important source of flat ware firstly by John Coakley 1828, who was followed by John Sutter(s) in 1835. Manchester also provided silversmiths who concentrated upon flat ware. Thomas Olivant of Manchester however sent his wares to London. Patrick Leonard of Salford (who also registered at Sheffield in 1835), seems to be the same person as the Patrick 'Landra' mentioned in the Plate Duty Books in 1835 (otherwise unknown). Manchester silversmiths were also asked to make medals, in particular John and Joseph Armstrong and Thomas Newton. Isaac Simmons from St. Anne's Square, Manchester registering his mark at Chester and also Sheffield in 1839. He was responsible for numerous badges, both for the masons and for members of Oddfellows' Societies. His mark which is found on Sheffield assayed medals as well and on Chester ones, an IS within a square. He also cast the coats of arms which occupy the centre of the medals and his name Isaac Simmons is found on some as part of the casting. These Manchester silversmiths were continuing a long tradition which had been established in the City in the 16th century when a Robert Welshman is found there and a Ralph Bexwick whose son Gyles was baptised in 'the old church' (now Manchester Cathedral) in 1612 ('late of Manchester'). Martin Cundlyve was buried there in 1620, (probably a relation of Edward Cunliffe 1568) and Richard Wayte had his children baptised there during the Commonwealth.

The Liverpool tradition was also of great antiquity. An early reference is made to Michael Ith in 1415. Edward Holme of Knowsley died 1628, and with the coming of Edward Lewis who settled in Water Street in 1672 and his assistant Robert Shields who took over his shop when Edward died in 1691. The Brancker family followed him and then the Jones and Walley partnership, maintaining the goldsmith tradition well into the 18th century. After the time of John Sutter there appears a goldsmith William Smith who used an incuse mark similar to those attributed to watchcase makers, but added an inscription 'W. Smith Sculpt' on the few elaborate and very eastern looking pieces made between 1875 and 1879 which were assayed at Chester.

In the very centre of this extraordinary century was the Great Exhibition of 1851 in Hyde Park. An enormous amount of work went into this, and almost every aspect of the machine age was on show. The silversmiths vied with each other to produce elaborate pieces and spent much time in presentation pieces and gigantic dinner services which could only have felt at home in an industrialist's mansion. Taste was sacrificed in the interests of over elaboration and price. The later Exhibition of 1862 seemed to dwell on the designs of the earlier, and glory once more in much repetition and the results of machine production.

There was soon to be a reaction to this and the exhibits displayed at the Great Exhibition. Although many felt strongly that a change was inevitable it eventually centred on William Morris and his group of like minded socialists, who within ten years of the exhibition had set up the Arts and Crafts Movement. This was a return to the satisfaction of hand made crafts. Ruskin shared this vision and formed the Guild of St George in 1871 on which he had spent a great deal of money.

It was a deliberate attempt to destroy the results that he saw in an impersonal industrial society. The Guild failed, but his ideals were taken up by others. Mistakes were made in the early years for their claim to return to a 'pure medieval style' with the accompanying 'satisfaction and joy' of the hand made. It could not compete with the demands for the produce. Victorian society was wholly different from the medieval one, and the joys of craftsmanship did not automatically guarantee quality. Arthur H. Mackmurdo and Selwyn Imago formed the Century Guild in 1881. The Art Workers' Guild followed in 1884, joined by 'the Fifteen' led by Lewis F. Day, and Walter Crane; its members included William Morris, Edwyn Lutyens and Roger Fry. They truned their hands to designs of many kinds, and let others produce them. Walter Crane had for a while been Director of Design at Manchester Municipal College (1883) before going to the Victoria and Albert Museum in 1887. His influence had far reaching effects upon the students who attended his lectures and in consequence smaller groups arose reflecting his influence. In Cheshire, Fred H. Crossley, working in wood and copper, together with Charles Bebington of Weaverham, was one such group that ceased working in 1914 due to the war. The Group was based upon the principles of William Morris which included 'handmade and no sandpaper'. Such persons did not use the larger commercial firms to retail their goods because their production was so limited and depended upon individual orders. The more ambitious turned to Liberty's of Regent Street, London. After the Paris Exhibition the Arts and Crafts movement became known as the 'Art Nouveau' and its influence was felt throughout Europe and the United States. Because of the commercial interests involved it led to the use of many of the principles and practices which William Morris and others had fought to defend.

Liberty's had been founded by Arthur Lazenby Liberty. He had bought the exhibits from the Japanese Exhibition (1862) after it had closed down in 1874. It had had some influence in curtailing the flambuoyancy of the Mid Victorians, and his shop became a useful means of handling the products of the craft guilds which had grown up throughout the country, on the continent and in America. Unfortunately the work done for Liberty's had to carry the Liberty mark when assayed and as such the name and work of many excellent silversmiths and designers did not survive. As the demands increased so did mass production. Original designs were sometimes changed to suit the trade or customer. Archibald Knox from the Isle of Man, Bernard Cuzner, Rex Silver, and Jessie King from Kirkcudbright were all associated with Liberty's who adopted the title 'Cymric' for their silver, a name derived from the decoration on the *Book of Kells* and other celtic sources. It is interesting to note that Iverna Cubbin, a Cheshire silversmith from Wirral developed some of the ideas enshrined in the Cymric style and registered her mark at Chester in 1922.

The attempt to popularise 'native' work was shown by Alex Ritchie who worked on Iona and used the trade name of Iona Celtic Art. He registered his incuse mark at Chester AR on 9 May 1910. He was sponsored by Saunders and Shepherd of Holborn Circus, London who had also registered at Chester.

A series of paddle-like oars is known assayed at Chester. They have sharp blades and paddle like knobs to the end of the handles. They display date letters around 1911. Their purpose is difficult to ascertain. It has been suggested that they may have been given as awards at regattas, but the sharp blades are against this idea. They were made by John Millward Banks (a Birmingham firm) and may perhaps have been an attempt at a type of Art Nouveau table knife.

A complete departure was made by the Birmingham based company of George Nathan and Ridley Hayes. They catered for the increased interest in the recent antiquarian finds in the middle east and other regions and produced a large series of reproduction articles usually in silver gilt, of the finds made by Schliemann and others. Although they registered their mark at Birmingham in 1894 they used a distinctive mark at Chester of GN above RH within an ornamental shield. This was used on all plate made in the antique style.

Nathan and Hayes were not alone in producing articles of antique interest. The firm of Frederick James Ross of Winchester registered first at London 3 December 1904 and then using a slightly different mark at Chester 28 August 1905. His firm traded as J. Ross and Sons at 43/44 High Street, Winchester. The mark used at Chester was F.J.R. within a rectangle. They produced small silver copies of the Winchester bushell which is kept at the City Museum. These were $2\frac{1}{2}$ inches in diameter. They also made spoons of seal top type having a figure of the trusty servant on the head which was a copy of the portrait hanging in Winchester College showing a composite figure made up of sheep, ass and pig with a human body holding a collection of utensils and having a padlock on his mouth. (see *Finial*, February 1994, the monthly journal of the Silver Spoon Society.)

Coronation spoons, copies in various sizes of the anointing spoon of silver gilt, date from the time of the coronation of Edward VII. Lowe and Son of Chester produced the spoon and two pronged fork which had been in the possession of the Duke of Rutland at the time of the jubilee of George V and Queen Mary.

In Cumberland, Canon Rawnsley one of the founding members of the National Trust, formed the Keswick School of Art in 1884. It developed into the Keswick Industries and Robert Hilton became the Director. He had moved from Meliden in North Wales and settled first at Allerford near Taunton and first registered his mark at Chester 11 May 1896. In 1905 he registered his new mark at Chester KSIA (Keswick School of

Industrial Arts) when he was working at Northgate, Chester and then moved to Keswick 12 April 1905.

The makers' CS*FS, for Cornelius Saunders and Francis Shepherd Limited, Bartlett's Passage Buildings, Holborn Circus, London who registered at Chester 25 January 1884 and 1 December 1899, made many miniature silver pieces based upon earlier designs. In the Glasgow Art Gallery is a curious nursery pepper pot in the shape of a child's horse on wheels with a cylindrical body dated 1903. (illustration 32)

After the First World War, the making of silver declined at Chester and the Assay Office relied upon the enormous quantity of silver which came from elsewhere including such large firms as Walker and Hall (Sheffield) Alfred E. Jones (Birmingham), Charles Horner (Halifax) etc.

When the Second World War ended, silver ceased to be made by Lowe and Sons at Chester and the other Chester based firms also relied upon larger manufacturers. There was however an encouraging growth in the number of individuals who were sending their work to Chester from outside the City. Among them Iverna Cubbin of Little Caldy in Wirral. She registered her mark at Chester in 1922 and when the Assay Office closed at Chester, at London. Specimens of her remarkable work can be seen at the Williamson Art Gallery, Birkenhead. Chester also attracted some remarkable silversmiths who like Iverna Cubbin worked alone. Among them John Christopher Webb, then working at St Albans who provided the two church-wardens staves for Bunbury which carry the Chester mark for 1961/2. When the office closed he turned back to London and in his later years concentrated upon making silver flutes, many of which went to Japan.

Commercially speaking the National festivals of the Jubilee of George V and Queen Mary helped the silver trade, but ironically the notice that the Chester Assay Office was to close in 1962 produced an enormous amount of Chester silver carrying the capital M date letter. Much older designs were reproduced for this. Lowe's issued two complete sets of Apostle spoons based upon traditional 17th century spoons, with a gold Christus, and a series of Armada dishes were also popular as well as tumbler cups and Georgian style candelabra.

Assay Masters at Chester

JOHN SCASEBRICK. Appointed 21 October 1763. Died in office 1 December 1784.

RICHARD RICHARDSON (4). Appointed 28 January 1785. Resigned 19 March 1791.

GEORGE WALKER (1). Appointed March 1791. Died in office 1809.

JOHN WALKER. Appointed 16 March 1809. Took oath 1819. Appointment revoked 1 April 1840.

GEORGE LOWE (1). Appointed 1 April 1840. Died in office 28 December 1841.

THOMAS LOWE. Appointed 30 December 1841. Resigned 27 October 1864.

JAMES FOULKES LOWE. Appointed 27 October 1864. Died in office 27 March 1911.

RICHARD EDWARD TATLER. Appointed 4 April 1911. Resigned 1915.

WILLIAM FOULKES LOWE. Appointed 1 July 1915. Died in office November 1931.

FRANK ERNEST CLARK. Appointed 19 November 1931. Resigned November 1954.

ARTHUR VINCENT WARD. Appointed 30 December 1954. Resigned on the closure of the Assay Office 24 August 1962.

Chester Assay Plates and Books

(Contributed by Philip Priestley)

1.	Plate Number 1	Makers' Marks and Assay Marks 1701 to 1840
2.	Plate Number 2	Makers' Marks and Assay Marks 1841 to 1860
3.	Plate Number 3	Makers' Marks and Assay Marks 1861 to 1883
4.	Plate Number 4	Chester Assay Marks 1883 to 1888
5.	Plate Number 5	Makers' Marks 1883 to 1898
6.	Plate Number 6	Chester Assay Marks 1888 to 1901
7.	Plate Number 7	Chester Assay Marks 1896 to 1897
8.	Plate Number 8	Chester Assay Marks 1897
9.	Plate Number 9	Makers' Marks 1898 to 1907
10.	Plate Number 10	Chester Assay Marks 1898 to 1906
11.	Plate Number 11	Chester Assay Marks 1902
12.	Plate Number 12	Chester Assay Marks 1902
13.	Plate Number 13	Makers' Marks 1902 to 1912
14.	Plate Number 14	Chester Assay Marks 1907 to 1916
15.	Plate Number 15	Makers' Marks 1912 to 1936
16.	Plate Number 16	Chester Assay Marks 1912 to 1922
17.	Plate Number 17	Chester Assay Marks 1915 to 1922
18.	Plate Number 18	Chester Assay Marks 1922 to 1935
19.	Plate Number 19	Chester Assay Marks 1923 to 1940
20.	Plate Number 20	Chester Assay Marks 1935 to 1954
21.	Plate Number 21	Makers' Marks 1936 to 1962
22.	Plate Number 22	Chester Assay Marks 1942 to 1962
23.	Plate Number 23	Chester Assay Marks 1954 to 1962
24.	Plate Numbers 24 to 33	Makers' Marks 1883 to 1885

25. Small Punch Book with Makers' Marks 1863 to 1877
    (Transliteration by Philip Priestley)
26. Large Punch Book with Makers' Marks 1877 to 1886
    (Transliteration by Philip Priestley)
27. Photographic facsimile of the large Punch Book
28. Register of Makers' Marks and their trade 24 April 1894 to 19 July 1905
29. Register of Makers' Marks and their trade 1905 to 1921
30. Register of Makers' Marks and their trade 1921 to 1962
31. Plate Duty Record Book 1784 to 1809
32. Plate Duty Record Book 1809 to 1837
33. Plate Duty Record Book 1837 to 1840
34. Day Ledger. Salaries etc., 1856 to 1882
35. Register of Assay Punches 1899 to 1921
36. Register of Assay Punches 1921 to 1935
37. Register of Assay Punches 1935 to 1962
38. Foreign and English Wardes Assayed. weights. 1913 to 1962
39. Watchcases. Numbers weights and value 1934 to 1962
40. Work Record Book. Numbers, weights and value 1937 to 1962
41. Silverwares. Makers' Type, numbers 1934 to 1947
42. Day Book Goldwares Makers' Type numbers 1960 to 1962
43. Day Book Silverwares Makers' Type numbers 1947 to 1962
44. Day Book Goldwares Makers' Type numbers 1934 to 1940
45. Day Book Goldwares Makers' Type numbers 1940 to 1954
46. Day Book Goldwares Makers' Type numbers 1954 to 1959

NOTE. The records 31 to 46 are at present housed in the Birmingham Public Library because the Assay Office is short of space.

Apart from the membership roster of the Chester Goldsmiths' Company which included only Chester workers, the earliest surviving written records of Goldsmiths who actually used the Chester Assay Office are the three Plate Duty Books covering the period from the end of 1784 to 1809, 1809 to 1837 and 1838 to 1840. Although there are no makers' marks in these books, the first volume does show watchcase makers and other workers names and the volume of business up to 1798 when duty was removed on watchcases. Thereafter the watchcase makers are mentioned only where they occasionally submitted both gold and silver boxes.

The first records showing the makers' mark, name and address, but not trade, started in 1863. The workers' trade was introduced for the first time in the 1894 register. Between these dates the trade of the silversmiths has been identified from Trade directories, and from the London and Birmingham Assay Office records. Additional information has been extracted from Jackson's publication and it seems clear that Jackson used the records of the Chester Goldsmiths Company, the Plate Duty Books and trade directories for most of his work on Chester. He may also have had access to the register covering the period 1886 to 1894 which book now seems to be missing. There exists however a copper plate number 5 covering 1883 to 1898 which overlaps this information gap. One helpful aspect has been the realisation that some workers used the same punch at several offices, presumably because punches were expensive.

Chester Plates 1 to 23 are made of copper, some are flat whilst others are curved. There is a curious mark on the reverse side of plate 1 which has been claimed as a makers' mark and been identified as such by Jackson. It was reported to be on a spoon then in Breadalbane Collection which Jackson had examined, and was reported to be associated with a pre 1700 date letter (A): it could not have been linked with the newly formed Assay Office and was therefore either a copper makers' mark or a deliberate link with the old regime.

The small and large punch books contain metal sheets (possibly lead or tin) on parchment or cartridge paper, and are very heavy. The makers' marks are punched both on to the sheets and onto the corresponding copper plate. The writing in the small and large books is deteriorating and will only be a matter of time before the writing is illegible, hence the reason for the computerised records of these two books. There is a photographic facsimile of the large punch book held in the Birmingham Assay Office.

The Registers of Makers' marks from 1894 contain trade details and a reference code (up to three digits) which enables a cross reference to be made to the corresponding plate. All copper plates are divided into squares. The first plate started with squares being allocated individually (to the early 1701 to 1780) Chester makers but later the plate was covered with sporadic markings to 1840. Other plates show makers' marks in alphabetically orientated squares.

Registrations at Chester

REGISTRATIONS OF SILVERSMITHS AT CHESTER AS RECORDED IN THE CHESTER DUTY BOOKS 1784-1840 (No watchcase makers after 1798).

Liverpool 49. Chester 13. Manchester 12. Birmingham 2 (doubtful) 6.

REGISTRATIONS AT THE CHESTER ASSAY OFFICE 1863-1876
(Some firms registered more than once)

Coventry 52. Liverpool 51. Manchester 12. London 11. Chester 6. Birmingham 5. Preston 2. Belfast 2. Bolton 2. Birkenhead 1. Whitehaven 1. Blackburn 1. Lancaster 1. Llandudno 1. Dublin 1. Southport 1. Kendal 1. Rochdale 1.

1877-1885

Birmingham 286. London 75. Coventry 45. Liverpool 27. Manchester 17. Bristol 4. Hull 3. Derby 3. Belfast 2. Newcastle on Tyne 2. Edinburgh 2. Chester 2. Dublin 1. Bradford 1. Halifax 1. Rugby 1. Bury 1. Leeds 1. Glasgow 1. Leamington Spa 1.

1894-1904

Birmingham 260. London 185. Manchester 64. Coventry 25. Liverpool 21. Glasgow 12. Sheffield 8. Halifax 5. Accrington 5. Newcastle on Tyne 4. Leeds 4. Middlesbrough 4. Chester 4. Bolton 4. Prescot 3. Bradford 3. Altrincham 3. Dublin 3. Hull 2. Grimsby 2. Belfast 2. Northampton 2. Worcester 2. Aberdeen 2. Melbourne (Australia) 2. Eton College 1. Taunton (later Rhyl) 1. Preston 1. Leek 1. Leicester 1. Wellington 1. Gloucester 1. Nottingham 1.

1905 - January 1921

By far the greater number came from Birmingham 523. The second highest from London 371. Manchester 69. Liverpool 42. Sheffield 31. Glasgow 23. Coventry 15. Leeds 13. Chester 15.

It should be remembered that a large number of the registrations at Chester were from minor silversmiths, jewellers, pipe makers and umbrella makers who preferred to put a mark on what might be a very small piece of silver, not normally requiring an assay mark, but who wished to advertise it as silver. In addition to these places of origin were a large number of centres sending from either one place or more. Bristol 9. Oldham 9. Belfast 8. Edinburgh 8. Bradford 6.

The Income and Expenditure of the Assay Office in the 19th Century

The Chester Plate Duty Books record the duty raised from assaying Gold and Silver between the end of 1784 and 1840.

The Report from the select Committee on Gold and Silver wares and the proceedings of the Committee including the minutes of Evidence, which were ordered to be printed by the House of Commons 1 May 1856 contain a report on the receipts and expenditure of the Assay Office for the years 1846 to 1855 and state that the income received from the Chester Office largely relied upon the assaying of watchcases. This varies (and increased) over the years stated. Watchcases certainly provided most of the income but as the accounts show this came from 'marking gold and silver watchcases, gold and silver plate, and private assays of gold and silver'

1846	£294.18.11$\frac{1}{2}$.
1847	£285.15.04.
1848	£292.12.09$\frac{1}{2}$.
1849	£291.12.09$\frac{1}{2}$.
1850	£617.00.09.
1851	£756.09.04.
1852	£814.13.02.
1853	£994.01.11$\frac{1}{2}$.
1854	£995.02.11.
1855	£965.18.02.

If one of these years is examined, (1850) it shows the year when there was a sudden rise in income. It also supplies the names of the Assay staff and their annual wage.

Thomas Lowe, assay master	£348.18.08
Joseph Green, assistant	£104.00.00
Edward Jones, clerk	£ 18.14.00
John Lowe and John Garner, wardens	£ 9.00.00
Mr Page, surgeon	£ 2.02.00
John Garner, scraper	£ 35.17.06
Rent and taxes	£ 13.18.04$\frac{1}{2}$
Stationery and printing	£ 5.01.04
Punches	£ 1.16.00
Ironmongery	£ 5.07.05
Assay apparatus	£ 4.06.03
Coal, coke and gas	£ 6.13.10
Travelling expenses	£ 4.19.00
Postage and carriage	£ 5.13.08
Mrs Scott and Mrs Edwards' interest	£ 10.00.00
Repairs and cleaning office	£ 4.17.06
Mr John Lowe, balance due to him at 1 February 1847	£ 32.08.08
Sundry small sums	£ 3.06.04
	£617.00.09

The Chester Plate Duty Books 1784-1840

There are three volumes of the same size now kept in the Birmingham Public Library as an overspill from the Birmingham Assay Office due to the lack of space for storage in the latter. Owing to a confusion in recording these volumes they were not known to the author when he wrote the two earlier volumes on Chester Silver, and it is due to the kindness of Philip Priestley who found them when working on his defintive book on the watchcase makers of London, Birmingham and Chester that their existence was made known. It is clear that Sir Charles Jackson knew of them, which accounts for several references to silversmiths and their dates which were otherwise unknown.

A note in the first volume records the expenditure in connection with the imposition of the plate duty at Chester.

Paid fee to two expresses being 2 punches 2/6 each 0.5.0.
Paid for this book to enter the duty   0.6.0.
Paid postage of 3 letters   0.1.4.
To the accountant 6d in the pound $0.5.1\frac{1}{2}./17/11\frac{1}{2}.$

The first Book begins to record on 27 November 1784. From then onwards the year is divided into four sections, January to the end of March, April to the end of June, July to the end of September and from November to the end of the year with occasionally a slight run over into the next quarter. Each page is separated into columns which record the date when items were submitted to receive their duty punch, the name of the goldsmith, a brief list of items submitted and the total gross weight in ounces, pennyweights, and grains. Silver and gold are not kept separately until 5 April 1815 when silver and gold are recorded in different compartments. At the end of each quarter the accountant was paid 6d which was deducted from the duty. The duty was then acknowledged and received by William Thomas (1784-93) then R. Pierce, and after 1814 by Thomas Huxley until 1835, when Joseph Price took his place. There is no acknowledgement after 1837 until 1840 when the third book ends.

The first book ends in 1809, the second (for which they paid £1.7.8¼) continues until 1837, and the third volume which is only partly used until 1840. There are no further records of this kind to be found at Chester. A great many records were destroyed about 1962 but other papers passed into private hands, many of them have been returned to the Company and are housed at the Town Hall, Chester amongst the City archives.

The omission of anyone to examine or receive the duty after 1837 may have had serious consequences which reflected in the dismissal of the Walkers from the Company and the Assay Office. From the beginning of the imposition of the duty marks there is evidence that all was not correct. On several occasions the secretary who compiled the duty books and recorded the names of the workmen submitting the silver and gold for assay and duty failed to record every piece which was stamped at the office. These mistakes can only be checked from surviving pieces which have passed through the Assay Office and on which the duty mark had been placed. An occasional

EXAMPLES OF THE FULL PAGE LAYOUT OF THE PLATE DUTY BOOKS

Date	Workman's name and Residence	Particulars of the goods	Weight Oz.	Dwt.	grs.	Gross Duty £	s	d	1/6 allow'd Oz.	Dwt.	grs.	Nett Duty £	s	d
1785 Dec 16	John Adamson, Liverpool	13½ pair silver Watchcases	30	13	—		15	4	5	2	4		12	9
	James France, Manchester	6 silver skewers	14	12	—		7	3½	2	8	16		6	1
(Total for the quarter)			622	9	12	18	10	10½	103	12	14	15	9	4¾

Total Duty for the quarter to 25 March 86   £   15   9   4¾
Less the accountants fee 6d pr £   7   8¾
                                  15   1   8   8

Date	Names	Species	Gross Oz.	Dwt.	grs.	1/6 allow'd Oz.	Dwt.	grs.	Nett Wt. Oz.	Dwt.	grs.	Nett Duty £	s	d
1832 Jan 12	Jno Coakley	SILVER 53 Tea Spoons	28	10	—	4	15	—	23	15	—	1	15	7½
1832 Jan 19	G. Lowe	GOLD 20 rings	1	8	—		4	16	1	3	8		19	10
(Total for the quarter) Silver			285	10	—	47	11	16	237	18	8	17	16	10½
Gold			13	12	6	2	5	9	11	6	26	9	12	10

(Total duty for the quarter) Silver   £17   9   16   12   10½   10
Do...... Gold   27   9   13   8½   9

To the accountant at 6d   £26   15   11

mistake may have happened but there seems to be so many examples of this that deliberate fraud must have been practiced.

The first example noted (by Mr Simon Davidson) was on the fully marked 'shaving canister or cream canister' exhibited and illustrated in the Sotheby Exhibition at Chester (July and August 1984). The canister is dated 1809/10 or 1831/32' and was made by Nicholas Cunliffe a Liverpool goldsmith. The Duty Books show that he submitted silver to Chester from 1798 to 1814. There is no reference to anything corresponding to this canister. This is not an isolated example, even if the goods were held back before being submitted. The same can be said of a basting spoon submitted in 1793/94 by Robert Bowers, and a basting spoon in 1803/4. The initials JC which were at one time thought to refer to J. Crossley (*C.S.*, p. 71) are now confirmed as those of J. Coakley (*C.S.*, p. 71). A fish slice (1828/29) and ladles (1828/29) by him. Nicholson Lee (*C.S.*, p. 95) made a gorget (1828/29) and a tipstave (*C.S.*, p. 95) and George Walker a bougie box (1790/91) a saucepan (1790/91) and a pap boat (1789/90) which all carry the duty marks but are not mentioned in the record.

One can only assume that if payment had been made by the silversmith the omission from the records would result in a considerable loss of revenue (or whether some private agreement had been made.).

A SUMMARY OF THE WEIGHTS AND DUTY RECORDED IN THE PLATE DUTY BOOKS

(A) The nett duty paid after the deduction of (1/5 in 1785) 1/6 allowed for the assay, here calculated to the nearest pound.

(B) Weight of silver and gold combined until 1814.

(C) From 14 April 1814 the duty and weights are listed separately.

		(A) £'s	(B) ounces
1784-85	Dec 25 - Mar 25	11	541
1784-85	March 25 - June 24	16	602
	June 24 - Sept 29	11	270
	Sept 29 - Dec 25	23	651
1785-86	Dec 25 - March 25	15	622
	March 25 - June 24	17	638
	June 24 - Sept 29	32	828
	Sept 29 - Dec 25	21	634
1786-87	Dec 25 - March 25	20	686
1787	March 25 - June 24	21	712
	June 24 - Sept 29	23	1002
	Sept 29 - Dec 25	30	1127
1787-88	Dec 25 - March 25	18	683
	March 25 - June 24	22	813
	June 24 - Sept 29	20	851
	Sept 29 - Dec 25	26	780
1788-1789	Dec 25 - March 25	17	803

		(A) £'s	(B) ounces
	March 25 - June 24	25	916
	June 24 - Sept 29	18	629
	Sept 29 - Dec 25	26	780
1789-1790	Dec 25 - March 25	11	408
1790	March 25 - June 24	14	197
	June 24 - Sept 29	14	354
	Sept 29 - Dec 25	14	364
1790-91	Dec 25 - March 25	13	248
	March 25 - June 24	15	229
	June 24 - Sept 29	16	305
	Sept 29 - Dec 25	9	185
1791-92	Dec 25 - March 25	10	157
1792	March 25 - June 24	14	120
	June 24 - Sept 29	14	179
	Sept 29 - Dec 25	8	88
1792-93	Dec 25 - March 25	14	120
1793	March 25 - June 24	11	216
	June 24 - Sept 29	11	268
	Sept 29 - Dec 25	12	265
1793-94	Dec 25 - March 25	12	334
1794	March 25 - June 24	17	436
	June 24 - Sept 29	16	394
	Sept 29 - Dec 25	16	461
1794-95	Dec 25 - March 25	24	660
1795	March 25 - June 24	25	778
	June 24 - Sept 29	29	984
	Sept 29 - Dec 25	29	983
1795-96	Dec 25 - March 25	26	883
1796	March 25 - June 24	37	1181
	June 24 - Sept 29	47	1518
	Sept 29 - Dec 25	39	1264
1796-97	Dec 25 - March 25	33	1291
1797	March 25 - June 24	48	1567
	June 24 - Sept 29	69	705

(6 July 1797 to Sept 29 1797 Duty now one shilling per ounce silver and gold sixteen shillings per ounce.)

		(A) £'s	(B) ounces
	Sept 29 - Dec 25	49	944
1797-98	Dec 25 - March 25	49	767
1798	March 25 - June 24	6	88
	June 24 - Sept 29	20	64
	Sept 29 - Dec 25	16	42
1798-1799	Dec 25 - March 25	18	61
1799	March 25 - June 24	19	116
	June 24 - Sept 29	26	51
	Sept 29 - Dec 25	15	43
1799-1800	Dec 25 - March 25	22	46
1800	March 25 - June 24	15	77
	June 24 - Oct 10	11	85
1800-01	Oct 10 - Jan 5	21	69
1801	Jan 5 - April 5	29	104
	April 5 - July 5	14	118
	July 5 - Oct 10	31	72
1801-02	Oct 10 - Jan 5	10	38
1802	Jan 5 - Ap 5	19	115
	Ap 5 - July 5	33	77
	July 5 - Oct 10	31	77

		(A) £'s	(B) ounces
1802-1803	Oct 10 - Jan 5	35	146
1803	Jan 5 - Ap 5	35	92
	Ap 5 - July 5	39	149
	July 5 - Oct 10	35	153
1803-04	Oct 10 - Jan 5	28	128
1804	Jan 5 - Ap 5	26	107
	Ap 5 - July 5	35	129
	July 5 - Oct 10	30	193
1805-06	Oct 10 - Jan 5	19	114
1806	Jan 5 - Ap 5	32	133
	Ap 5 - July 5	19	75
	July 5 - Oct 10	38	74
1806-07	Oct 10 - Jan 5	25	61
1807	Jan 5 - Ap 5	31	82
	Ap 5 - July 5	22	64
	July 5 - Oct 10	26	73
1807-08	Oct 10 - Jan 5	41	72
1808	Jan 5 - Ap 5	27	136
	Ap 5 - July 5	17	46
	July 5 - Oct 10	33	100
1808-1809	Oct 10 - Jan 5	12	45
1809	Jan 5 - Ap 5	31	79
	Ap 5 - July 5	28	77
	July 5 - Oct 10	25	82
1809-10	Oct 10 - Jan 5	26	44
1810	Jan 5 - Ap 5	24	54
	Ap 5 - July 5	31	30
	July 5 - Oct 10	24	43
1810-1811	Oct 10 - Jan 5	30	71
1811	Jan 5 - Ap 5	37	196
	Ap 5 - July 5	32	86
	July 5 - Oct 10	20	50
1811-1812	Oct 10 - Jan 5	28	60
1812	Jan 5 - Ap 5	32	70
	Ap 5 - July 5	25	45
	July 5 - Oct 10	25	66
1812-13	Oct 10 - Jan 5	25	59
1813	Jan 5 - Ap 5	20	40
	Ap 5 - July 5	34	71
	July 5 - Oct 10	37	124
1813-14	Oct 10 - Jan 5	25	55
1814	Jan 5 - Ap 5	33	59

		SILVER	GOLD	SILVER	GOLD
		Duty (To the nearest pound)		Duty (To the nearest ounce)	
	Ap 14 - July 14	2	33	31	20
	July 14 - Oct 14	1	43	16	63
1814-15	Oct 14 - Jan 15	2	43	40	64
1815	Jan 15 - Ap 15	1	34	25	50
	Ap 15 - July 5	4	32	68	48
	July 5 - Oct 5	4	43	80	65

(Memorandum. From 31 August 1815 the old duties on Gold and Silver were repealed and new duty 17/- per oz on gold and 1/6 per oz on silver were imposed by Act of Parliament.)

To old duty on silver and god £4.3.9³₄, £43.0.1¹₂

To new duty on silver and gold (31 August 1815) 9s 11¹₄, £22.14.11.

		SILVER	GOLD	SILVER	GOLD
		Duty		Duty	
		(To the nearest pound)		(To the nearest ounce)	
1815	Aug 31	8	32		
1815-16	Oct 5 - Jan 5	3	38	48	54
1816	Jan 5 - Ap 5	3	40	44	57
	Ap 5 - July 5	5	29	82	81
	July 5 - Oct 5	5	41	73	57
1816-17	Oct 5 - Jan 5	3	26	50	36
1817	Jan 5 - Ap 5	5	31	74	44
	Ap 5 - July 5	4	27	61	37
	July 5 - Oct 5	3	36	19	51
1817-18	Oct 5 - Jan 5	1	33	22	46
1818	Jan 5 - Ap 5	6	33	5	47
	Ap 5 - July 5	2	17	36	25
	July 5 - Oct 5	1	39	21	56
1818-19	Oct 5 - Jan 5	2	41	28	57
1819	Jan 5 - Ap 5	1	27	17	38
	Ap 5 - July 5	1	31	10	43
	July 5 - Oct 5	2	39	32	55
1819-20	Oct 5 - Jan 5	1	43	9	61
1820	Jan 5 - Ap 5	1	38	21	54
	Ap 5 - July 5	1	37	10	53
	July 5 - Oct 5	2	34	37	47
1820-21	Oct 5 - Jan 5	3	28	51	39
1821	Jan 5 - Ap 5	2	25	27	35
	Ap 5 - July 5	2	37	33	53
	July 5 - Oct 5	1	40	18	56
1821-22	Oct 5 - Jan 5	3	24	54	33
1822	Jan 5 - Ap 5	2	29	27	41
	Ap 5 - July 5	2	29	27	40
	July 5 - Oct 5	3	36	43	51
1822-23	Oct 5 - Jan 5	2	21	30	30
1823	Jan 5 - Ap 5	1	23	14	33
	Ap 5 - July 5	2	31	29	44
	July 5 - Oct 5	1	23	21	32
1823-1824	Oct 5 - Jan 5	2	32	31	45
1824	Jan 5 - Ap 5	2	25	38	36
	Ap 5 - July 5	2	33	34	46
	July 5 - Oct 5	4	41	41	30
1824-25	Oct 5 - Jan 5	2	38	44	54
1825	Jan 5 - Ap 5	1	23	22	32
	Ap 5 - July 5	7	36	105	51
	July 5 - Oct 5	4	41	57	58
1825-26	Oct 5 - Jan 5	5	19	75	27
1826	Jan 5 - Ap 5	4	29	70	41
	Ap 5 - July 5	6	14	96	19
	July 5 - Oct 5	2	20	40	28
1826-27	Oct 5 - Jan 5	4	34	62	34
1827	Jan 5 - Ap 5	3	28	48	40
	Ap 5 - July 5	3	19	41	26
	July 5 - Oct 5	7	24	113	33

		SILVER	GOLD	SILVER	GOLD
		Duty		Duty	
		(To the nearest pound)		(To the nearest ounce)	
1827-28	Oct 5 - Jan 5	6	21	88	29
1828	Jan 5 - Ap 5	10	31	158	32
	Ap 5 - July 5	6	24	101	34
	July 5 - Oct 5	35	34	559	48
1828-1829	Oct 5 - Jan 5	33	19	539	48
1829	Jan 5 - Ap 5	33	37	518	37
	Ap 5 - July 5	47	15	777	21
	July 5 - Oct 5	42	21	678	30
1829-30	Oct 5 - Jan 5	32	20	514	28
1830	Jan 5 - Ap 5	33	20	435	18
	Ap 5 - July 5	40	6	634	8
	July 5 - Oct 5	37	13	592	18
1830-31	Oct 5 - Jan 5	32	19	505	27
1831	Jan 5 - Ap 5	37	8	597	11
	Ap 5 - July 5	29	17	456	24
	July 5 - Oct 5	32	7	510	11
1831-32	Oct 5 - Jan 5	23	17	376	24
1832	Jan 5 - Ap 5	18	10	286	14
	Ap 5 - July 5	21	16	343	23
	July 5 - Oct 5	10	11	159	15
1832-33	Oct 5 - Jan 5	21	10	360	14
1833	Jan 5 - Ap 5	11	4	179	5
	Ap 5 - July 5	2	3	32	4
	July 5 - Oct 5	13	7	212	10
1833-34	Oct 5 - Jan 5	7	9	110	12
1834	Jan 5 - Ap 5	1	5	22	7
	Ap 5 - July 5	9	5	138	8
	July 5 - Oct 5	3	5	47	8
1834-35	Oct 5 - Jan 5	4	9	68	12
1835	Jan 5 - Ap 5	4	6	72	8
	Ap 5 - July 5	18	5	296	7
	July 5 - Oct 5	26	8	406	11
1835-36	Oct 5 - Jan 5	25	8	398	32
1836	Jan 5 - Ap 5	16	8	252	12
	Ap 5 - July 5	4	12	57	17
	July 5 - Oct 5	22	14	351	20
1836-37	Oct 5 - Jan 5	39	22	627	17
1837	Jan 5 - Ap 5	46	11	730	
	Ap 5 - July 5	27	9	431	12
	July 5 - Oct 5	47	11	748	
1837-38	Oct 5 - Jan 5	42	16	673	22
1838	Jan 5 - Ap 5	51	8	817	12
	Ap 5 - July 5	57	8	913	11
	July 5 - Oct 5	54	8	564	12
1838-39	Oct 5 - Jan 5	24	6	376	8
1839	Jan 5 - Ap 5	26	5	418	7
	Ap 5 - July 5	37	5	574	7
	July 5 - Oct 5	36	5	484	6
1839-40	Oct 5 - Jan 5	50	13	794	18
1840	Jan 5 - Ap 5	31	9	500	13

Silversmiths mentioned in the Chester Plate Duty Books with Dates when their Names appear 1784-1840

J. Abbott, Liverpool, 1817-1826.
Abbott and Jones, Liverpool, 1808-1816.
(Jones and Abbot), Liverpool, 1812-1814.
Hugh Adamson, Liverpool, 1805-1833.
John Adamson, Liverpool, 1785-1798.
J. Adamson and Son, Liverpool, 1798.
R. Adamson, Liverpool, 1833.
Thomas Appleby, Manchester, 1791.
Thomas Armitt, Manchester, 1831-1834.
John and Joseph Armstrong, Manchester, 1833-1839.
J. Atker, 1819.
William Ball, Liverpool, 1823-1826.
James Barton (and Co.), Liverpool, 1785-1798.
David Beyendorfe, Liverpool, 1786-1792.
Richard Boulger, Liverpool, 1787.
T. M. Bowen, Liverpool, 1831.
Robert Bowers, Chester, 1787-1814.
John Brooks, Liverpool, 1831-1832.
Samuel Bryans, 1831.
Burrell and Co., Liverpool, 1809.
C. Careless, 1815.
Edward Christian, Liverpool, 1825-1830.
John Clarke, Liverpool, 1813-1830.
John Clifton, Liverpool, 1785.
Henry Close, Liverpool, 1839.
Samuel Close, Liverpool, 1838.
John Coakley, Liverpool, 1828-1833.
Crompton and Parry, Liverpool, 1815-1816.
William Crumpsty, Liverpool, 1822-1823.
Thomas Cubbin, Liverpool, 1837-1839.
Nicholas Cunliffe, Liverpool, 1798-1814.
James Dixon, Chester, 1785-1788.
James Duke, Manchester, 1816.
Joseph Duke, Chester, 1838-1840.
Joseph Dutton, Chester, 1836-1838.
John Ellison, Liverpool ?, 1794-1807.
Ellison and Co., Liverpool, 1824-1837.
W. Ellison, Liverpool ?, 1815.
Joseph Falconer, Chester, 1790.
John Fisher, Liverpool, 1784-1790.

Richard Fisher, Manchester, Liverpool, 1795-1804.
Henry Fishwick, Liverpool, 1838.
J. Fowler, Manchester, 1813-1816.
E. Foxall, 1821.
Thomas Foxall, 1820-1822.
Elizabeth France, Manchester, 1819-1824.
James France, Manchester, 1785-1819.
John Gilbert, Liverpool, 1786-1797.
James Glover, Manchester, 1810-1813.
Robert Green, Liverpool, 1791-1803.
Thomas Green, Liverpool, 1785-1799.
John Hack, 1833.
Isaac Hadwin, Liverpool, 1792.
Richard Harper, Liverpool, 1799-1800.
Thomas Harrison, Liverpool, 1785.
John Helsby, Liverpool, 1830-1834.
John Helsby and Sons, Liverpool, 1826.
Thomas Helsby and Son, Liverpool, 1816-1827.
William Helsby, Liverpool, 1830.
James Hemming, Liverpool, 1837-1839.
William Hemming, Liverpool, 1827-1836.
John Hemmingway, Manchester, 1813-1814.
James Hemmingway, Manchester, 1827-1836.
Hemmingway and Glover, Manchester, 1808-1810.
Joseph Hewett, Liverpool, 1790-1793.
Thomas Hill, Chester, 1788-1789.
N. Hort, 1834.
William Hull, Liverpool, 1785-1801.
H. M. and S. Huntingdon, Chester, 1822-1830.
Mary Huntingdon, Chester, 1815-1822.
The Jones Family:
    Robert Jones, Liverpool, 1788-1822.
    R. Jones and Son, Liverpool, 1813-1832.
    C. Jones also C. Jones and Co., Liverpool, 1825-1831.
    Jones and Walley also Walley and Jones, Liverpool.
    W. Jones and Abbot, Liverpool, 1812-1814.
    Jones and Reeves, Liverpool, 1821-1822.
    William Jones, Liverpool, 1806-1813.
Richard Kilshaw, Liverpool, 1802.
John Kind, 1821-1822.
E. Kirkman, Liverpool, 1832-1839.
Patrick Landra, 1835 (see Patrick Leonard p. 123).
Nichs Lee, Liverpool, 1796-1817.

Joseph Lewis (Samuel), Liverpool, 1834-1839.
David Lloyd, Liverpool, 1828-1831.
The Lowe Family:
    George Lowe 1 and George Lowe 2, Chester, 1791-1840.
    Robert Lowe, Preston, 1830-1837.
Richard Lucas, Liverpool, 1832-1839.
Edward Maddock, Liverpool, 1798-1815.
William Maddock, Liverpool, 1831-1832.
John Miller, Newcastle on Tyne, 1825-1826.
Peter Molyneux, Liverpool, 1793-1797.
Richard Morrow, Liverpool, 1786-1792.
Thomas Morrow, Liverpool, 1798.
Joseph Morton, Manchester, 1811.
Newton and Hyde, Manchester, 1822-1840.
Thomas Newton, Manchester, 1827-1840.
Edward Nightingale, 1826-1828.
John Parsonage, Liverpool, 1831.
Thomas Pierrepoint, Liverpool, 1831.
Robert Preston, Liverpool, 1787-1792.
William Pugh, Birmingham (goldworker) 1810-1814.
Reeves and Jones (see Jones and Reeves), Liverpool, 1820-1822.
James Richards, Liverpool, 1798.
Richard Richardson, Chester, 1784-1790.
Henry Rigby, Liverpool 1785-1787.
Joseph Lewis Samuel (and Co.), Liverpool, 1834-1839.
M. Solomon, 1814-1815.
John Sutter(s), Liverpool, 1835-1840.
William Tarlton, Liverpool, 1785-1786.
J. Taylor, Chester, 1825.
John Twemlow, Chester, 1814-1833.
William Twemlow, Chester, 1787-1823.
Vale and Co., Birmingham, 1819.
The Walker Family:
    C. B. Walker, Chester, 1837.
    George Walker, Chester, 1785-1805.
    John Walker, Chester, 1805-1830.
    Thomas Walker, Chester, 1830-1834.
Walley and Jones, Liverpool (see Jones and Walley).
Thomas Woolfield, Liverpool, 1832-1837.
(J. Wemlow, see Twemlow).

Record of the Work Registered in The Chester Plate Duty Books, 1784-1840

ABBOTT and JONES, Liverpool, 1808-1818.
See under the JONES family.

J. ABBOTT, Liverpool.
See ABBOTT & JONES (JONES & ABBOTT) under **Jones.**

The partnership between Abbott and Jones seems to have ceased and in 1817 J. Abbott seemed to be working alone.

1817	2 snuff boxes (one of which was rejected as not being sterling).
1819	A masonic medal.
1821	2 medals. 11 gold rings.
1822	1 gold ring. 2 medals. A 'plate for mounting.'
1823	3 masonic medals. 2 'ferrils for canes'. 1 cane top. A jug rim.
1824	2 medals.
1826	11 gold rings. A medal.

HUGH ADAMSON, Liverpool, 1805-1833.
Probably the son of John Adamson (qv).

1805	1 silver medal.
1808	4 silver medals.
1811	18 gold rings.
1817	31 gold rings.
1820	A snuff box.
1829	1 gold ring.
1833	12 tea spoons, 2 table spoons.

JOHN ADAMSON, Liverpool, 1785-1798. Watchcase Maker.
He lived at 25 North Street, Liverpool and in 1790 moved to 18 Johnson Street. He also registered at Birmingham after 1773. He was one of four watchcase makers who were warned about putting too much solder on joints and mouldings which may have prompted him to transfer his work to Birmingham for a while.

1785	78 watchcases and 2 half cases.
1786	174 watchcases and four half cases.
1785	1 snuff box.
1786	4 snuff boxes.
1787	203 watchcases and 6 half cases ($5\frac{1}{2}$ not sterling). 8 snuff boxes.
1788	202 watchcases and 14 half cases. 15 boxes.
1789	98 watchcases and four half cases.
1795	138 watchcases. 37 boxes.
1796	181 watchcases. 6 boxes.
1797	143 watchcases (2 not sterling). 5 boxes.
1798	4 pr watchcases. 1 box. (and 2 boxes and 1 watchcase not sterling).

JOHN ADAMSON & SON, Liverpool, 1796-1798. Watchcase makers.

1796	34 watchcases.
1797	16 watchcases.
1798	8 watchcases. 2 boxes.

R. ADAMSON, Liverpool, 1833.
1833   24 tea spoons. 2 salt spoons. 1 caddy spoon. 6 table spoons.

THOMAS APPLEBY, Manchester, 1791.
An earlier attribution of the mark TA within a shaped rectangle to Thomas Appleby has now been amended on the evidence of the Chester Duty Books where there is

only a single reference to him in 1791. Jackson reports that he was a watchcase maker but there are no references to him as such in 1798 as one might expect. Otherwise the references to Thomas Appleby under the TA mark (Ridgway. *Chester Silver*, p. 57) are correct. The mark is now attributed to Thomas Armitt who made various badges (see Thomas Armitt).

1791   21 gold rings and 2 pairs of gold buttons.

THOMAS ARMITT, Manchester, 1832-35.

The Chester Duty Books refer to him as a medal maker. The reference to the TA mark as that of Thomas Appleby is incorrect and should now be taken as the mark of Thomas Armitt. In Pigot's Manchester Directory from 1824 to 1843 Thomas Armitt is listed as a 'glass and china dealer' moving from 65 Chapel Street to 37 Smithy Door, Manchester, Bridge Street and 12 Victoria Street. Unfortunately there is no directory for the crucial period 1833-35, nor is he mentioned as a metal worker.

1832   57 medals.
1833   26 medals.
1834   44 medals.
1835   31 medals.

Several badges can now be attributed to Thomas Armitt. Representative of these is a badge engraved . . .

> Presented by the Officers and Brothers of the Loyal Shakespeare Lodge to P. G. George Lovitt on the 16th Decr 1834 for his valuable services to the said Lodge.

A portrait of Shakespeare is in the centre of the badge with the name Shakespeare Lodge. The badge is cut from sheet silver and the back has two attachments. There are six marks on the reverse side including the Chester mark, the duty mark, maker's mark and the date letter.

Length 4.7 inches. Width 3.6 inches. Weight 2.5 ounces.

JOHN ARMSTRONG and JOSEPH ARMSTRONG, Manchester 1833-39

Joseph Armstrong appears in 1833 and seems to have taken over from John Armstrong who first records in 1833. They were watchcase makers but also were involved in making medals for masonic lodges and other similar bodies. Joseph Armstrong was attached to St Mary's Church (now demolished) where from 1829 to 1830 six of his children were baptised. His wife was Sarah and he was described as of Deansgate, Manchester.

John Armstrong:
1833   9 medals.
1834   45 medals and 20 rims for horns, 20 mounts for horns and 3 mustard pot lids.

Joseph Armstrong:
1833   8 medals.
1835   10 medals.
1836   17 horn mounts.
1838   6 medals.
1839   10 medals.

J. ATKER, 1819.
1819   21 gold rings.

WILLIAM BALL, Liverpool, 1823-26.
1823   A pencil case.
1824   2 gold rings.
1826   A trowel.

JAMES BARTON, Liverpool, 1786-1798
According to the Liverpool Trade Directory, James Barton in 1787 is listed as an engraver of Cumberland Street, and from 1790 to about 1814 as a watchcase maker

having moved to Key Street in 1811. He transferred his work to Birmingham Assay Office in 1789 but returned to Chester in 1795. He died in 1816 aged 79 and was buried at Plumbe Street.

1786	72 pair (7 broke down), 2 half cases.
1787	306 pair. 3 half cases.
1788	1 buckle (not sterling), 156 pair, 4 half cases.
1789	1 box. 54 pair (12 not sterling). 3 half cases. 1 box (broke).
1795	259 pair. 26 boxes. 10 cases.
1796	246 pair. 8 boxes.
1797	355 pair (12 broke down). 14 boxes (one not sterling). 6 watchcases not sterling.
1798	134 pair. 8 boxes.

J. BARTON & Co., Liverpool, 1785.

1785	8 pair.

DAVID BEYENDORFE (Byendoff. Beyendroff), Liverpool, 1786-1792.

Apprenticed in 1753 in the Clockmakers' Company to Richard Payne of London. He settled in Liverpool at St John's Square, as a spring maker and watchase maker. He married Ann the widow of Thomas Pierrepoint (q.v.).

1786	44 and four and a half cases.
1787	128 and five and a half cases. 1 gold watchcase.
1788	193 and two and a half cases (32 broke).
1789	180 and five and a half cases, 31 boxes.
1790	130 and four and a half cases. Two pair of watchcases not sterling.
1791	129 (& 16 not sterling). 20 boxes and one and a half cases.
1792	7 watchcases. 1 box.

RICHARD BOULGER, Liverpool, 1787.

(see Ridgway. *Chester Silver,* p. 66.)

He married Susanna Charnock 26 July 1784 at St Nicholas Parish Church, Liverpool and was responsible for the Church clock at St Peter's, Chester.

1787	9 pair watchcases.

T. M. BOWEN, Liverpool, 1831.

1831	48 spectacle frames.

ROBERT BOWERS, Chester. Goldsmith. 1787-1814.

Robert Bowers of Eastgate Row, Chester had been a practicing goldsmith at Chester before the time of the Lowes, but in the Lowe Day Book which begins in 1792 he is often mentioned as working closely with George Lowe. (see Ridgway, *Chester Silver,* p. 64 f.).

1787	pair of buckles.
1793	10 motto rings. 28 gold rings. A pair of gold buttons.
1794	16 gold motto rings.
1795	A silver box. 56 gold rings.
1797	37 gold rings. 9 motto rings. 24 lables. 12 shoe clasps.
1798	35 gold rings, one pair of show clasps and a gorget.
1800	16 gold motto rings, 3 breast plates, 2 dog collars, 93 gold rings and 5 skewers.
1801	27 gold rings, 9 motto rings, 36 lables, 2 silver plates (coffin plates?), 8 pair gold buttons, 16 coat buttons.
1802	5 silver nipperkins. (a measure).
1803	3 soup ladles, 6 sauce ladles, 8 butter ladles, 1 pr of clasps, 12 marrow spoons, (5 of which rejected as not sterling), 12 salt ladles, 7 skewers, 1 toast rack, 1 silver buckle, 11 egg spoons, (6 rejected), 6 table spoons, 42 ladles, 2 coffin plates, 45 gold rings.

1804	8 coffin plates, 138 tea spoons, 3 skewers, 97 gold rings, 1 castor frame, 2 silver cups, 34 salt (?spoons), 1 tumbler, 8 mustard ladles, 12 pr tea tongs, 4 pr clasps, 1 'panikin', 57 table spoons, a knife blade, 4 salt spoons, 6 dessert spoons, 2 gravy spoons.
1805	1 liquor frame, 44 table spoons, 12 dessert spoons, a foot and rim for a cocoa nut shell, 153 tea spoons, 6 gravy spoons, 1 soup ladle, 7 skewers, 1 'panikin', 1 coffin plate, 24 salt ladles, 1 ladle, 1 handle, 6 pr sugar tongs, 103 gold rings.
1806	12 table spoons, 55 teo spoons, 1 gravy spoon, 1 dessert spoon, 1 butter ladle, 1 skewer, 3 coffin plates, 71 gold rings.
1807	1 gold ring.
1808	2 coffin plates, 18 'nozils', 51 gold rings.
1809	2 coffin plates, 5 marrow scoops.
1810	66 gold rings.
1811	2 coffin plates.
1812	1 belt plate, 1 coffin plate.
1813	45 tea spoons, 19 dessert spoons, 2 salt spoons, 2 coffin plates, 3 gold hoop rings, 32 gold rings.
1814	20 dessert spoons, 13 tea spoons, 1 coffin plate, 2 knife rests, 32 gold rings.

JOHN BROOKS, 1831-1832.

1831	2 medals.
1832	5 medals.

SAMUEL BRYANS, 1831.

1831	16 medals.

BURRELL & Co., Liverpool, 1809.

1809	4 silver knife rests.

C. CARELESS, 1815.

1815	16 gold rings.

EDWARD CHRISTIAN, Liverpool, 1825-1830.

1825	68 gold rings.
1826	1 jug mounting, 70 gold rings.
1827	3 salt ladles.
1829	11 gold rings.
1830	28 gold rings.

JOHN CLARKE, Liverpool, 1813-1830.

1813	53 gold rings.
1814	12 gold rings, 139 silver rings.
1815	275 gold rings.
1816	527 gold rings.
1817	268 gold rings, 1 pr buckles.
1818	222 gold rings.
1819	177 gold rings, 1 shell mount.
1820	89 gold rings. A mounting for a cane.
1822	2 lancet cases, 1 gold ring.
1823	4 salt ladles. 19 gold rings.
1824	50 gold rings.
1825	52 gold rings.
1826	39 gold rings.
1829	22 gold rings.
1830	1 jug top.

JOHN CLIFTON, Liverpool, 1785.

He is listed as a clock and watchmaker but also as a supplier of groceries. There are two long cased clocks by John Clifton in the Liverpool Museum. He was born 1742 and lived at Fazakerley Street, Liverpool where he died aged 51.

1785   23 pairs of watchcases (6 were rejected as not sterling).

HENRY CLOSE, Liverpool, 1828-1839.

1828	a 'cathetor'.
1829	Soap box.
1830	A medal.
1831	Tooth brush box.
1835	A top for a pepper castor. 2 table spoons. 2 medals.
1836	5 medals.
1837	1 medal. 12 table spoons. 12 dessert spoons. 12 tea spoons.
1839	A box lid.

SAMUEL CLOSE, Liverpool, 1838.

1838   2 medals.

JOHN COAKLEY, Liverpool, 1828-1833.

(See Ridgway. *Chester Silver,* p. 71.)

It seems clear that the JC mark within a rectangle which provisionally was attributed to John Crossley (and others) is now established as the mark of John Coakley and his work appears in the Plate Duty Books. The Trade Directory of 1829 lists him as a silversmith of 18 Arley Street, Liverpool. The appearance of John Sutter(s) in the Chester Plate Duty Books in 1835 (see 'Finial' October 1993) and the last appearance of John Coakley in 1833 may be related as John Sutter produced an enormous amount of flatware in Liverpool. Jackson refers to a John Coakley at Exeter in 1828 but the Exeter Museum cannot add anything to this information.

1828   762 tea spoons. 85 dessert spoons. 54 table spoons. 93 sugar tongs. 12 caddy spoons. 192 salt spoons. 42 mustard spoons. 1 gravy spoon. 3 sugar spoons. 6 egg spoons. 3 butter knives. 37 forks.

1829   6 mustard spoons. 16 sugar spoons. 2 sauce ladles. 6 caddy spoons. 9 ladles. 76 dessert spoons. 7 egg spoons. 13 gravy spoons. 245 salt spoons. 194 tongs. 246 table spoons. 2025 tea spoons. 48 pickle forks. 7 forks. 2 mustard pots. 2 boxes. 1 pencil case. 3 cups. 1 bottom of cruet frame. 1 mustard mount. 1 patch box. 2 bottle tops. 4 cork mounts. 2 butter knives. 2 skewers.

1830   1 cream jug. 2 half pints. 14 caddy spoons. 6 gravy spoons. 4 butter knives. 6 butter ladles. 4 fish slice. 35 mustard spoons. 124 sugar tongs. 1718 tea spoons. 156 table spoons. 222 salt spoons. 5 sugar spoons. 16 sauce ladles. 45 dessert spoons. 34 forks (dessert). 2 mustard tops. 3 glass mounts. 4 medals. 6 bottle tickets. 3 box lids. 4 fish knives.

1831   4 caddy spoons. 2 butter ladles. 1 sauce ladle. 4 ladles. 98 sugar tongs. 1302 tea spoons. 122 table spoons. 96 mustard spoons. 5 sugar spoons. 166 salt spoons. 32 dessert spoons. 1 ink stand mount. 18 dessert forks. 15 pickle forks. 6 table forks. 12 forks. 10 tumblers (cups).

1832   25 sugar tongs. 673 tea spoons. 34 table spoons. 2 (toast) racks. 14 pickle forks. 15 dessert spoons. 11 mustard spoons. 2 caddy spoons.

1833   9 sugar spoons. 23 salt spoons. 13 egg spoons. 8 dessert spoons. 8 forks. 6 table forks. 3 caddy spoons. 311 tea spoons. 22 table spoons.

CROMPTON & PARRY, Liverpool, 1815-16. (Cumpton).

1815	63 gold rings. 2 jug mounts.
1816	43 gold rings. 4 wires (see p. 72).

WILLIAM CRUMPSTY, 1822-1823.

1822	41 gold rings.
1823	20 gold rings.

THOMAS CUBBIN, 1837-1839.

1837   1 gold ring.

1839   1 medal.

NICHOLAS CUNLIFFE, Liverpool, 1798-1814.

Nicholas Cunliffe, a silversmith from Liverpool, registered his mark twice in square 28 on the first copper plate, NC within an oval frame. His work was carried on first at 4 Castle Street (1790) at Sir Thomas's Buildings (1794) and in 1825 at Daulby Street. The Liverpool Directory locates him there in 1835. In 1837 Isabella Cunliffe is mentioned there which might mean that he had died there.

1798   41 gold rings.

1799   36 gold rings.

1800   2 cross keys. 1 cross pen. 6 small spoons. A pair of sugar tongs. 2 skewers. 1 wine funnel stand. 7 skewers. 3 pr compass tops. 5 masons medals.

1801   5 masons medals. 5 masonic medals.

1802   1 medal. 4 lables. 2 silver medals. 9 lables.

1803   6 masonic medals. 1 gold stock buckle. 18 silver coat buttons. 4 vest buttons.

1804   3 labels. 1 medal. 1 pr of buckles. 1 egg cup.

1805   'One dozen cruet tops'.

1806   One pr gold buttons and a thimble.

1807   9 Masons medals. 6 lables. 1 box.

1808   1 pr of buckles. 12 nozils. 1 boatswains call. 1 whistle. 2 lables.

1809   1 table spoon. 17 gold rings. 3 medals (not sterling and rejected). 3 silver medals.

1810   2 silver boxes. 2 hoops for jugs. 1 cruet frame. 43 gold rings. 3 medals.

1811   24 buttons. 1 egg cup. 3 medals. 46 gold rings. 1 cruet frame. 2 hoops for jugs. 2 salt ladles. 1 pr gold sleeve buttons.

1812   Silver box. 61 gold rings.

1813   45 gold rings.

1814   22 gold rings.

JAMES DIXON, Chester, 1785-1788.

(See Ridgway, *Chester Silver,* p. 75).

1785   24 coat buttons.

1788   4 spoons. 8 sauce ladles.

JAMES DUKE, Manchester, 1816.

1816   34 gold rings.

JOSEPH DUKE, Chester, 1838-1840f.

The early history of the Duke family is found in Ridgway's *Chester Silver,*. The second Joseph Duke was admitted to the Chester Goldsmiths Company in 1818 but does not appear in the Company books until the annual meeting 5 July 1835. He appears thereafter until 1840, when he was appointed Assistant Assay Master under George Lowe to replace John Walker and Arthur Davies Walker. He remained Assistant Assay Master until 1849. His mark has not been verified but there is a plain I.D. mark in square 8 of the copper plate which might be his.

1838   30 gold rings. 2 salt spoons. 1 horn mount. 2 pair sugar tongs. 1 mustard spoon. 6 tea spoons.

1839   36 gold rings. 2 medals. 6 lables. 8 knife rests. 6 tea spoons. 1 pair sugar tongs.

1840   1 caddy spoon. 2 mountings for horns. 8 gold rings.

JOSEPH DUTTON, Chester, 1836-1838.

(See Ridgway, *Chester Silver,* p. 81).

Joseph Dutton may have been the son of Henry Dutton of Eastgate Street, Chester, then living according to the 1782 Directory at Eastgate Street, a silversmith. He is listed as a watch and clock maker in the Chester General Directory of 1840 but also as a 'Silversmith and Jeweller'. A paid account exists from Joseph Dutton to John Walker date Chester, 31 August 1837 showing that in 1835 he supplied 'To cleaning clock 2/- a funnell glass 1/-, and in 1837 steel scissor 2/6'.

1836	16 gold rings. 2 medals.
1838	2 salt spoons. 3 horn mounts.

JOHN ELLISON, Liverpool, 1794-1807.

The Ellison family seem to be associated with 5 Crosshall Street, Liverpool (1796). There was a John Ellison at 148 New Scotland Road, Liverpool as a case maker in 1821. John Ellison senior died in 1823.

1794	86 watchcases. 3 boxes.
1795	307 watchcases. 20 boxes.
1796	373 watchcases. 23 boxes.
1797	434 watchcases. 2 boxes.
1798	86 watchcases. (28 of these had duty returned).
1807	1 gold ring.

ELLISON & Co., Liverpool, 1824-1837.

1824	1 gold ring.
1826	1 gold ring.
1829	1 box.
1832	2 lockets.
1837	1 gold ring.

W. ELLISON, Liverpool, 1815.

1815	Mounting for shell box.

JOSEPH FALCONER, Chester, 1790.

1790	Soup ladle. 4 tea spoons. Wine funnel.

JOHN FISHER, Liverpool, 1784-1790.

1784	20 coat buttons. 1 skewer, 2 half pint mugs.
1785	1 small cup. 7 pair of knee buckles. 1 pair of show buckles. 238 coat buttons.
1786	9 gold rings (rejected as below standard). 90 buttons. A spatula.
1787	6 skewers (broken down as below standard). 42 buttons.
1788	14 coat buttons. 12 breast buttons (broken down). 14 coat buttons and 12 buttons (accepted later in September).
1790	A pair of buckles and 16 buttons (rejected in 2 August) were accepted on 16 August). 16 coat buttons. 19 breast buttons. 163 gold rings.

RICHARD FISHER, Manchester/Liverpool, 1795-1804.

1795	38 gold rings.
1796	30 plain gold rings.
1799	37 gold rings.
1800	99 gold rings.
1804	7 pair gold buttons.

HENRY FISHWICK, Liverpool, 1838.

1838	1 gold ring.

J. FOWLER, Manchester, 1813-1816.

1813	39 gold rings.
1816	29 gold rings.

E. FOXALL, 1821.

1821   1 gold ring.

THOMAS FOXALL, 1820-1822.

1820   66 gold rings.
1821   19 gold rings.
1822   19 gold rings.

ELIZABETH FRANCE, Manchester, 1819-1822.

The work of James France (q.v.) of Manchester passed to Elizabeth France in 1819. She was only a ring maker and her skill had probably been linked with James France long before she submitted to Chester in 1819.

1819   898 gold rings.
1820   1542 gold rings.
1821   1221 gold rings.
1822   1474 gold rings.

JAMES FRANCE, Manchester, 1785-1819.

(See Ridgway, *Chester Silver,* p. 83.)

Without the evidence of the Plate Duty Books the output of James France would not have been known. The record shows that until 1796 he was capable of adding general silverware to his production, but after that date he seems to have concentrated upon making gold wedding rings. He occasionally made buttons (1799), a gold box (1806) and a staff head (1812) until he ceased working as a silversmith in 1819.

1785   376 gold rings. 13 skewers, 2 gold buttons. 24 breast buttons.
1786   523 gold rings. 15 skewers (and 4 not sterling). 1 pair sleeve buttons. 9 gold sleeve buttons. 52 lables (and 75 not sterling). 1 coat button.
1787   308 gold rings. 642 tea spoons. 14 caddy spoons. 64 coat buttons. 97 breast buttons. 18 lables. 12 table spoons.
1788   422 gold rings. 216 tea spoons. 1 pap boat. 12 tea tongs. 12 dessert spoons. 12 caddy spoons. 64 coat buttons. 2 pair of buttons.
1789   117 gold rings. 2 pair of stock clasps. 6 skewers.
1790   396 gold rings. 140 coat buttons. 17 breast buttons. 2 staff heads. 5 skewers. 15 lables. 56 buttons.
1791   772 gold rings. 175 coat buttons. 7 caddy ladles. 1 button hook.
1792   1143 gold rings. 218 coat buttons. 116 breast buttons. 6 gold buttons. 1 link.
1793   828 gold rings. 33 coat buttons.
1794   550 gold rings.
1795   591 gold rings.
1796   816 gold rings. 6 skewers.
1797   687 gold rings and 35 not sterling.
1798   317 gold rings.
1799   717 gold rings. 72 coat buttons.
1800   512 gold rings.
1801   667 gold rings.
1802   1282 gold rings.
1803   1544 gold rings.
1804   1530 gold rings.
1805   1435 gold rings.
1806   1349 gold rings. 1 gold box.
1807   1194 gold rings.
1808   723 gold rings.
1809   1133 gold rings.
1810   873 gold rings and 89 not sterling.
1811   1223 gold rings and 171 not sterling.
1812   1092 gold rings. 1 staff head.
1813   1019 gold rings.

1814	1982 gold rings. 2 silver rings.
1815	1793 gold rings and 123 gold rings not sterling.
1816	1234 gold rings and 78 not sterling.
1817	1167 gold rings and 78 not sterling.
1818	1469 gold rings.
1819	(part) 331 gold rings.

JOHN GILBERT, Liverpool, 1786-1797.

1786	52 plain gold rings.
1787	65 plain gold rings.
1788	128 gold rings.
1790	60 gold rings. (41 not sterling).
1791	35 gold rings. 6 silver forks.
1792	55 gold rings.
1794	35 gold rings.
1797	120 gold rings.

JAMES GLOVER, Manchester, 1810-1813.

1810	39 gold rings.
1811	128 gold rings.
1812	113 gold rings.
1813	28 gold rings.

ROBERT GREEN, Liverpool, 1791-1803.

(See Ridgway, *Chester Silver,* p. 83).

The Duty Books show that he was responsible for a number of interesting pieces in addition to those already known by him.

1791	31 gold rings (which were rejected as not being sterling). A silver arrow. 16 coat buttons.
1792	A tobacco box. An Argyle.
1793	2 skewers. A cream jug. 6 boatswains calls (rejected as not sterling).
1794	1 bottle stand. 1 butter tub.
1796	1 silver bow. 1 silver panakin.
1799	1 silver saucepan.
1802	1 silver cup.
1803	1 small cup. 2 beakers. 4 skewers. 6 'calls' (boatswains' calls) rejected as not being sterling.

THOMAS GREEN, Liverpool, 1785-1790.

(See Ridgway, *Chester Silver,* p. 85).

Thomas Green was the son of James Green a watchcase maker of Nantwich, Cheshire. He is listed variously as clockmaker, watchmaker, watchcase maker and tool maker. His address is given as Wyke's Court, Dale Street, Liverpool. Wyke was the name of his famous partner John Wyke (see Ridgway, *Chester Silver,* p. 215, 217). He severed his connection with John Wyke 24 June 1782 but carried on his business at Wyke's Court. The Liverpool Street Directories show that from 1790 he also used Sir Thomas's Buildings as a manufactory and from 1796-1804 at Wire Works at Brownlow Hill near the China Houses. He also submitted silver to the Birmingham Assay Office by 1792, but returned to Chester about 1795.

1785	2 boxes. 262 watchcases.
1786	2 boxes. 169 watchcases and three half cases.
1787	349 and 3 half cases.
1788	309 watchcases and a half case.
1789	173 watchcases. 6 watchcases 'turned down and broke'. 1 box.
1790	145 watchcases and two and a half cases.

JOHN HACK, 1833.
1833   5 silver boxes.

ISAAC HADWIN (Hadwen), Liverpool, 1792.
The Liverpool Trade Directories state that he worked in Pool Lane from 1766 until 1794 when he is linked with Thomas Hadwin as silversmith of 34 Pool Lane. From 1796 to 1804 he is listed as a 'gentleman' of 1 Rose Place, St Anne's and then until 1827 as a 'gentleman' of 1 Great Nelson Street. His early years lable him as 'silversmith and watchmaker'.
1792   45 gold rings.

RICHARD HARPER, Liverpool, 1799-1800.
1799   32 gold rings.
1800   66 gold rings.

THOMAS HARRISON, Liverpool, 1785.
Born about 1750 and listed as a watch and clock maker, but in 1785 the only reference to him in the Plate Duty Books was to watchcase making. He may have used cases made by others. He is listed at 1 Finney Lane, Thomas Street, Liverpool (1774-1803). He was employed by Joseph Finney before 1772 and married Elizabeth, the daughter of Joseph Finney. He had a son, Finney Harrison, who was brought up in the clock-making business and from 1804 the Company was named Harrison and Son.
1785   7 pr. watchcases.

The HELSBY Family, Liverpool. (Illustration 28-29)
(See Ridgway, *Chester Silver*, p. 85f.).
The Helsby family of Liverpool used the Chester Assay Office from the end of the 18th century and were principally watchcase makers, but expanded their work to include other silver wares. Their ability to make hinges for watchcases provided the expertise to make hinged gold and silver boxes.
In the Liverpool Trade Directories, Thomas Helsby is listed as a watchcase maker of Trueman Street in 1794. By 1800 he was at Vauxhall Road where he remained until 1832 being joined by his sons in a manufactory at 28 Vauxhall Road. He was probably responsible for introducing engine turning which became a hallmark of Liverpool cases. He also made repousse gold cases.
Thomas Helsby first appears in the Chester Plate Duty Books in 1793.
1793   133 silver watchcases. 1 gold pair of watchcases.
1794   1 silver case. 9 boxes.
1795   307 watchcases. 20 boxes (3 additional watchcases as 'not silver').
1796   209 watchcases (16 rejected as not silver). 16 pair of gold watchcases and 1 case and 33 boxes.
1797   328 watchcases (9 rejected as not silver). 18 pair in gold and 42 boxes.
1798   105 silver pair of watchcases. 3 gold cases. 3 boxes. 1 gold box.
1811   1 gold medal.

THOMAS HELSBY and SON, Liverpool, 1816-1826.
1816   1 gold ring.
1817   1 snuff box.
1819   1 snuff box.
1820   1 gold toothpick case. 17 mounts for shells. 2 boxes.
1821   1 tea spoon. 1 snuff box. 1 pair gold sleeve buttons.
1822   2 snuff boxes. 1 gold cane head.
1824   2 gold rings.

THOMAS HELSBY and SONS, Liverpool, 1827.
1827   1 snuff box lid.

J. HELSBY and SON, Liverpool, 1826.

1826   1 snuff box.

WILLIAM HELSBY, Liverpool, 1830.

1830   1 box.

JOHN HELSBY, Liverpool, 1830-.

He appears to be the son of Thomas Helsby (along with William) and are the Son and Sons mentioned above. He worked independently after 1830.

John Heslby appears in the Liverpool Trade Directory in 1823 as a watchcase maker at 45 Bevington Hill but moved to several addresses in the years following. He was in Trueman Street until 1837, Hunter Street, 42 Springfield until 1857, Moss Street 1860-2 and in 1864 is listed as 'Assayer of gold and silver in Pembroke Gardens'.

An unusual example of his work was sold at Sotheby's Beresford Adams at Chester 2 December 1980. This was a silver mounted Mearshaum pipe. The bowl was covered by a hinged lid applied with a monogram and crest within floral scroll work above the pierced legend 'In fumo vivimus'. Inscribed around the mouthpiece acanthus borders. 7 inches long and dated Chester 1843. It was presented in a leather case. Carries the inscription 'In commemoration of skiff race won by George Bentham at Chester Regatta August 10 1843'.

1830   1 shell snuff box top. 2 cream jugs. 1 box.
1831   1 coffin plate.
1832   359 tea spoons. 32 table spoons. 80 salt spoons. 3 caddy spoons. 15 pairs sugar tongs. 15 mustard spoons. 17 'spoons'. (also 35 tea spoons. 7 table spoons and 5 salt spoons not sterling and rejected, 'no intention to fraud'.)
1833   25 'silver tickets'. 1 gold ring.
1834   1 watch swivel in gold. 1 medal. 1 pencil case.
1835   2 gold rings. 2 medals. 2 'instruments'.

JAMES HEMMING, Liverpool, 1837-1839.

Lived in 13 Tarlton Street, Liverpool. He apparently took over from William Hemming and combined the work of watchcase maker with that of making gold rings.

1837   3 gold rings.
1838   1 gold ring. 2 seals. 2 silver boxes.
1839   A badge.

WILLIAM HEMMING, Liverpool, 1827-1836.

William Hemming lived at 13 Tarlton Street, and was a watchcase maker.

1827   2 small boxes. 3 bottle tops rejected in May were replaced by three in June which were approved.
1828   2 boxes.
1830   1 gold ring.
1831   2 silver boxes.
1833   4 gold rings. 2 horn mounts.
1836   3 boxes and under W. J. Hemming a gold ring.

JOHN HEMMINGWAY, Manchester, 1813-1814.

1813   63 gold rings.
1814   126 gold rings.

HEMMINGWAY & GLOVER, Manchester, 1808-1810.

1808   39 gold rings.
1809   95 gold rings.
1810   39 gold rings.

JOSEPH HEWETT, Liverpool, 1790-1793.

1790   A dram bottle. 2 cups. A pocket bottle.

1791   A pocket bottle. 10 skewers. 34 coat buttons. 44 wine tickets (32 wine tickets were rejected.)

1792   A chalice (rejected as not sterling) but one accepted a month later. 32 wine tickets. 12 vest buttons. 16 coat buttons.

THOMAS HILL, Chester 1788-1789.

1788   9 pair of buskles. 3 pr knee buckles. 4 pr shoe buckles.

1789   39 pair plain buckles. 70 pr knee buckles. 45 pr shoe buckles. 1 stock buskle. 4 nozils. 7 seals. 16 bottle lables. A pair of clasps. 20 skewers. 52 sugar tongs. A wine funnel. 12 gold rings. A fork. 8 masonic lables. 1 masonic square. A gorget. 38 tea spoons. 7 tables spoons. 13 gravy spoons. 9 sauce ladles. A plain ladle. 1 dessert spoon.

N. HORT, 1834

1834   6 toy tea spoons (not allowed) as they were in a finished state.

WILLIAM HULL, Liverpool, 1785-1801.

He is listed as at Crosshall Street (1779), Tarlton Street (1784), Wyke>s Court (1785), Cheapside (1788), Tythebarn Street (1794), 65 Highfield Street (1796). He was one of four watchcase makers who transferred his work to Birmingham in 1789. (Chester had warned him of added solder in a letter quoted in the Minute Book). He returned in 1798 and died in 1818, aged 75.

1785   27 watchcases.

1786   50 and a half case.

1787   129 watchcases but six rejected as not sterling. 2 boxes.

1789   163 (seven rejected). 2 boxes. 2 half cases.

1793   2 watchcases.

1794   106 (4 not sterling). 5 boxes. 1 box (rejected).

1795   95 watchcases. 9 boxes.

1796   486 watchcases. 11 half cases. 13 boxes.

1797   244 watchcases. 12 half cases (6 watchcases rejected.).

1798   104 watchcases. 4 half cases. 5 boxes. 7 medals.

1801   1 gold ring.

H. M. & S. HUNTINGDON, Chester, 1822-1830.

(See Mary Huntingdon).

Mary Huntingdon apparently began this firm but was later linked with S. Huntingdon from 1822.

1822   A cream ladle.

1823   4 salt ladles. 33 gold rings.

1824   2 sugar tongs. 4 skewers. A castor top. 94 gold rings.

1825   126 gold rings. 2 coffin plates. 2 bottle tickets.

1826   32 gold rings. 6 egg spoons. 6 rims for drinking horns. A pap boat.

1827   2 toast racks. 37 gold rings. 2 castor tops. 4 horn mounts.

1828   1 pair of tongs. 1 silver clasp. 2 butter knives. 2 pickle forks. 82 gold rings

1829   A mount for glass. 2 coffin plates.

1830   2 coffin plates. 17 gold rings.

MARY HUNTINGDON, Chester, 1815-1822.

(See Ridgway, *Chester Silver*, p. 89).

1815   3 cream jugs. 1 'foot for coco'.

1821   3 coffin plates. 8 bottle tickets. 4 skewers. A knife blade. 4 salt spoons. 90 gold rings.

1822   4 coffin plates. 8 bottle tickets. Pair of spurs.

The JONES Family, Liverpool.
(See Ridgway, *Chester Silver,* p. 90-94 and 205f.).

According to the Chester Duty Books several Jones submitted their wares for duty from Liverpool, most of them related. Some were linked with the Walley family and others to the Reeves. Apart from the work of Joseph Walley (1785-88), one Reeves (1820-21) and William Jones and Abbot (1814) or Abbott and Jones (1812), they seem to have worked together. (See Jones and Son, R. Jones & Co., C. Jones & Co., Jones and Walley (Walley & Jones), Robert Jones, William Jones, W. Jones and Abbot, Jones and Reeves.)

ROBERT JONES, Liverpool, 1788-1822.

1788   19 skewers. 6 plain funnels. 18 blades. 18 forks. 5 salad forks. 27 labels. 84 gold rings.

1789   48 coat buttons. 36 forks. $12^1{}_2$ pairs of sleeve buttons. 29 bottle lables. 4 salad forks.

1790   1 toast rack. 6 funnels. 15 skewers. 2 dish crosses. 10 calls (boatswains calls). A cane head. 10 gold rings. 24 gold sleeve buttons. A parcel of children's clasps.

1791   18 skewers. 241 gold rings.

1792   12 pair gold buttons. 196 gold rings. 24 silver seals. 42 pair buttons. 17 pair silver clasps. 5 dish crosses. 5 skewers. 5 punch ladles. 6 wine funnels. 1 pair of studs. 18 servers. 12 boatswains calls.

1793   60 boatswains calls. 177 gold rings. 9 skewers. 18 dessert forks. 3 funnels. 1 pap boat. 2 salad forks. 27 pair buttons. 2 dish crosses. 4 seals.

1794   210 gold rings. 2 cheese scoops. 3 'toast trays'. 9 pair gold buttons. 12 pair clasps. 28 pair buttons. 3 skewers. 36 bottle tickets. 1 funnel.

1795   24 pair coat buttons. 38 links of buttons. 1 gold stock button. 11 pair gold buttons. 100 pair sleeve buttons. 1 chalice cup and cover. 1 silver case. 7 seals. 3 toast racks. 1 toast tray. 13 skewers. 198 gold rings.

1796   258 gold rings. 21 skewers. 3 cruet tops. 2 toast racks. 1 pair shoe buckles. 4 plates for furniture. 16 calls.

1797   7 pair gold buttons. 18 seals. 16 skewers. 154 gold rings. 12 waist coat buttons. 16 coat buttons. 24 calls. 1 dish cross. 1 butter stand. 6 pair sleeve buttons. 1 dram bottle. 10 bottle tickets.

1798   21 skewers. 74 gold rings. 18 calls. 13 clasps. 97 link buttons were rejected as not sterling.

1799   1 gold spectacle. 346 gold rings. 18 skewers. 5 pair of clasps. 40 pair buttons. 36 calls. 1 gold mount for a snuff box.

1800   11 skewers. 190 gold rings. 1 pr. spectacles. 25 calls.

1801   394 gold rings. 11 pair of $^3{}_4$ gold buttons. 18 pair of silver clasps. 30 skewers. 29 pr of sleeve buttons. 14 calls.

1802   34 skewers. 1 pair gold spectacles. 325 gold rings.

1803   270 gold rings. 5 skewers. 1 shell mount.

1804   Mounting for a sugar basin.

1805   6 pairs of saddle mounts. 42 pairs sleeve buttons. 447 gold rings.

1806   2 pair gold spectacles. 130 gold rings. 12 silver seals. 1 trowel.

1807   352 gold rings.

1808   4 pair gold sleeve buttons. 8 pair gold buttons. 14 skewers. 60 gold rings.

1809   6 gold salt spoons. 170 gold rings.

1810   98 gold rings.

1811   23 skewers. 180 gold rings.

1812   (Under the name R. Jones and Co., the only entry under that title) 142 gold rings.

1812   9 gold rings (for R. Jones and Son, see below.).

1814   1 pr gold spectacles. 1 pr gold knee buckles.

1815   178 gold rings.

1816   9 prs spectacles.

1817   193 gold rings.

1818	131 gold rings.
1819	107 gold rings. 'A cocoa nut mount'.
1821	139 gold rings.
1822	139 gold rings.

R. JONES & SON also R. JONES Co., Liverpool, 1813-1832.

1813	7 prs sleeve buttons. 1 plate. 131 gold rings.
1814	1 pr spectacles. Silver breast plate. 139 gold rings.
1815	26 gold rings.
1816	A nutmeg grater. 6 prs spectacles. 267 gold rings.
1817	168 gold rings.
1820	454 gold rings.
1821	148 gold rings.
1822	A mount for an ink stand. Mount for a cane head. A caddy handle. 165 gold rings.
1823	A pair of sleeve buttons. 275 gold rings.
1824	A mounting for a cup. 402 gold rings.
1825	A ferule. 275 gold rings. A cane head in gold. 3 prs spectacles in gold. 152 gold rings.
1826	Pr spectacles in gold. 152 gold rings.
1827	151 gold rings. 9 lables. 10 fish knives.
1828	4 sauce boats. 4 toast racks. An extinguisher. 22 fish knives. 6 skewers. 137 gold rings.
1829	271 gold rings.
1830	142 gold rings.
1831	111 gold rings.
1832	114 gold rings.

R. JONES & CO., 1811-1831.

1811	142 gold rings.
1828	12 butter knives.
1830	264 gold rings. 1 trowel.
1831	128 gold rings.

C. JONES, Liverpool, 1825-1831.
(also C. JONES & Co., 1830-1831, Liverpool.)

1825	1 gold ring.
1830	1 snuff box.
1831	2 castor tops.

JONES and WALLEY also WALLEY and JONES Liverpool.
In 1785 and 1786 the partnership was Walley and Jones. From September 1786 to 1788 it became Jones and Walley.
(See Ridgway, *Chester Silver*, p. 205).

1785	4 salad forks. 6 skewers 2 toast racks. 3 punch ladles. 2 pap boats. 3 dish crosses. 12 seals. 72 dessert spoons. 48 buttons. 1 funnel. 1 barrel.
1786	14 prs plain gold buttons. 7 funnels. 1 pannikin. 6 skewers. 30 waist buttons. 36 coat buttons. 3 child's boats. 3 dish crosses. 2 gold stock buckles. 1 stand. 11 seals. 36 dessert spoons. 3 doctors instruments .58 gold rings.
1787	3 salad forks. 6 pap boats. 132 dessert spoons. 174 gold rings. 42 salt ladles. 2 children's cups. 2 toast stands. 6 funnels .12 skewers. 2 toabcco boxes. 1 silver barrel. 1 dish cross. 2 pannikiins. 6 calls. 2 cheese diggers. 1 saucepan. 2 cups.
1788	2 children's cups. 1 dish cross. 12 gold buttons.

W. JONES and ABBOTT, Liverpool, 1812-1814.

(also ABBOTT and JONES).

1812   66 gold rings.
1813   7 gold rings.
1814   20 gold rings.

JONES and REEVES, Liverpool, 1821-1822.

(REEVES and JONES, 1820).

1820   Mount for box. A box. 5 medals.
1821   A snuff box.
1822   2 salt ladles. A mount for glass. An ear trumpet.

WILLIAM JONES, Liverpool, 1806-1813.

1806   99 gold rings. 8 links sleeve buttons.
1807   71 gold rings.
1808   A lamp and stand. 8 gold buttons. 138 gold rings.
1809   1 seal. 1 coffin plate. 1 dairy spoon. 250 gold rings.
1810   103 gold rings.
1811   132 gold rings.
1812   43 gold rings.
1813   20 gold rings.

RICHARD KILSHAW, Liverpool, 1802.

Richard Kilshaw was apprenticed to William Hull for five years in 1792.

1802   12 silver seals.

JOHN KIND, 1821-1822.

1821   78 gold rings. 30 gold rings were rejected as 'not sterling'.
1822   30 gold rings.

E. KIRKMAN, Liverpool, 1832-1839.

1832   2 gold rings.
1839   1 busk.

PATRICK LANDRA, 1835.

This is the only appearance of Patrick Landra in the Chester Duty Books when he submitted 6 tea spoons. It is possible that this is a mistaken reference to Patrick Leonard, well known as a flat ware maker. 1835 was the year Leonard registered his mark at Sheffield and also at Chester. (See under Patrick Leonard, p. 123).

NICHOLSON LEE, Liverpool, 1796-1817.

Described as a watchmaker or watchcase maker. Listed as Nicholas Lee at 7 Ray Street, Liverpool (1796) and at 29 Ray Street (1810), 32 Ray Street (1818), 36 Ray Street and 143 Scotland Road (1823-1825) where he died in 1834. Will proved at Chester 1835. He married Grace Spencer in c. 1792. His two sons also became watchcase makers for M. I. Tobias of London and Liverpool.

1796   47 watchcases. 5 boxes.
1797   131 watchcases. 6 boxes.
1798   37 watchcases (3 rejected). 1 box. Duty had been paid on 18 of the watch-cases and was refunded after 25 March 1798.
1799 to 1806   Supplied watchcases as usual but are not now listed.
1807   7 boxes.
1817   1 gold ring.

JOSEPH LEWIS, 1834.

(See Joseph Lewis Samuel, CO Liverpool.)

DAVID LLOYD, Liverpool, 1828-1831.

1828   19 gold rings.
1831   36 gold rings.

THE LOWE FAMILY, Chester.

The earlier members of the Lowe family are dealt with in full in *Chester Silver 1727-1837* but the following is a resumé of George Lowe 1 and George Lowe 2, his son. His other sons, John, Thomas and Robert also appear in the Chester records of marks but only Robert in the Plate Duty Books.

George Lowe (2) moved to Gloucester and appears to have used a mark which is recorded at Chester. He later returned to Chester and the entry George Lowe and son appears to include on that of his father by him.

In November 1837 the record changes to George Lowe and sons which may mean that from then on, when George Lowe (1) was ill the other sons had joined to form a family business. The repeat of type 1 mark which is recorded on the 1840 copper plate may indicate that the aged father still wanted his mark recorded. George Lowe 2 was not officially admitted to the Company until 1847, and John Lowe and Thomas appear from 1839/40 record their marks on the first copper plate (compartment 11) and on the second copper plate in compartment L.

Thomas remained in Chester working with his brother John, but Robert had moved to Preston but recorded his own mark at Chester and recorded work in the Plate Duty Books from 1830 to 1837, of a very limited amount.

Although John registered a separate mark in 1864 shortly before he died, but after this date although many Lowes registered their separate marks on the copper plates, the firm appeared as Lowe and Sons which remained in the family in Bridge Street Row, Chester until well into the twentieth century.

Later members of the Lowe family appear on page 124).

GEORGE LOWE (1), Chester and GEORGE LOWE (2), Chester and Gloucester.

(See also JOHN, THOMAS, sons of George Lowe (1) p. 18) also (Ridgway, *Chester Silver,* p. 97f).

1791   114 gold rings. 30 breast buttons.
1792   92 gold rings. 3 skewers. 1 'scissors'. 1 pr buckles. 20 coat buttons. Pair of gold buttons.
1793   88 gold rings. 1 knife blade. 19 seals. 2 pap boats. 4 sauce ladles. 3 boxes. a basin. 18 bottle tickets. 24 silver buttons. 28 salt spoons. 2 table spoons. 6 caddy spoons. 2 beakers. (2 not sterling). 3 cups. 4 butter trowels 3 medals. 1 coffee urn cover. 1 muffineer.
1794   135 gold rings. 18 seals. 1 silver cup. 1 cream jug. 4 salt spoons. 30 pairs silver buttons. 3 pairs knee buckles. 2 pairs sugar tongs.
1795   153 gold rings. 4 spoons. 6 small spoons. 1 muffineer. 1 fork. 4 prs sugar tongs. 19 coat buttons. 20 pairs buttons. 1 mustard pot lid. 2 cream jugs. 16 seals. 1 purse mount. 1 pr buckles. 1 pr boot buckles. 1 pr knee buckles. 1 butter trowel. 1 coffin plate. 1 chalice and cover. 2 prs clasps. 1 wine strainer. 1 boat (?cream boat).
1796   148 gold rings. 1 cream ladle. 1 cream boat. 3 boats. 1 punch ladle. 38 prs sleeve buttons. 1 coffin plate. 3 forks. mustard ladle. 1 chalice. 1 tumbler. 1 pr sugar tongs. 1 sauce boat. 5 spoons. 1 handle. 1 pr tongs plus 'anchors'. 7 blank seals. 1 beaker. 1 jug. 1 trowel. 3 cream jugs. 2 caddy ladles. 1 caddy shell. 1 wine strainer. 15 buttons.
1797   284 gold rings. 13 pr sugar tongs. 3 jugs. 1 cream jug. 1 pr goblets. 39 pairs buttons. 1 sauce pan. 1 silver cup. 1 seal. 1 candle box.
1798   164 gold rings. 5 skewers. 1 saucepan. 1 small waiter. 1 punch bowl and ladle. a wax candle box. 2 sauce ladles. 1 apple scoop. 1 coffin plate.
1799   gold rings. A silver box.
1800   232 gold rings. 1 fork. 2 boxes. 4 ladles. 6 punch ladles. 29 coat buttons. 12 breast buttons. 2 castor tops. 1 butter knife. 4 prs clasps. A wax candle box.

1801	244 gold rings. 8 small tumbler ladles. 12 small ladles. 2 ladles. 4 toast racks. 1 bottle. 1 skewer. 1 strainer. 1 coffin plate. 4 ladles. 1 'scissor' sheath. 5 caddy spoons. 2 boxes.
1802	393 gold rings. 6 lables. 3 castor tops. 4 silver pap boats. 11 bottle rings. bottle ticket. 1 'cream'. 6 caddy ladles. 1 silver foot for a cocoa hull. 12 pair coat buttons. 2 skewers.
1803	375 gold rings. A mustard pot lid. 10 bottle rings.
1804	334 gold rings. 4 knife and fork stands. 4 skewers. bottle rings. 15 ladles. 4 castor tops. 1 panakin. 8 belt plates. 1 toast rack. 2 bottle tickets. 4 forks. 1 toasting fork. 24 coat buttons. 1 nipple. 3 ladles.
1805	424 gold rings. 15 caddy ladles. 1 tea spoon. 26 prs buttons. 13 bottle tickets. 1 dog collar. 11 belt plates. 17 sugar tongs. 1 ear trumpet. 14 seals. 2 skewers. 1 tea pot stand. 1 'corral'. 4 cream jugs. 1 fork. 1 box. 2 cans. 1 extinguisher. 6 mustard spoons. 4 bottle rings.
1806	389 gold rings. 3 forks. 1 comb. 3 cream ladles. 1 box. 1 coffin plate. 1 'corral'. 1 silver mace. 2 cruet tops.
1807	525 gold rings. 2 jug tins. a wax candlestick (rejected). 9 forks. 2 jug mounts. 3 spoons. 10 skewers. 7 pr sleeve buttons. a tea pot lid. 6 cans. 6 small spoons. cocoa shell mount.
1808	480 gold rings. 1 box. 3 caddy shells. A foot and rim to cocoa shell. 14 prs sleeve buttons. 6 skewers. 1 lable. A $\frac{1}{2}$ pint can. cream jug. 2 cocoa mounts 2 castor tops. 2 seals. 2 forks. 1 knife. 4 bottle tops. 4 knife rests.
1809	434 gold rings. 4 ladles. 1 cup cover. 1 goblet foot. 54 pair sleeve buttons. 2 coffin plates. 10 skewers. 4 forks. 2 spoons. 5 pair belt clasps. 1 mustard spoon. 1 chamber candlestick. 5 cocoa nut foot. 4 'bugles' (Buckles ? or hunting bugle?).
1810	833 gold rings. 4 pair belt clasps. silver medals (not sterling). 1 book case. 3 medals. skewers.
1811	649 gold rings (30 not sterling). 3 medals. 2 cream pans. 1 sugar muller. 1 mount for cup. 6 skewers. 4 bottle tickets (not sterling)). 6 ladles. 1 spoon. 3 bottle tickets.
1812	593 gold rings. 2 bottle tickets. 2 sugar spoons. 2 ladles. 10 prs sleeve buttons. 2 skewers. 1 mustard spoon. 12 tea spoons. 4 egg spoons. 6 small silver spoons. 1 pr gold knee buckles.
1813	613 gold rings. 3 cocoa nut mount. 7 egg spoons. 1 box. 4 cruet tops. 4 pair sleeve buttons. 2 silver coffin plates.
1814	726 gold rings. 1 bottle ticket. 2 castor tops. 3 sugar tongs. 1 mustard pot mounting. 1 buckle. 1 tube. 8 coffin plates. 1 butter ladles. 1 snuff box. mustard spoons. 7 small toy spoons.
1815	701 gold rings. 3 mountings for a cocoa nut shell. 5 skewers. 6 bottle rims. 5 toast racks. 6 pickle forks. 2 coffin plates. 11 mounts for jugs. (2 mounts for jugs rejected). 6 caddy spoons. 23 sugar tongs. 7 spoons. 1 snuffer tray. 1 cream ewer. 3 cream jugs. 1 'foot for coco'.
1816	620 gold rings. (and 52 rejected as not sterling). 82 coffin plates. 10 cream jugs. 11 mustard spoons. 1 dessert fork. 13 sugar tongs. 1 tea pot. 1 toast rack. 2 sugar spoons. 2 lables. 4 snuffer trays. 2 snuffer stands. 9 pap boats. 5 habit clasps. 2 jug mounts. 14 egg spoons. 6 pair sleeve buttons. 7 caddy ladles. 2 forks. 6 horn mounts. 4 knife rests. 1 button book. 5 skewers. 2 salt shovels. 1 box.
1817	462 gold rings. 23 skewers. 13 small skewers. 1 box. 2 snuff boxes. 2 fillets (and 2 fillets refused). 4 pickle forks. (and 4 pickle forks rejected). 2 cocoa nut mounts. 4 coffin plates. 17 caddy shells. 4 bottle rings. 10 decanter labels. 2 cream ladles. 3 jug mounts. 9 horn mounts. 6 mustard spoons. 1 bottle mount. 3 'save calls'. 2 dog couplers. 1 pair dog couplers. 3 cream ladles.
1818	732 gold rings. 1 mustard (top). 1 castor top. 6 jug mounts. 3 pap boats. 6 spoons. 2 coffin plates. 8 pr tongs. 3 pr gold buttons. 14 ladles.
1819	817 gold rings. 4 coffin plates. 2 ladles. 1 lemon strainer. 1 box. 1 shell mount. 6 skewers. 3 pap boats.

1820	796 gold rings. 1 mount for mustard pot. 3 cream jugs. 3 coffin plates. 9 sugar spoons. 4 skewers. 1 fork. 1 bottle ticket. 2 prs dog couplers.
1821	759 gold rings. (48 rejected as not sterling). 1 pair dog couplers. 4 mustard spoons. 10 pairs of sleeve buttons. 7 coffin plates. 6 pickle forks. 1 cocoa nut mount. 8 mounts for horn. 7 sugar ladles. pair of buckles. 1 pap boat. 12 shoe clasps. 3 pairs of gold sleeve buttons.
1822	650 gold rings (and 17 rejected). 6 pickle forks. 2 forks. 1 pair of clasps. 19 pairs shoe clasps. 1 coffin plate. mustard lid. 4 skewers. 1 medal. 6 sauce ladles. 20 mustard spoons. 6 sugar spoons.
1823	518 gold rings. 33 egg spoons. (9 egg spoons rejected). 2 pairs sugar tongs. 2 mustard spoons. 4 mounts for jug. 1 tobacco box. 3 coffin plates. 6 punch ladles. 4 ladles. 2 sauce ladles. 1 toast rack. 1 medal. 1 horn mount.
1824	608 gold rings. 9 coffin plates. 12 tea spoons. 5 pairs clasps. 2 toast racks. 4 skewers. 1 jug cover. 1 horn rim. 7 bottle tickets. 8 mustard spoons. 12 pairs sleeve buttons. 1 chamber candlestick. 1 extinguisher. 2 medals. 9 shoe clasps.
1825	676 gold rings. 12 bottle tickets. 18 egg spoons. 7 skewers. 2 medals. 8 coffin plates. 1 purse top. 1 pair sugar tongs.
1826	558 gold rings. 14 lables. 3 toast racks. 18 caddy spoons. 25 egg spoons. 2 coffin plates. 1 seal. 6 skewers. 6 mustard pot mounts (and 3 rejected as not sterling). 1 jug. 1 panikin. 3 jug mounts. 1 pickle frame. 2 bottle rings. 1 fork. 1 mount for horn drinking. 1 butter knives.
1827	460 gold rings. 1 pickle frame. 1 collar. 1 horn mount. 5 coffin plates. 2 mustard spoons. 13 spoons. 2 tea spoons. 2 toast racks. 4 bottle tickets. 10 labels. 2 sugar tongs. 1 fork. 18 egg spoons. 12 caddy spoons. 1 medal. 4 knife rests. A trowel. 1 'nipperkins'. 1 cover and handle for coffee pot. 1 apple scoop. 1 jug mount.
1828	573 gold rings. 6 horn mounts. 7 coffin plates. 2 salt spoons. 27 sugar tongs. 26 egg spoons. 18 lables. 6 mustard mounts. 18 caddy spoons. 1 box cover. 1 box. 4 knife rests. 24 sleeve buttons. 12 funnels. 2 wine labels. 1 gravy spoon. 1 sugar basin. 1 soup ladle. 5 horn mounts. 9 skewers. 9 pickle forks (and 3 rejected as not sterling). 6 pairs shoe clasps.
1829	479 gold rings. 8 horn mounts. 4 coffin plates. toast racks. 5 large and 2 small skewers. 29 bottle tickets. 6 lables. 6 sugar spoons. 6 toy tea spoons. 24 salt spoons. 2 wine lables. 2 silver tubes 1 box. 1 butter knife. 2 apple scoops. 1 mount for mustard pot. 1 mustard mounts. 1 cup and saucer.
1830	271 gold rings. 8 small sugar tongs. 21 sugar tongs. 7 sugar spoons. 4 toast racks. 8 caddy spoons. 6 coffin plates. 1 cream ladle. 2 bottle tickets. 1 cream jug. 2 pap boats. 6 small funnels. 24 mustard spoons. 2 apple scoops. 2 mustard pot mounts. 1 box lid. 1 box. 1 horn mount. 1 dessert spoon. 1 tea spoon (refused 1/6 as in a finished state). 12 spectacle frames.
1831	478 gold rings. 5 cream jugs. 6 sugar spoons. 2 table spoons. 2 tea spoons. 1 fork. 1 saucepan lid. 1 sugar breaker. 3 toast racks. 2 horn mounts. 12 mustard spoons. A handle for a shaving brush. 6 small funnels. 7 coffin plates. 5 mustard pot mounts. 28 salt spoons. 6 pickle forks. 1 pair salts. 1 box. 6 butter knives. 3 skewers. 1 tea pot handle.
1832	477 gold rings. 4 coffin plates. 1 paperknife. 1 silver jug. 1 water jug. 9 ladles. 2 pap boats. 1 mustard spoon. 5 wine labels. 19 egg spoons. 3 skewers. 8 sugar tongs. 2 mustard pot mounts. 1 medal.
1833	342 gold rings. 16 wine labels. 1 mount for foxes head. 2 coffin plates. 12 sugar tongs. 2 toast racks. 5 horn mounts. 1 gold mount for a cane. 1 mount for glass.
1834	395 gold rings. 1 cane mounting. 2 lids for inkpots. 23 bottle labels. 3 mustard pot mounts. 4 coffin plates. 3 toast racks.
1835	348 gold rings. 8 coffin plates. 2 small jug mounts. 2 ladles. 1 cream ladle. 6 caddy spoons. 1 snuff box. 1 cap for whip. 1 medal. 1 butter knife. 1 horn mount. 4 pickle forks. 1 mustard pot.
1836	342 gold rings. 6 coffin plates. 2 mustard pot lids. 4 mustard pot mounts. 2 toast racks. 6 sugar spoons. 1 water pot. 2 sugar ladles. 1 teapot.

1837	463 gold rings. 9 castor tops. 3 sugar spoons. 45 salt spoons. 32 salts. 1 cream ladle. 9 coffin plates. 4 butter knives. 1 egg spoon. 2 toast racks. 8 caddy spoons. 2 pap boats. 1 wafer box. 2 mustard spoons. 1 beaker cup. 1 lid. 1 cup. 8 pair sleeve buttons.
1838	460 gold rings. 2 ladles. 21 mustard spoons. 1 mustard pot lid. 2 trowels. 2 crump trowels. 5 tea spoons. 11 castor tops. 5 sugar spoons. 24 pr sugar tongs. 1 jug mount. 22 egg spoons. 12 salt spoons. 2 sugar crushers. 5 bottle tops. 3 butter knives. 1 coffin plate. 2 pickle forks. 1 buckle. 1 box lining. 1 lining for cup.
1839	441 gold rings (7 rejected as not sterling). 38 sugar tongs. 6 horn mounts. 1 snuff box lining. 1 crump trowel. 1 trowel. 48 spoons. 4 butter knives. 1 coffin plate. 1 pair spectacles. 10 labels. 10 bottle labels. 5 pickle forks. 1 medal. 9 castor tops. 2 cheese knives. 1 cheese 'scope'.
1840	(to March 13)
	6 gold rings. 2 coffin plates. 1 tumbler. 1 cup cover and handle. 2 mountings for snuff boxes. 6 pairs of sugar tongs.

A third mark (now recorded) belonging to George Lowe (1) appears on six toy tea spoons and a pair of tongs. They are fiddle back, $2^1{}_2$ inches long, and appear to be the 'seven spoons' mentioned in 1815 weighing 3 ounces. They have four marks. GL with mid way pellet in square frame with sloping right edge, lion passant guardant, duty mark and date letter U.

ROBERT LOWE, Preston, 1830-1837.
Robert Lowe was the fourth son of George Lowe (1) born 1 September 1796 and baptised at Holy Trinity Chester 16 October 1796. He became a goldsmith though apparently not a member of the Company. He dealt mainly in watches and moved to Preston where his business was not particularly good. He had married Jane Colley Hunt of Hockley near Birmingham and had three children. These are referred to in a journal kept by George Lowe Whitehouse in 1836 and 1841 to 1843. One of whom was the Reverend William Lowe and there were two girls.

Robert Lowe was helped by his brothers particularly John Lowe. His work was further handicapped by an ailing wife. There is a mark recorded at Chester of RL within a rectangle 'which appears about the time when the firm added and sons' and he may have been included in this along with John and Thomas. His mark does not appear in Jackson and he is referred to as a watchmaker, as watchcase makers were no longer required to have duty paid on their work at this time and there are no references to this kind of work, though his submission of various silver goods between 1830 and 1837 appear in the Plate Duty Books.

1830	12 caddy spoons. 3 sugar spoons. 1 silver ladle. 3 pair of sugar tongs (and 5 rejected as not sterling). 6 sugar ladles. 2 butter knives.
1831	13 sugar tongs. 1 toast rack. 6 sugar crushers. 2 butter knives. 15 bottle labels. 7 egg spoons.
1832	12 pair sugar tongs. 3 caddy spoons. 8 egg spoons. 4 butter knives. 4 sugar spoons.
1833	6 pair sugar tongs. 8 egg spoons.
1837	1 trowel.
1839	1 trowel.

RICHARD LUCAS, Liverpool, 1832-1839.

1832	4 masonic medals.
1839	2 medals.

EDWARD MADDOCK, Liverpool, 1798-1815. Watchcase maker. Son of William Maddock.
Born about 1768. A watchcase maker from Cumberland Street, Liverpool (1791), Plumb Street (1793), Edmund Street (1795) and Ormond Street (1807-1830). He married Alice Harrison.

1798	13 watchcases and 1 half case.
1815	Snuff box.

WILLIAM MADDOCK, Liverpool, 1831-1832. Watchcase maker.

22 Sawney, None Street, Liverpool. Also seems to have registered his mark at Birmingham 1836.

1831   1 gold ring.

1832   1 trowel.

JOHN MILLER, Newcastle, 1825-1826. (Illustration 22)

Although it is not stated in the Chester Plate Duty Book where John Miller came from, Margaret Gill, *A Dictionary of Newcastle Goldsmiths* p. 173 reports a goldsmith of that name at Newcastle, saying that he was the son of William Miller of Newcastle yeoman and that he was apprenticed to Thomas Watson for seven years 28 December 1809. He was excused the apprenticeship fee as his father provided 'meat, drink, washing, lodging and wearing apparel during the said term'. He was admitted a freeman of the town 7 October 1816 and of the Company 6 December 1831. If this identity is correct it would account for the two years he is found assaying at Chester in 1825-26.

Only one mug with the marks JM and the Chester assay are known along with the date letter for 1825/26. It is a plain mug 3^1_2 inches high, diameter of rim 2^3_4 inches and base 3 inches which is reeded. There are no examples of his work in the Laing Art Gallery at Newcastle with any Newcastle marks. The mark is illustrated in the *Archaeologia Aeliana*, 4th series, vol. xlvii, p. 101f and illustrated no. 276 as found on the Newcastle copper disc The surviving example is evidently one of the 'eightieth cans' 1825 or one of the '12 cans' submitted in 1826 (see illustration p.   ).

1825   1 gold ring. 18 cans. 1 porringer. 2 salts. 10 ladles. 1 goblet. 1 pair of nut-crackers. 6 pr sugar tongs. 7 mustard mounts. 9 mug mounts. 5 skewers. 2 cayenne spoons. 2 muffineers. 2 cream ewers. 1 toast rack. 1 spoon. 4 jug mounts.

1826   8 jug mounts. 12 cans. 1 punch ladle 1 mustard   mount. 18 bottle mounts. 1 tumbler. 2 goblets. 5 pr sugar tongs (and of these 3 not sterling). 1 mustard spoon. 9 jug rims.

PETER MOLYNEUX, Liverpool, 1793-1796.

1793   24 gold rings.

1794   12 gold rings.

1796   42 gold rings.

RICHARD MORROW, Liverpool, 1786-1792.

1786   25 gold rings. 4 buckles.

1787   30 gold rings. '7 masons jewels'. 2 pair buttons.

1788   4 seals.

1789   15 gold rings. 1 pair buckles. 16 coat buttons

1790   40 gold rings.

1792   6 masons medals.

THOMAS MORROW, Liverpool, 1796.

1796   7 pairs of gold buttons. 37 gold rings.

JOSEPH MORTON, Manchester, 1811.

1811   48 gold rings.

NEWTON and HYDE, Manchester, 1822-26.

(See also Thomas Newton.)

1822   178 gold rings.

1823   1176 gold rings.

1824   1194 gold rings.

1825   1079 gold rings.

1826   549 gold rings.

THOMAS NEWTON, Manchester, 1827-1840.

(See Newton and Hyde). Ridgway, *Chester Silver,* p. 118.

Thomas Newton first appears in the Chester Plate Duty Books in 1822 in partnership with Samuel Hyde. Their period together was limited and they produced a large number of gold rings presumably wedding rings. (q.v.).

In 1827 Thomas Newton appears alone. The mark used in partnership with Samuel Hyde appears to have been NH within a rectangle and later when working alone TN within a rectangle, both marks are found on the Chester copper plate in compartment 19.

Thomas Newton married Margaret Johnson Owen 27 July 1824. In Bains Directory, Manchester and in the Manchester Directory of 1833 he is described as a working jeweller and a silversmith at 9 Chapel Walks, Manchester. In 1851 he had moved to 68 Bradshaw Street, Hulme where he is described as a house agent and where his two daughters, Frances Mary and Eleanor were provision dealers. His son, Frederick, emigrated to Australia, became a mounted policeman at Ararat and died young.

By 1861 Thomas Newton had moved to 3 New York Street, Chorlton on Medlock as a house agent where he died 20 June 1872. He left in his will about £6,000 which included houses in New York Street and Little Rumyard Street, Chorlton.

1827	460 gold rings. 12 Masonic medals. 31 medals.
1828	911 gold rings. 3 escutcheons. 39 medals. 8 pieces of cane mounts.
1829	609 gold rings. 1 gorget. 29 medals.
1830	50 gold rings. 2 mustard glass mounts. 8 medals.
1831	29 gold rings.
1832	194 gold rings. 8 medals.
1835	119 gold rings.
1836	532 gold rings. 1 staff head. 2 cane heads.
1837	420 gold rings.
1838	60 gold rings.
1839	1 box.
1840	59 gold rings.

EDWARD NIGHTINGALE, 1826-1828.

1826	71 gold rings.
1827	18 gold rings.
1828	71 gold rings.

JOHN PARSONAGE, 1831.

1831	2 box lids.

THOMAS PIERREPOINT, Liverpool, 1785-1786.

Thomas Pierrepoint was born about 1757 and lived at 12 Southside, St Paul's Square, Liverpool He married Ann Atkinson in 1778 and died on Chirstmas Day 1785. Later David Beyendorfe (q.v.) married Thomas Pierrepoint's widow, Ann. The five watch-cases submitted in January 1786 were probably sent by his widow.

1785	22 silver watchcases and 13 were broke down. They weighed 26 oz. 4 dwt.
1786	5 silver watchcases.

ROBERT PRESTON, 1787-1792.

1787	1 silver tun.
1792	16 coat buttons. 13 breast buttons.

WILLIAM PUGH, Birmingham, 1810-1814.

(See Ridgway, *Chester Silver,* p. 128.)

The registration of William Pugh on the Chester Plate is interesting as there was a ban on gold and silver being taken from Birmingham at this time. He appears to have produced several items apart from the gold boxes which are listed at Chester. There is known silver registered at Birmingham where he recorded his mark from 1773 to 1801. The gold boxes have not been traced.

At Birmingham he lived in Suffolk Street where he made a butter knife and a gold snuff box in 1807.

1810   3 gold boxes.
1813   3 gold snuff boxes.
1814   3 gold snuff boxes.

REEVES and JONES (Jones and Reeves), Liverpool, 1820-1822.
(See Jones and Reeves, p. 87).

JAMES RICHARDS, Liverpool, 1795. Watchcase maker.
Lived at Marybone, Bevington Bush Road in 1796.
1795   77 watchcases. 5 gold watchcases. 1 gold watchcase 'broke'. 6 boxes.

RICHARD RICHARDSON, Chester, 1784-1790.
(See Ridgway, *Chester Silver,* p. 179f.)

1784   2 pair of buckles. 14 buttons. 1 bailiff's mace. 1 wide funnel. 1 pap spoon. 1 caddy spoon.

1785   5 table spoons. 37 dessert spoons. 33 tea spoons. 9 gravy spoons. 4 spoons. 8 punch ladles. 14 sauce ladles. 20 skewers. 7 ladles. 3 coconut shell mounts. 2 pair buckles. 2 stock buckles. 58 salt ladles. 1 sugar ladle. 4 labels. 1 bottle label. 3 gold rings. 80 buttons. 3 pr shoe buckles. 3 knee buckles. 13 coat buttons. 1 patch box. 1 butter knife. 4 saddle buttons. 1 mustard spoon. 1 cheese knife. 1 pr shoe clasps. 3 cheese diggers. 6 children's spoons. 1 pap spoon. 1 panikin. 1 fork. 1 coffin plate. 1 gold motto ring. A gold cup (weighing 10 oz 5 dwts at 8/- an ounce). 2 tumblers.

1786   6 table spoons. 14 gravy spoons. 8 ladles. 78 salt ladles. 1 mustard spoon. 2 coconut feet. 26 salt shovels. 2 apple scoops. 48 tea spoons. 2 cups. 4 saddle buttons. 1 knife and fork. 2 pr shoe buckles. 17 pr knee buckles. 6 skewers 2 castor tops. 1 knife blade 1 box lid. 2 boxes. 1 half pint. 2 panikin. 3 pap boats. 3 pap spoon. 1 communion cup. 1 pair clasps. 2 corks. 2 coffin plates. 1 salad fork. 1 pr buckles. 4 medals. 2 plain medals. 47 gold rings. 3 wine funnels. 1 nozil. 1 snuff. 1 stock buckle. 1 seal. 14 coat buttons. 1 waistcoat buttons. 8 sauce ladles.

1787   66 gold rings 10 soup ladles. 12 gravy spoons. 2 cups. 1 gold cup. 1 cheese knife. 135 pair buttons. 5 labels. 3 coffin plates. 11 punch ladles. 12 spoons. 2 table spoons. 2 tea spoons. 2 skewers. 5 pair buckles. 43 salt ladles. 34 coat buttons. 2 coat badges. 1 sugar spoon. 17 pr of clasps. 2 bridle buckles. 6 dessert spoons. 2 whip heads. 1 coconut feet. 1 pap boat.

1788   121 gold rings. 2 cruet tops. 2 mustard ladles. 16 sauce ladles. 8 nozils. 17 gravy spoons. 43 tea spoons. 13 table spoons. 87 buttons. 2 pannikins. 8 skewers. 1 small candlestick. 4 pap boats. 2 wine funnel stands. 76 salt ladles. 14 salt spoons. 1 coconut mount. 6 pr shoe buckles. 1 pr shoe clasps. 4 saddle buttons. 2 marrow scoops. 2 sugar spoons. 1 knife blade. 2 pr clasps. 1 pr buckles. 12 dessert spoons. 4 tureen ladles. 1 pr knee buckles.

1789   2 pr buckles. 2 quarter pints. 1 gravy spoon. 7 marrow scoops. 5 mustard ladles. 1 mustard spoon. 12 salt ladles. 12 sauce ladles. 37 labels. 1 cream ladle 1 gold cup (weighing 9 ounces 19 dwts). 1 bugle horn. 3 gold sleeve buttons. 2 ferrules. 4 forks. 3 knives. 34 gold rings. 1 whip head. 1 saucepan. 12 waistcoat buttons 4 coffin plates. 2 caster tops. 1 pr shoe buckles. 15 pr knee buckles. 14 buttons. 28 pr clasps. 27 tea spoons. 20 spoons. 2 ladles. 1 salt spoon. 6 punch ladles.

1790   38 tea spoons. 17 dessert spoons. 49 salt spoons. 2 mustard spoons. 4 marrow spoons. 1 tureen ladle. 2 snuffer stands. 2 castor tops. 1 punch ladle. 1 sauce ladle. 13 gravy spoons. 8 table spoons. 2 salad forks. 1 pr boot buckles. 3 pr shoe buckles. 1 pr shoe clasps. 6 pair buckles. 4 coffin plates. 3 knee buckles. 1 hat buckle. 10 pr clasps. 3 cups. 1 stay hook. 4 pap boats. 3 skewers. 1 gold cup. 15 lables. 20 buttons. 44 **gold rings.**

HENRY RIGBY, Liverpool, 1785-1787.

Henry Rigby's address seems to have been 76 Cable Street (1774), John Street (1777) and Tarlton Street (1777). It is possible that as a finisher he may have sent other people's watchcases for assay at Chester in 1785. There are two variations of the HR mark seen on Chester watchcases but none on the first Chester plate. This also applied to David Beyendorfe, to Wyke and Green. Thomas Pierrepoint and Gabriel Smith. Henry Rigby died in 1787.

1785   171 watchcases and half case. 2 boxes.
1786   34 watchcases.
1787   26 watchcases and one half case.

JOSEPH LEWIS SAMUEL Co., Liverpool, 1834-1839.

1834   1 gold medal.
1838   1 medal. 1 gold ring.
1839   4 silver rings.

M. SOLOMON, ? Liverpool, 1814-1815.

1814   81 gold rings.
1815   28 gold rings.

JOHN SUTTER (S), Liverpool, 1835-1840 f.

(See Ridgway, *Chester Silver,* p. 193f).
(See Gill, *Dictionary of Newcastle Goldsmiths*).
(Illustration 14)

The name of Sutter has been linked with Scotland and it is possible that the family moved from there to Newcastle on Tyne. It is here that he registered his mark on the circular copper plate, but according to Gill his output was very small being four penny weights of plain gold rings, and eighty five ounces of silverware, including butter knife, lid for a snuff box, sugar tongs, egg spoons, salt spoon and tea spoon. Jackson (1921 Edition) records his name at Newcastle but due to a misprint he appears as John Sutler. He used the Newcastle Office for a very short time between 31 August 1832 and 18 June 1833. Unfortunately the punch books for that period at Newcastle have not survived, and there is no record of his address, nor do the local trade directories for 1830 list him as a resident in Newcastle and we may assume that he moved to Liverpool where the trade directories list him in 1839 living at 29 Standish Street and working as a silversmith. By 1843 he had moved to 8 Fleet Street from 1857 to 1860 at 12 Williamson Street, in 1868 and 1874 he is in College Lane. It is also possible that if his Scottish ancestry became known the Newcastle rules for 1536 may have still applied which forbade any Scotsman to be apprenticed or to work in Newcastle.

When he moved to Liverpool he registered his mark at Chester and first appears there in the Plate Duty Books 16 April 1834 on which he paid 11/8½ duty their weight being 7 ounces 15 dwts and 20 grains. From then on he produced a very large quantity of silver. The plural 's' is dropped in October 1836. The revenue which the Chester Office received from the watchcase makers ceased in 1798 and from then on no duty was paid. It did not apply to other silver and gold articles and the income from John Sutter, a newcomer to Liverpool would be most welcome. Although the Chester Plate Duty Books only record his work for a period of four and a half years, his turn over was very considerable, and it continued for long after 1840.

His mark at Chester was stamped five times in compartment 7 of the first copper plate.

John Coakley had been responsible for much flatware made in Liverpool at this time and he ceased to submit to Chester about the time John Sutter came to Liverpool. It is possible that he may have joined his firm (see p.   ).

His first entry at Chester was in 1834 on which he paid 11/8½ duty their weight being 7 ounces 15 dwts and 20 grains. From then on he produced a very large quantity of silver.

1834   A gravy spoon. Tea spoon. 1 sauce ladle. 1 pepper caster.

1835	784 tea spoons. 75 dessert spoons. 39 table spoons. 40 table forks. 20 forks. 105 salt spoons. 14 caddy spoons. 16 sugar spoons. 23 pairs sugar tongs. 18 mustard spoons. 4 butter spoons. 6 toddy ladles. 15 pickle forks. 2 ladles. 1 honey knife. A pair of scales (see C. B. Walker 1837 '2 scale panes'). A small hammer.
1836	604 tea spoons. 40 'spoons'. 175 table spoons. 69 dessert spoons. 26 table forks. 15 dessert forks. 25 'forks'. 92 salt spoons. 12 pickle forks. 9 caddy spoons. 60 'shells'. 8 ladles. 6 egg spoons. 7 toddy ladles. 12 mustard spoons. 4 prs sugar tongs. a 'sugar'. 1 pepper ladle.
1837	1216 tea spoons. 12 'spoons'. 243 dessert spoons. 126 table spoons. 143 salt spoons. 3 mustard spoons. 12 toddy ladles. 32 'ladles'. 24 egg spoons. 120 pr sugar tongs. 8 caddy spoons. 163 dessert forks. 140 table forks. A 'dole' spoon. A toast rack. A child's jug. 1 gold ring. (this record has been damaged).
1838	1307 tea spoons. 236 table spoons. 177 dessert spoons. 31 mustard spoons. 29 sugar spoons. 52 ladles. 12 caddy spoons. 1 oar. 4 sauce spoons. 2 gravy spoons. 133 salt spoons. 24 egg spoons. 174 table forks. 83 dessert forks. 27 'forks'. 60 pickle forks. 37 prs sugar tongs. 6 toddy ladles. 1 medal.
1839	1013 tea spoons. 324 table spoons. 12 'spoons'. 140 dessert spoons. 48 mustard spoons. 18 sugar spoons. 306 salt spoons. 28 egg spoons. 49 ladles. 30 caddy spoons. 17 gravy spoons. 1 cheese knife. 1 cream spoon. 38 'forks'. 263 dessert forks. 91 table forks. 1 'busk for stays'. A mustard pot cover. A box mounting. 4 skewers. A nipple plate. A 'Royal Crown for Africa' (see note below).
1840	(record until 5 April 1840) 210 tea spoons. 72 dessert spoons. 48 salt spoons. 24 'forks'. 25 dessert forks. 11 pickle forks. 3 ladles. 2 ladle spoons. 1 butter knife. 12 pr sugar tongs.

In this short record the production of over 5000 tea spoons and over 1600 table and dessert spoons, 1000 table and dessert forks indicates a considerable output and the large number of staff employed. He appears to have worked until about 1850.

The reference to the making of 'a Royal Crown for Africa' in 1839 is of special interest. It is known that Liverpool carpenters were called on to make thrones for African chiefs who had been elevated to kings at the time of colonial expansion and that before the First World War, Waring and Gillows were asked to furnish palaces overseas even to the extent of supplying portraits for the walls. For whom this crown was provided is not known.

Among the references to single 'forks' in 1838 is one of that date which combines both fork and knife, used presumably by a person with an amputated arm.

It is of interest to note that two brass forks have been found with fiddle pattern handles which were made from the same mould as a silver fork. The marks on the brass forks have a strange form of lion passant, a type of crown and one of an anchor. There is also a JS within an oval but also the mark used by John Sutter on silver. The presence of such a mark on brass needs some explaining. (see *The Finial*, Journal of the Silver Spoon Society, 1993.)

Very few Chester caddy spoons have been recorded though quite a number are listed. A caddy spoon by John Sutter is reported by Captain John Norie as having been found with full hall marks (dated 1839) by a collector of caddy spoons living in Baltimore (with the head of Queen Victoria on the Duty mark.)

WILLIAM TARLETON, Liverpool, 1785-1787.

Born about 1740. Lived in Bixteth Street (1766), Church Street (1769), Lime Street (1800). Was apprenticed to John Parker, a watchmaker of Liverpool. He gave evidence to the Royal Commission on taxing watches and clocks (1798) but though his output at that time was twenty a week his last appearance in the Plate Duty Books was in 1787 when he submitted only gold rings. He died about 1815.

J. TAYLOR, 1825.

1825	23 gold rings.

JOHN TWEMLOW, Chester, 1814-1833.

(See John Wemlow, 1833).

John Twemlow joined his father William Twemlow after they moved to Chester and established his workshop at Broughton on the east side of the city. For twenty years he made a variety of goods including flat ware and wedding rings. In the Chester General Directory (1840) he is listed as 'silversmith' and working jeweller in 'Spital, Broughton'.

1814	6 tea spoons.
1823	7 caster mounts. 1 cream jug. 119 gold rings.
1824	9 jug mounts. 10 salt ladles. 2 mustard mounts. 3 gold rings.
1825	6 tea spoons. 4 salt spoons. 1 mount for a snuff box. 25 gold rings.
1826	3 mustard pot mounts. mount for a jug rim. 4 bottle tickets. 22 gold rings.
1827	28 gold rings. 4 egg spoons. 4 cups.
1828	90 gold rings. 1 mouth piece.
1829	6 tea spoons. 1 toast rack. 1 salt frame. 52 gold rings.
1830	12 forks. 20 gold rings.
1831	1 wine coaster. 104 gold rings.
(1833	17 gold rings but see J. Wemlow.)

WILLIAM TWEMLOW, Nantwich and Chester, 1787-1823.

(See Ridgway, *Chester Silver,* p. 194.)

William Twemlow was living in Nantwich in south Cheshire in 1786 and at first appears to have made minor pieces of silver and gold rings, but between 1799 and 1800 tumbler cups and flat ware. He moved to Chester with his son (John Twemlow) about 1814.

1787	46 gold rings (and 17 broke as not sterling.)
1788	25 gold rings.
1790	1 caddy spoon. 14 gold rings.
1791	22 gold rings.
1792	2 tumblers. 29 gold rings.
1793	18 gold rings.
1797	2 prs buckles. 1 'jill cup'. 1 nutmeg grater. 1 punch ladle. 2 pr watchcases and a watchcase. 34 tea spoons. 1 caddie spoon.
1798	6 nozils.
1799	2 punch ladles. 1 bottle stand. 1 quarter pint. 6 tea spoons. 12 gold rings.
1800	1 panakin. 4 table spoons. 6 tea spoons. 4 salt ladles.
1801	1 table spoon, 2 spoons. 4 salt ladles. 1 punch ladle.
1802	2 child's saucepan. 3 small maces. 1 toast rack. 1 pr sugar tongs. 1 saucepan. 12 tea spoons. 3 table spoons. 52 gold rings.
1803	14 coat buttons. 1 saucepan. 4 salt ladles. 1 barrel. 1 soup ladle. 1 pr buckles. 30 tea spoons. 1 pr spurs. 2 table spoons. 3 cantels.
1804	12 tea spoons. gun furniture. 1 cream jug.
1805	18 tea spoons. 10 table spoons. 1 cream jug. 1 skewer. 2 beakers .
1806	1 ear trumpet. 2 cups. 44 spoons. 1 half pint. 1 salt ladle. 4 sugar tongs. 1 box. 1 table spoon.
1807	1 ladle. 4 salt ladles. 1 beaker. 3 skewers. 20 gold rings.
1808	1 gravy spoon. 2 table spoons. 2 dessert spoons. 18 tea spoons. 4 salt ladles. 1 cup. 1 coconut foot.
1809	2 table spoons. 1 saucepan. 1 large cane head. 1 cup.
1810	1 skewer. 1 coconut foot. 18 tea spoons. 2 cups. 3 medals. 1 coffin plate.
1811	3 coffin plates. 6 tea spoons. 3 medals. 1 cup. 1 'scutcheon'.
1812	2 cream 'tubbs'. 8 salt ladles. 'set of book ornaments'. 37 book ornaments. 1 pr buckles. 1 cup. 57 gold rings.
1813	13 tea spoons. 1 cup. 1 dog collar.
1814	12 tea spoons. 1 cup. 1 dog collar. 2 coffin plates.
1815	5 coffin plates.
1816	12 tea spoons. 11 gold rings. 2 pr sugar tongs. 1 coffin plate.

1817	6 table spoons. 1 skewer. 1 pr sugar tongs. 2 gravy (spoons). 6 tea spoons. 2 cups. 1 snuffer tray.
1818	1 lable. 1 plate (?coffin plate). 2 table spoons. 1 buckle.
1819	4 salt spoons.
1820	34 gold rings. 7 lables. 1 coffin plate. 5 skewers.
1822	6 salt spoons.
1823	A mount for a box. 25 gold rings.

VALE AND CO., 1819.

| 1819 | 111 gold rings. |

THE WALKER FAMILY

(See Ridgway, *Chester Silver*, p. 196f.)

The first of the family to become goldsmiths at Chester was George Walker who obtained his freedom in 1767. He married Sarah Bagg (who died in 1825). He had served his apprenticeship under Richard Richardson (2) and was admitted to the Company 29 July 1770 becoming Warden in 1771 and remained as one of the Wardens until 1791 when he became Assay Master. He remained as Assay Master until his death in 1809 when his son John succeeded him. In the *Chester Chronicle*, 18 February 1777 appears an advertisement saying George Walker had 'at great expense purchased a method of mending broken china', he also states that he was living in Eastgate Street and that he was an agent to the Manchester Fire Office, yet he heads his advertisement 'China mended without rivets . . . Goldsmith, Jeweller and Engraver.' Although his other son, George, as well as William Sanderson both served their apprenticeship, there is no question that the son was a goldsmith for although he was the elder son he became a wine merchant and lived eventually at Castle Hill House, Kingsley where he died 22 October 1844, aged 67. This makes him five years older than his brother John. This George should not be confused with George Walker who was his brother-in-law having married Elizabeth, his youngest sister. The two Georges were made free on the same day 23 March 1799 and both were wine merchants. The evidence seems to show that all the GW silver so far located belongs to George Walker (1). The period covered by the Chester Plate Duty Books is later than the porringers which were made by him.

There is a break in the Company's Minute Book at 1796 and when it is resumed John Walker appears 5 July 1809 when it is stated that he had served his apprenticeship under his father and this was witnessed by both George Walkers.

When George Walker (1) died in 1809 of dropsy it seems that John had already taken over the family business. He submitted silver under his name in 1805. He became Assay Master in 1834 when his own son, John Walker (2) registered his mark. This mark has not been identified as the family fell from favour in 1840 and all had been ejected from the Company. John Walker lived at Broughton, Chester after his disgrace and died a bankrupt. (15 January 1841, *Chester Chronicle*.)

In the Duty Book is the name of C. B. Walker in 1837. This was Charles Burton Walker, son of John Walker (1) who submitted 'a spectacle frame,' and '2 scale panes' in 1837. Thomas Walker was another son of John Walker (1) who submitted plate between 1830 and 1836.

John Walker (2) was admitted a brother 'the elder son of a brother and having been bound by indenture to a brother of the company for seven years' was admitted on the same day as his brother Thomas 5 July 1834. He is not mentioned in the Chester Plate Books.

At a meeting of the Company 1 April 1841, the Walkers were directed to deliver up 'all books, papers, stamps, dies, punches, scales, weights and other implements belonging to the said Company' and the family were dismissed from the Company. Charles Burton Walker 'he not being a freeman at the time of his admission and not being brought up to the trade of a goldsmith but that of a bookseller and not having his admission entered on a stamp as by law required'. Henry Walker, son of George Walker (2) for 'not having served his apprenticeship to a brother of the Company as by law required and not having been sworn in, 'he refusing to qualify' was also dismissed. After this date the Walkers were no longer involved in Company matters.

C. B. WALKER, Chester, 1837.
(Charles Burton Walker)
1837   Spectacle frame. '2 scale panes'.

GEORGE WALKER, Chester, 1785-1805.
(See Ridgway, *Chester Silver,* p. 196).

1785   7 pair buckles. 10 breast buttons. 28 buttons. 4 pairs knee buckles. 3 pairs shoe buckles. 4 funnels. 2 nipperkins. 1 small cup. Cups.
1786   4 salt ladles. 14 breast buttons. 7 cream boats. 3 cups. 1 skewer. 1 gold ring.
1787   2 cream boats. 1 cup. 3 pairs buckles. 3 pairs knee buckles. 2 tea canisters. 3 skewers. 128 gold rings. 2 tumblers. 1 tea pot.
1788   1 tankard lid. 1 pair buckles. 1 pair buttons. 12 waist coat buttons. 4 cream boats. 27 coat buttons. 368 gold rings.
1789   15 coat buttons. 149 gold rings.
1790   1 pair sleeve buttons. 16 coat buttons. 14 buttons. 1 dog collar. 329 gold rings.
1791   1 hair slide. 2 pairs clasps. 12 seal blanks. 34 coat buttons. 2 tobacco boxes. 1 dessert spoon. 1 table spoon. 21 tea spoons. 6 toy tea spoons. 1 knee buckle. 1 patch box. 1 gold cup. 1 nozil for candlestick 1 pair buttons. 20 breast buttons. 1 punch ladle. 5 tooth brush cases. 3 salt ladles. 11 skewers. 4 sugar ladles. 1 dog collar. 1 coffin plate. 1 scratch back. Pair salts. 3 table spoons. 1 pair tongs. 242 gold rings. 6 dessert forks.
1792   12 seals. 1 wax candle box. 6 labels. 16 tea spoons. 1 toy spoon. 5 dessert spoons. table spoons. 1 cheese tester. 1 hat buckle. 2 snuffer pans. 9 breast buttons. 1 knife blade. 4 marrow spoons. 1 castor top. 2 skewers. 1 butter ladle. 3 coffin plates. 58 coat buttons. 1 pepper box. 3 gravy spoons. 1 sauce pan. a knife and fork. cream ladles. 2 salad forks. 1 pair clasps. 2 cheese diggers. Salt ladles. 1 cream boat. 1 pair sleeve buttons. 1 knee buckle. 2 small boxes. 9 breast buttons. 2 'Quaril Arrows'. 270 gold rings. 2 'spung boxes'. 4 salt shovels.
1793   11 seals. 9 chaise plates. 3 coffin plates. 8 salt ladles. 4 candlestick nozils. 1 wine funnel. 3 cream boats. 11 tea spoons. 1 punch ladle. 7 skewers. 2 sauce ladles. 2 candle boxes. 3 tables. 2 pairs buckles. 1 dessert spoon. 1 hat buckle. 1 scrape tongue. 2 salt spoons. 1 fruit knife. 2 buttons. 1 butter ladle. 2 canister tops. 20 gold rings. 2 nozils. 3 sugar ladles. 8 salt ladles.
1794   3 butter trowels. 2 buckles. skewers. 23 sauce ladles. 2 cheese scoops. 3 pairs gold buttons. 2 funnels. 1 knife blade. 1 pair buttons. 4 caddy spoons. 2 pairs shoe clasps. 1 punch ladle. 7 table spoons. 3 tea spoons. 14 dessert spoons. 4 pr sugar tongs. 1 sugar ladle. 13 bottle tickets. 1 tongue scrape. 11 seals. 1 muffineer. 1 salad fork. 22 coat buttons. 24 breast buttons. 356 gold rings. 1 tobacco stopper. 9 silver blanks. 1 jug cover. 1 pap boat. 2 labels.
1795   1 pepper ladle. 1 seal. 1 snuff box. 1 cruet foot. 2 coffin plates. 1 dog collar. 6 skewers. 5 links of gold buttons. 2 nozils. 1 toy spoon. 4 pairs clasps. 1 cheese digger. 4 castor tops. 2 watchcases. 251 gold rings. 1 mustard spoon. 1 handle.
1796   1 pepper ladle. Sugar ladle. 1 cream. 2 castor tops. 1 nutmeg grater. 2 seals. 4 blank seals. 3 coffin plates. 1 silver cup. 2 buttons. 3 coat buttons. 5 pairs sleeve buttons. 3 pairs clasps. 13 tea spoons. 2 honey ladles. 4 labels. 4 mustard spoons. 1 knee buckle. 1 tube. 1 butter trowel. 2 pencil cases. 3 caddy spoons. 1 toast rack. 18 salt ladles 20 pairs sugar tongs. 2 dessert spoons. 1 gold cane head. 1 pair gold buttons. 302 gold rings. 1 cup.
1797   1 'Save' all. 4 coffin plates. 1 hat plate. 5 sugar tongs. 1 cheese scoop. 2 butter trowels. 3 tea spoons. 2 mustard spoons. 2 sauce ladles. 1 sugar ladle. 1 punch ladle. 1 whip cap. 13 coat buttons. 1 skewer. 388 gold rings. 1 watch-case. 1 apple scoop. 3 spoons. 2 cane heads. 1 watch box.

1798	2 skewers. 14 coat buttons 1 funnel. 1 pair knee buckles. 2 sauce ladles. 1 pin cushion case. 1 clasp. 1 small cup. 1 seal. 236 gold rings.

1798   2 skewers. 14 coat buttons 1 funnel. 1 pair knee buckles. 2 sauce ladles. 1 pin cushion case. 1 clasp. 1 small cup. 1 seal. 236 gold rings.

1799   1 medal. 1 salve box. 3 coffin plates. 1 ladle 1 pair gold sleeve buttons. 1 apple scoop. 1 small cup. 1 child's spoon. 2 pair sugar tongs. 1 gold motto ring. 286 gold rings.

1800   3 coffin plates. 1 extinguisher. 1 pair clasps. 1 hair comb. 1 apple scoop. 1 shoe buckle. A pair of small spurs. 278 gold rings.

1801   1 barrel. 2 sugar ladles. 2 small ladles. 6 buttons. A seal. 1 ear trumpet. 'A foot cover and spoon to cocoa shell'. 1 knife blade. 1 cup. 2 coffin plates. 439 gold rings.

1802   2 coat buttons. 22 breast buttons. 3 coffin plates. 1 crucible. 6 dessert forks. 1 label. 3 skewers. 1 gorget. 1 snuff box. 2 boxes. 1 spectacle case. '2 plates to a barrel'. 1 salt ladle. 430 gold rings.

1803   'A foot and cover to a cocoa shell'. 1 mustard ladle. 3 coffin plates. 1 crucible. 2 lables. 3 skewers. 3 ladles. 4 bottle stands. 30 breast buttons. 1 small cup. 545 gold rings.

1804   16 coat buttons. 1 salt ladle. 1 sugar ladle. 1 mustard spoon. 4 egg spoons. 15 breast buttons. 2 gravy spoons. 1 coffin plate. 4 cruet tops. 1 tea spoon. 537 gold rings.

1805   318 gold rings. 2 cocoa shell feet. 3 lables. 3 cruet tops. 13 coat buttons. 1 butter knife. A music mouthpiece.

JOHN WALKER, Chester, 1805-1836.

(See Ridgway, *Chester Silver,* p. 204.)

1806   521 gold rings. 3 coffin plates. 1 cup. 4 salt shovels. 5 pairs sugar tongs. 24 breast buttons. 36 coat buttons. 2 buckles. 4 castor tops.

1807   370 gold rings. 1 pipe tube. 12 tea spoons. 4 table spoons. 1 coffin plate. 6 table forks. 33 salt ladles.

1808   386 gold rings. 5 coconut mounts. 4 coffin plates. 5 tea spoons.

1809   220 gold rings. 3 salt spoons. 2 table spoons. 2 coffin plates. 1 cup. 2 castor tops. 2 skewers. 1 dairy spoon. 1 seal.

1810   278 gold rings. 3 coconut mounts. 1 coffin plate. 1 pair shoe buckles.

1811   225 gold rings. 2 gravy spoons. 2 coffin plates. 4 'salts'. 51 tea spoons. 7 table spoons. 1 soup ladle. 4 sauce ladles.

1812   307 gold rings. 1 castor top.

1813   180 gold rings.

1814   232 gold rings. 1 sugar spoon. 9 tea spoons. 10 dessert spoons. 10 table spoons. 1 medal. 14 salt ladles.

1815   155 gold rings. 2 table spoons. 4 table forks. 1 castor stand. 6 knife rests. 1 coffin plate. 2 dessert forks.

1816   196 gold rings. 3 salt ladles. 1 half pint. 2 table forks. 1 muffineer.

1817   113 gold rings. 4 coffin plates. 3 mustard spoons. 5 dessert spoons. 1 gravy spoon. 3 sugar spoons. 1 table fork. 4 butter ladles.

1818   71 gold rings. 1 nozil. 1 cup. 1 cup mount. 3 medals. 1 coffin plate.

1819   83 gold rings. 6 table spoons. 3 dessert spoons. 9 salts. 4 mustard spoons.

1820   34 gold rings. 3 dessert spoons. 2 dessert forks. 1 tea spoon. 1 salt spoon. 1 coffin plate.

1821   122 gold rings. 4 bottle tickets. 8 salt ladles. 5 table spoons. 4 table forks.

1822   76 gold rings. 1 medal. 2 castor tops. 10 salt spoons. 1 coffin plate. 2 sauce ladles.

1823   55 gold rings. 1 coffin plate. 1 caddy mount.

1824   108 gold rings. 1 top to muffineer. 8 medals. 10 salt ladles. 1 trowel. 2 coffin plates. 5 tea spoons. 93 dessert forks.

1825   19 gold rings. 6 table spoons. 3 egg spoons.

1826   57 gold rings. 2 tea spoons. 1 coffin plate. 2 salt ladles.

1827   20 gold rings. dessert spoons. 5 mustard spoons. 1 tea spoon. 1 coffin plate. 1 sugar spoon.

1828   48 gold rings. 3 medals. 6 tea spoons.

| 1829 | 99 gold rings. Tea spoons. 1 soup ladle. 3 skewers. 3 table spoons. |
| 1830 | 29 gold rings. 18 salt spoons. |

THOMAS WALKER, Chester, 1830-1834.

1830	1 coffin plate. 22 table spoons. 18 dessert spoons. 32 gold rings.
1831	64 gold rings. 24 table forks. 12 dessert forks. 2 skewers. 72 tea spoons. 24 salt spoons.
1832	1 mustard pot mount. 23 gold rings.
1833	35 gold rings.
1834	36 gold rings. 1 half pint.
1836	1 medal.

WALLEY AND JONES, Liverpool.

(See Jones and Walley.)

J. WEMLOW

(See J. Twemlow.)

THOMAS WOOLFIELD, Liverpool, 1832-1837.

1832	1 mount for a tray. 1 mount for soap. 1 mount for ink stand. 4 silver covers for boxes.
1833	7 pomatum pot covers.
1834	4 salt mounts (1/6 not allowed being finished work). 12 covers for dressing cases. 4 bottle stands and bottoms.
1835	Rack for honey stand. 1 silver box. 5 mountings for shells.
1836	1 shoe horn.
1837	2 spoons. 2 forks. 1 cup.

Unfamiliar words used in The Chester Plate Duty Books

ANCHORS	(George Lowe 1795) It is suggested that this may refer to a bar attached to a watch chain or clasp to hold it in position, or to a knife rest (George Lowe 1827).
ARGYLE	(Robert Green 1792) A spouted pot fitted with an inner jacket to contain hot water and with a compartment to hold heated gravy.
BARRELL	(Walley and Jones 1785) A vessel formed in the shape of a barrel or tun showing the ribs of construction and a bung hole. Usually divided into two beakers and used at picnics or given as awards.
BUGLEHORN	(Richard Richardson 1789) Originally the horn of a wild ox sometimes adapted for drinking, or as a musical instrument (hence bugle). Probably used in this district as a hunting horn.
BUSK	(John Sutter 1839) A strip of wood, whalebone or metal (here silver) passed down the front of a corset to stiffen or support it hence 'Busk or stays'.

CADDY SHELLS	(R. Adamson 1815) Shell may refer to the shape, otherwise a caddy spoon but why '6 caddy shells and 6 caddy spoons')
CALLS	(Jones 1792) Short for Boatswains' calls. A signalling whistle.
CORROL	(Lowe 1804) A coral inserted into a babies rattle to assist teething.
CANISTER	(George Walker 1787) A container for tea.
CANTEL	(W. Twemlow 1803) A segment or corner used in book binding. Also '37 silver book ornaments' (W. T. Twemlow.)
CAP FOR WHIP	(George Lowe 1835) A hunting reference.
CATHETER	(N. Close 1828) A tube for passing into the bladder.
CAYENNE SPOON	(John Miller 1825) Spoon to serve pungent red pepper of capsicum.
CHAISE PLATE	(George Walker 1792) ? A silver plate for a carriage.
CHEESE DIGGER	(Richard Richardson 1785) A curved spoon to dig into a cheese.
COFFIN PLATE	(John Walker 1806) A plate on which information was engraved about the deceased, and attached to the coffin.
CRUMP TROWEL	(George Lowe 1839) A trowel or slice for serving crumpets.
DISH CROSS	(R. Jones 1797) A stand with four adjustable feet for warming plates.
DOG COUPLERS	(George Lowe 1821) A chain to link two dogs. Silver collars are also referred to.
DOLE SPOON	(J. Sutter 1837) A serving spoon.
EGG CUP	(N. Cunliffe) This is the only reference to a silver egg cup from 1784 to 1840. (Unless '1 cup' refers to one.)
ESCUTCHEON	(Scutcheen) (W. Twemlow 1811) A small shield.
EXTINGUISHER	(R. Jones & Co. 1828) A cone shaped article for putting out candle flames.
FERRILE	(Ferril, Ferrule) (Richard Richardson 1789) A ring or cup of metal to strengthen the end of a stick.
GORGET	(T. Newton 1829) Originally a military term indicating a throat guard and used as an insignia.
MARROW SCOOP	(R. Bowers 1809) Impliment designed to remove the marrow from bones.
MOUTH PIECE	(John Walker 1805) For a musical instrument.
MUFFINEER	
MULLER	(George Lowe 1811) See SUGAR MULLER/BREAKER.
NAPPERKIN	(Nipperkin) (George Walker 1785) Of Dutch origin. A measure or vessel for liquor containing $\frac{1}{2}$ pint.

NOZIL	(Nozzle) (Richard Richardson 1788) A socket on the top of a candlestick.
PANIKIN	(R. Richardson 1785) A small pan or drinking vessel.
PAPBOAT	(R. Richardson 1786) A vessel with an extended spout for feeding a baby or sick person.
PAP SPOON	(Walley & Jones 1785) A spoon to accompany a papboat.
PIPE TUBE	(George Lowe 1814)
POMATUM POT	(Thomas Woolfield 1834) A pot to hold toilet preparations.
SCARCALL	(George Walker 1797) Short form of whistle.
SCRAPE TONGUE	(George Walker 1793) As descriped.
SCRATCH BACK	(George Walker 1791) A back scratcher.
SHELLS	(See CADDY) '60 Shells' which weighed 12 oz 10 dwts.
SPATULA	(J. Fisher 1786) Medical, for depressing tongues.
SPUNG BOX	(George Walker 1792) A container for a sponge.
STOPPER	(George Walker 1794) For pressing tobacco into a pipe.
SUGAR MULLER	(George Lowe 1811) A disc on the end of a stem having a circular handle to break sugar.
TROWEL	(George Walker 1796) Often used with butter, but could mean a larger instrument.
TUMBLER	(George Walker 1785) Usually accompanied with the word cup. The bottom rounded to prevent spilling.
TONGUE SCRAPE	(See Scrape Tongue) (George Walker 1794).
WAX CANDLE BOX	(George Walker 1792) A Bougie box (see *Chester Silver*, p. 198/9).
WHIP HEAD	(See Cap for Whip) (Richard Richardson 1789).
WIRES	(Crompton and Parry 1816) '4 wires' they weighed together 15 dwts. Used in making watchcases.

Weights of Silver and Gold Assayed at Chester

According to the last Assay Master at Chester, Mr A. Vincent Ward, the records of silver and gold assayed at Chester before 1889 were destroyed during the 1939-45 War. Many others were destroyed shortly before the closing of the Assay Office in 1962, making research difficult. If his statement had been true, he had forgotten about the Plate Duty Books, or believed they had been destroyed. They supply an accurate picture of the silver and gold assayed at Chester from the end of 1784 to 1840.

The earliest surviving record of the amount of plate, which presumably includes both gold and silver, is found in the 1773 Report to Parliament which gives the figures for seven years (found in Appendix No. 3 of the report, p. 73).

1766	824 ounces
1767	331 ounces
1768	314 ounces
1769	161 ounces
1770	2176 ounces
1771	2429 ounces
1772	2348 ounces

The introduction of a special mark to record the payment of duty led to the introduction of the Plate Duty Books. Three of these books remain. Each year is divided into quarters occasionally overlapping so that some run from Christmas and others from January. It has been found that occasionally slight mistakes have been made in the arithmetic by the book keeper and where this has been noted the correction has been made in the following table.

From 18 December 1784 until 1814 gold and silver weights are recorded together, after that date, gold and silver are listed separately. A note reads

NB. The Commissioners of his Majesty's Stamp Duties having a different form for the return of the Plate Duty, distinguishing betwixt the Gold & Silver. We have altered our form of Keeping the acc^t as above distinguishing the Silver from the Gold & leaving the net weight & net Duty a facsimile of the acc^t sent to the Commissioners.

The first entry was made by Richard Richardson on 18 December 1784 when he submitted a 'wine funnel, a pap & a cady spoon' which weighed 5 ounces 10 Pennyweights. The figures which follow are to the nearest ounce.

	Silver	Gold
1785	1995	66
1786	2645	57
1787	3464	63
1788	3058	68
1789	2571	42
1790	1244	79
1791	856	111
1792	495	124
1793	766	102
1794	1526	89
1795	3749	116
1796	4689	158
1797	4849	164
1798	877	83

	Silver	Gold
1799	168	102
1800	193	85
1801	221	112
1802	31	72
1803	347	175
1804	466	157
1805	506	152
1806	189	152
1807	129	164
1808	206	121
1809	157	156
1810	28	219
1811	230	156
1812	92	149
1813	202	265
1814	12	88
	(From 5 January to 21 April 1814)	
	(From 21 April to end of the year)	
	56	128
1815	229	142
1816	249	191
1817	206	179
1818	90	185
1819	68	197
1820	119	193
1821	132	176
1822	127	162
1823	95	154
1824	157	166
1825	259	168
1826	268	122
1827	288	128
1828	1352	153
1829	2471	117
1830	2168	72
1831	1940	70
1832	1148	66
1833	534	31
1834	275	35
1835	1172	35
1836	1287	63
1837	(incomplete)	

	Silver	*Gold*
1838	2970	43
1839	2956	38
1840	(incomplete)	

After 1840 five years are preserved which show that in these years there was more gold assayed at Chester than silver.

	Silver	*Gold*
1850	106 ounces	207 ounces
1851	186	204
1852	115	190
1853	106	221
1854	124	188

It appears that until 1880 the Royal Mint did not receive the diets from Chester. In the nineteenth annual report of the Deputy Master of the Mint (1888) appears the statement . . .

> As a result of a conference held at the Treasury between representatives of that Department, the Board of Trade, and the Mint, their Lordships directed in November last that the 'diets' from the Chester Office should be examined by this Department, and they will for the future be tried with those from Birmingham and Sheffield.

'As a result of representations of the Departmental Committee, after its visit to the several Assay Offices in Great Britain and Ireland . . . arrangements will be made for conducting this joint examination in the course of July next.' In the 1889 annual report from the Royal Mint the figures for Chester appear with those of Birmingham and Sheffield for the first time, access having been given to the figures for 1885, 1886, 1887 and 1888. The year ran from 1 July to 30 June.

	Silver	*Gold*
1885	84,639 ounces	46,937 ounces
1886	123,380	49,426
1887	145,315	42,773
1888	195,190	40,310
1889	233,121	41,883
1890	248,212	51,166
1891	246,909	53,715
1892	233,491	55,789
1893	209,388	41,318
1894	227,250	62,442
1895	311,624	73,283
1896	473,887	97,281

	Silver	*Gold*
1897	556,801	109,187
1898	592,783	130,480
1899	741,044	148,895
1900	889,953	164,958
1901	965,166	173,631
1902	1,017,148	160,902
1903	900,384	167,934
1904	864,152	148,883
1905	788,282	131,989
1906	831,636	134,114
1907	1,020,341	132,384
1908	888,528	138,084
1909	923,255	130,108
1910	992,362	175,480
1911	946,674	166,954
1912	966,319	176,389
1913	981,108	184,624

After 1913 the Royal Mint report gives only the receipts and trial of the diets. There are slight discrepancies in some of these figures and it is possible that no account was given for wares which were 'broke'.

Ronald E. Wilson, *A History of the Sheffield Smelting Company Limited 1760-1960* was given information about some of the Assay Offices, and on interviewing Mr A. Vincent Ward the last Assay Master at Chester, he was informed that 'the earlier Chester Records had been destroyed in the 1939-45 war.' This view is in accord with the note attached to a typed copy of weights which was given to the Board of Trade Departmental Committee on Hallmarking (known as the Stone Report) in April 1956 where it states . . .

> The gaps in the tables are caused by the loss of old records and books stored in cellars, which were at one time during the last war badly damaged.

More documents were destroyed on the eve of the closure of the Assay Office or shortly afterwards.

Ronald E. Wilson could however produce the figures from 1889 given for silver every five years, which are reproduced in his book.

1889	233,121
1894	227,250
1899	741,044
1904	864,152
1909	925,708
1914	975,063

He also adds the figure for 1959 (the year before the book was published.)

1959   63,313

The typed copy preserved in the Chester Town Hall Archives, deposited by the Chester Goldsmiths Company, does not claim to be the final copy but it was submitted to the Board of Trade and was used by the Stone Committee in their report to Parliament. These figures are of considerable interest as they appear to have been taken from the lost or destroyed documents. They run from 1901 to 1955 with an added note for 1956.

For year ending June 30th	Silver	Broken	Number of gold and silver wares assayed
1901	966,885	—	—
1902	1,017,631	—	—
1903	900,745	357	—
1904	864,702	550	—
1905	788,807	524	—
1906	832,035	397	—
1907	1,020,894	552	—
1908	889,354	825	—
1909	925,714	495	—
1910	1,100,956	606	—
1911	948,569	2,639	—
1912	971,820	1,098	—
1913	980,498	811	—
1912	975,367	264	—
1915	549,154	304	—
1916	632,215	57	—
1917	420,925	—	2,388,911
1918	292,472	—	1,629,434
1919	472,247	2	2,064,990
1920	585,980	—	2,545,054
1921	374,676	—	—
1922	377,232	—	—
1923	374,473	—	—
1924	380,743	—	—
1925	421,368	—	1,108,724
1926	360,183	—	859,887
1927	323,384	—	667,293
1928	226,320	—	563,386
1929	212,835	—	563,173
1930	188,423	—	543,318
1931	160,317	9	367,010

For year ending June 30th	Silver	Broken	Number of gold and silver wares assayed
1932	126,788	78	342,193
1933	118,524	30	294,575
1934	148,629	37	410,240
1935	122,764	10	381,835
1936	132,128	49	396,480
1937	140,153	19	390,306
1938	136,537	35	438,619
1939	146,610	46	362,835
1940	124,207	185	349,822
1941	46,229	13	208,195
1942	30,687	21	154,022
1943	9,162	28	105,254
1944	15,832	7	114,074
1945	48,586	8	160,881
1946	66,808	—	187,179
1947	68,279	9	195,733
1948	53,201	6	262,411
1949	34,129	8	181,673
1950n	22,808	29	143,226
1951	24,446	—	132,619
1952	29,147	25	120,970
1953	34,730	38	150,254
1954	45,092	43	236,546
1955	48,980	10	280,148
1956	54,995	—	—

Return made at the request of the Board of Trade Departmental Committee on Hallmarking.   Chester, April 1956

Year ending June 30th	Gold wares (ounces)	Broken	Number of assays made
1901	157,089	—	—
1902	162,560	—	123,583
1903	169,765	1,831	135,373
1904	150,221	1,548	135,764
1905	132,905	969	128,905
1906	135,290	1,175	134,489
1907	133,180	796	—
1908	139,010	940	—
1909	132,500	915	155,668
1910	175,989	2,651	175,085

Year ending June 30th	Gold wares (ounces)	Broken	Number of assays made
1911	165,903	2,322	167,626
1912	177,651	2,096	—
1913	186,613	1,701	—
1914	188,566	2,040	169,462
1915	126,671	1,372	109,831
1916	192,204	1,839	117,122
1917	134,543	1,968	80,613
1918	121,762	2,531	59,962
1919	152,426	935	—
1920	180,541	—	—
1921	105,061	—	—
1922	91,433	—	—
1923	71,245	—	—
1924	69,038	—	—
1925	78,786	—	—
1926	71,635	—	—
1927	54,238	—	—
1928	49,346	—	32,500
1929	51,443	—	28,517
1930	45,275	—	27,107
1931	39,757	125	—
1932	25,664	78	—
1933	20,716	86	—
1934	30,309	68	19,033
1935	31,193	76	18,894
1936	30,100	64	18,586
1937	34,568	81	18,796
1938	36,368	66	18,973
1939	32,904	78	18,656
1940	33,271	47	14,739
1941	20,308	12	8,274
1942	13,490	31	4,620
1943	12,775	71	2,463
1944	11,661	2	2,526
1945	11,661	83	3,918
1946	14,017	17	5,636
1947	19,158	136	6,038
1948	16,632	30	5,481
1949	13,143	98	4,984
1950	9,254	53	4,376
1951	9,126	22	5,499

Year ending June 30th	Gold wares (ounces)	Broken	Number of assays made
1952	8,583	50	3,952
1953	9,569	13	4,697
1954	19,313	22	7,098
1955	25,497	175	8,942
1956	20,269	—	—

When the Stone report was presented to Parliament these figures were compared with the total amount of silver and gold assayed at the six Assay Offices and reduced to percentages for Chester. They gave the figures for 1919 to 1928 and from 1946 to 1957.

SILVER

			Chester %
1919	Total weight	8,879,594	7.2
1920		6,829,370	7.2
1921		4,819,759	7.6
1922		5,395,759	7.1
1923		5,652,981	6.5
1924		5,779,124	6.8
1925		5,808,703	7.0
1926		5,449,791	6.1
1927		5,919,718	4.5
1928		5,919,948	3.6
1946		2,817,928	2.8
1947		2,771,074	1.9
1948		2,122,486	2.4
1949		1,369,671	2.0
1950		1,207,997	1.7
1951		1,361,114	2.3
1952		1,062,892	2.8
1953		1,058,564	4.0
1954		996,395	4.3
1955		1,271,684	4.3
1956		1,326,148	4.1
1957		1,497,453	4.3

GOLD

Year		Total weight	Chester %
1919	Total weight	1,153,240	16.7
1920		1,045,398	20.2
1921		550,864	16.8
1922		538,682	15.1
1923		520,497	12.5
1924		583,289	12.8
1925		669,967	12.4
1926		504,411	11.0
1927		512,235	9.6
1928		526,319	10.0
1946		242,750	7.2
1947		371,902	4.5
1948		184,990	8.3
1949		183,796	6.0
1950		333,471	2.7
1951		553,330	1.6
1952		623,152	1.4
1953		279,067	3.9
1954		238,258	10.5
1955		278,957	9.2
1956		281,354	7.2
1957		309,787	7.9

Some Silversmiths who used the Chester Assay Office
(Other than those who were mentioned in the Plate Duty Books.)

William Aitken, Birmingham.
John Millward Banks, Birmingham.
Herbert Edward Barker & Frank Ernest Barker, Frederick Wallis Barker.
Barnett & Scott, Hull.
S. Blackensee, Birmingham.
Francis Butt, Chester.
Alfred Butt, Chester.
Walter Coulthard, Birmingham.
Iverna Cubbin, Wallasey and Bidston, Wirral.
James Deakin & Sons, Sheffield.
Noble Haseler & Edward John Haseler, Birmingham.
J. & R. Griffin, Birmingham.

Hilliard & Thomason, Birmingham.
Robert Hilton, Taunton, Dyserth, Chester & Keswick. (Keswick School of
    Industries)
Charles Horner, Halifax.
James Charles Jay, London.
Alfred E. Jones, Birmingham.
Grahame Jones, Chester.
Patrick Leonard, Salford.
The later Lowes.
    Francis Maurice Lowe, Chester.
    Peter J. Lowe, Chester.
    James Foulkes Lowe, Chester.
    John Lowe (1).
    John and Thomas Lowe, Chester.
    Thomas Lowe, Chester.
    George Bennett Lowe, Chester.
    John Lowe (2).
    William Foulkes Lowe, Chester.
    John ffoulkes Lowe, Chester.
    John Cecil Lowe, Chester.
    George Frederic Lowe, Chester.
    Martha Lowe, Chester.
    Joyce and John Lowe, Chester.
Joseph Mayer, Liverpool.
Sampson Mordan and Co., London.
Berthold Muller, London.
Nathan and Hayes, Birmingham.
Alexander Ritchie (Iona Celtic Art), Iona.
George Roseater, Devon.
Frederick James Ross, Winchester.
Cornelius Sanders and Francis Shepherd, London.
Isaac Simmons, Manchester.
William Smith, Liverpool.
Richard John Wakefield, Birmingham.
Wakely and Wheeler, London.
Walker and Hall, Sheffield.
Hugh Wallace, Altrincham, Cheshire.
Alfred Vincent Ward, Chester.
George Ward, Manchester.
J. F. Wathew, Chester.
John Christopher Webb, St Albans.
Alfred Wilcox, Birmingham.
Thomas Woolley, Chester.

WILLIAM AITKEN, Birmingham.

William Aitken is listed as a silversmith at Eagle Works, 78 Sumner Row, Birmingham, when recording his mark at Chester, fifteen times for a large version and fourteen times for a smaller version on 15 February and 7 November 1899. He also appears in the London record in 1912 and at Birmingham in 1907. He was a manufacturing silversmith and his claim was 'to make everything in silver', the motto of his house being 'nothing is too large, nothing is too small'. He made silver bowls, vases, card cases, peppers and mustard pots, tea services, stands, sugar tongs, and many other items.

JOHN MILLWARD BANKS, Birmingham. (Illustration 19, 20, 34)

John Millward Banks, silversmith and jeweller of 6 and 7 Northampton Street, Birmingham, registered his mark at Chester, 29 July 1898. He had already registered his mark at London in 1894 and at Birmingham 1902. After his death in 1911 the business was continued under the title of his eldest son, Francis M. Banks until 1926 when it was sold.

J. M. Banks specialised as a manufacturing goldsmith, silversmith and diamond mounter, manufacturer of coloured and bright gold, silver and gem set bracelets and lockets etc., patentee of J. M. Banks, patent bracelet fastener. He manufactured a wide range of goods including various types of jewellery, salts, muffineers, sugar spoons, sifters and match boxes.

Examples have been recorded of a bun-top dredger $1\frac{1}{4}$ inches high.

A small parcel gilt oblong box with rounded corners and slightly concave sides 1 1˙6 by $\frac{1}{2}$ inch deep having an engine turned top surrounding an oval on which are engraved initials.

Six similar pieces of flatware but with different dates (about 1905) of unknown use. These are $8\frac{3}{4}$ inches long and resemble a canoe paddle in shape. The blade 4 inches long is beaten flat and is sharp, the handle is round and has a heart shaped end. Each carries the Chester mark and the date letters. It has been suggested that they may have been given as awards for rowing, or canoeing, or were made as an experiment in producing dinner knives, or letter openers.

HERBERT EDWARD BARKER, FRANK ERNEST BARKER, (FREDERICK WALLIS BARKER) Birmingham

The three brothers registered their mark at Chester, 31 July 1906. They came from Constitution Hill, Birmingham and had showrooms at 292 High Holborn, London and at Glasgow. The firm claimed to have an early history in Mary Barker, who worked in a repair shop in Crego Street, Holloway Head, Birmingham, manufacturing buttons and small wares. The work expanded under her sons and became Barker Brothers by 1860. Later the firm became known for its E.P.N.S. products and had wide interests in the

United States to where much of its work was exported. It is believed that when the duty on silver was abolished in 1890, there was an increased demand for objects in silver and the firm developed that side of their work and produced some interesting silver including jam spoons and larger silver of generous quality.

In Birmingham their mark in 1871 was BB and later BB above S.Ld within a shaped shield but at Chester their mark from 1906 was H.E.B. above F.E.B. within a shaped shield.

A jam spoon with oval bowl and indented as it reaches the stem which is plain and curved. Length $5\frac{1}{6}$ inches. There are four marks on the stem including the Chester mark, the date letter Script K (1910/11) and maker's mark, and a small silver bell — Script U (1920/21).

BARNETT AND SCOTT, Hull.

It seems likely that the mark belongs to Barnett and Scott who resided at 45 Whitefriars, Hull, though their mark is lacking the Co. in the register at Chester. It is however known from a small silver funnel $2\frac{1}{2}$ inches high with an egg shaped bowl $1\frac{1}{2}$ inches deep, and $1\frac{1}{4}$ inches diameter. It is marked with the Chester mark, lion passant, and date letter E for 1888/89. Its size probably avoided the duty.

S. BLACKENSEE, Birmingham.

The firm was established in 1826, grew to enormous proportions and spread abroad to Australia in the years that followed. In London and Birmingham they registered several marks but at Chester the S.B. & S. mark appears on 6 August 1879. On 29 November 1910 the S.B. & Co. was recorded and the S.B. & S. Ltd. 25 February 1913.

Blackensee were one of the larger silver and jewellery manufacturers and bought up many well known firms including Nathan and Hayes in the early 1920s. (A full description of the firm and names is in Culme, *Gold and Silversmiths*).

In the Bristol Museum is a pair of cream boats having a reeded foot and scroll handle with the Chester marks, the maker's mark, lion passant and the date H for 1933/34.

FRANCIS BUTT, Chester.

In the Chester Trade Directories, Francis Butt is listed as a watch and clockmaker at 69 Eastgate Row, Chester. In 1870 he is described as a gold and silversmith, in 1874 the word 'Optician' is added, and in 1882 as a watchmaker and jeweller of 32 Eastgate Street Row South.

He registered his mark at Chester in 1865 in two forms. Again in 1867, and 1880 and as Butt&Co 7 March 1906 with 33 Eastgate Row, and 42 High Street, Wrexham as addresses.

The mark of 1880 was recorded by his son Alfred Matthew Butt at 69 Eastgate Row, Chester.

Francis Butt married the daughter of J. F. Wathew and succeeded him. He was Alderman and Sheriff of the City in 1856 and in 1869 presented the Sheriff's Chain of Office to the City.

ALFRED BUTT, Chester.

Alfred Butt was the son of Francis Butt and registered his mark at Chester, 16 June 1880 from 69 Eastgate Row, Chester.

In 7 March 1906 when the firm became a Limited Company a new mark B & Co was registered at 33 Eastgate Row, Chester and 42 High Street, Wrexham.

WALTER COULTHARD, Birmingham.

The mark was registered at Chester, 31 July 1900. He was working at 59 Northampton Street, Birmingham and 48 Hampton Road, Birmingham. His partners were Henry Porter and Nathaniel Porter and they traded as W. Coulthard and Co. An alternative mark was registered at the same time.

They made a variety of objects including small spoons.

The firm had already registered their mark at Birmingham in 1897.

A spoon with an oval bowl and round handle ending in a finial of a large ball. One is known with the first of the marks and the date letter Script D for 1914/15.

IVERNA CUBBIN (1895-1976), Wallasey and Bidston, Wirral.

(Illustration 40)

Iverna Cubbin was born in 1895, the daughter of a Manx blacksmith who had a ship repair yard in Birkenhead where Iverna was born. Later the family moved to Wallasey and then to Bidston. Until the death of her father she lived and worked at home in Little Caldy where she lived with her sister Eveline. Iverna died in 1976 and is buried at Rake Lane Cemetery, Wallasey.

She trained as a silversmith at the Liverpool School of Art from 1914 under the Swiss silversmith, J. Hodel, and exhibited at the Liverpool Autumn Exhibition and also at the British Empire Exhibition 1924-1925 at Wembley.

She registered her mark at Chester in 1922 and after the closure of the Chester Assay Office at London. Her work is described as follows . . .

'She particularly favoured simple flower and scroll designs, often cast and patterns made with applied wire work, plain areas of metal being left with a hammered finish'.

There is a collection of her work in the Williamson Art Gallery and Museum, Birkenhead which she presented to the gallery before she died.

The bowl (illustrated) is one of her more elaborate pieces, $10\frac{1}{2}$ inches in diameter, dated 1922, marked at Chester, was exhibited at Wembley in 1924 and subsequently given to the Williamson Art Gallery.

JAMES DEAKIN AND SONS, Sheffield. (Illustration 37-38)

James Deakin and Sons of Sidney Works, Sheffie!d registered their mark at Chester on 21 January 1908. They had already registered their mark at London in 1865 and at Sheffield 15 November 1895. They worked at Matilda Street, where their works were situated which is where they began in about 1865. James worked with his sons William, John and Albert. They opened in London in 1888 and also in Glasgow and Belfast. The first was large and made cutlery, small silver articles and chased work known as Alexandra.

Among the variety of goods assayed at Chester are small pintrays, cigarette cases and miniature cand!esticks.

J. & R. GRIFFIN, Birmingham.

J. & R. Griffin registered at Chester 5 October 1905. The firm was at 105 and 109 Rockley Street, Birmingham and were registered as jewellers. As such, they dealt in small articles in silver and amongst the more usual articles were responsible for napkin clasps. An account of such clasps appears in the February 1992 number of *Antique Collecting* by Eve Eckstein and June Firkins entitled 'A holder for napery'. From this we learn that Griffin also registered at Birmingham.

Other napkin clasp makers who registered at Chester (and also Birmingham) were Adie and Lovekin (Chester 8 August 1883 and 16 February 1895), Robert Pringle (Chester 26 August 1896), John W. Rolason (Chester 1 May 1903), Thomas Henry Vale, William Unite and William John Cross trading as William Vale and Sons (Chester 16 October 1895), Villiers and Jackson (Chester 15 April 1905), G. E. Walton (Chester 29 January 1902). Among London based silversmiths who also registered at Chester were H. J. Cooper and Co. Ltd. (Chester 30 May 1899), Thomas Edward Natty in partnership with Edward Thomas Natty and Herbert Natty who traded as Gourdel Vales & Co. (5 October (1901).

Many of these persons also concentrated on silver pencils as also did Saunders and Shepherd who also made napkin clasps and clips.

NOBLE HASELER and EDWARD JOHN HASELER, Birmingham.

The firm traded as Haseler Brothers from 53 Branston Street, Birmingham and registered their mark at Chester on 6 June 1895 with two punches. They had previously registered at Birmingham in August 1888 without cerifs to the capitals; they again registered at Birmingham in 1908 with cerifs.

A very heavy cast bell height weighing $3\frac{3}{4}$ ounces showing a grotesque head on the side and a handle showing a hand holding a billet with Chester marks and date letter B for 1902.

HILLIARD & THOMSON, Birmingham.

The firm of Joseph John Richardson and William Edwin Thomson trading as John Thomson and Nephews and Hilliard and Thomson, silversmiths 1.3.5 Spencer Street, Birmingham registered at Chester 20 January 1898. Their mark was H. & T. within a rectangle. A similar mark had been recorded at Birmingham in various forms in 1847, 1859, 1861, 1875 and 1888. They were responsible for a number of caddy spoons which bear the anchor mark of Birmingham and it is interesting to have a caddy spoon recorded with the Chester assay mark in 1898. There was an H. & T. mark similar to the Chester mark of Hilliard & Thomson, registered at Dublin by Henderson and Thomson of Belfast 1900 might be confused only the Chester records confirms its Chester origin. This could cause confusion but the Chester records confirm the Hilliard and Thomson mark.

ROBERT HILTON, Taunton, Dyserth, Chester and Keswick (Keswick School of Industries).

Robert Hilton is first mentioned in the Chester record of marks as an artist of Allerford, Taunton and also of Meliden, near Rhyl, North Wales. He registered his mark 11 May 1896. He later became responsible for work in the Arts and Crafts Tradition and in 1905 registered as the Director of the Keswick School of Industrial Arts (KSIA) at Northgate, Chester and at Keswick.

Robert Hilton does not appear to have used any Assay Office other than Chester. He is buried at Beetham, near Milnthorpe (Kendal) 1915.

Examples of his work may be seen at the Merseyside County Museum where there is a Communion Cup and Paten which came from St Paul's Church, Prince's Park. This is $8\frac{1}{2}$ inches high of chalice form and a base diameter of $6\frac{3}{4}$ inches. The base has a repousse decoration of vine on a matt surface and the bowl is cased with applied vine. The knop is hexagonal with applied decoration. It has the Chester mark of RH and the date letter 1904/05. (Exhibited at Sotheby's Exhibition, Chester 1984. Illustrated fig. 229.)

CHARLES HORNER, Halifax.

Charles Horner of 21/23 Northgate, and 1 Crossley Street, Halifax became famous as the maker of silver thimbles and hat pins which were stamped with the initials CH. He registered at Chester in 1884. The popularity of the Dorcas thimble established the firm at the turn of the century. Most of their thimbles were sent to Chester together with hat pins. This trade was shared with Henry Griffiths of Birmingham and James Walker who between them monopolised the thimble trade, and completely dominated other persons selling thimbles. It would appear that about forty other silversmiths who marked their goods with their own names relied heavily upon Horner to supply them with thimbles. He seemed to have no objection to the other silversmiths imposing their own marks on his thimbles. This seems to have been the case with the Turner Brothers of Warstone Lane, Birmingham and the Turnbull Brothers of Northampton Street, Birmingham.

Charles Horner died in 1896, his sons, James Dobson Horner and C. Harry Horner, became managing partners and built a new factory at Mile Cross, Gibbet Street, Halifax. Most of their work continued to be assayed at Chester and included in addition to thimbles and hat pins, gold and silver jewellery with enamel on the brooches and blouse pins. The firm became a Limited Company in December 1909. Their chief designer was Edgar Simpson.

There is an interesting model of Halifax Parish Church preserved in York Minster.

(See Culme, *Dictionary of Gold and Silversmiths*, p. 238. *The Thimble*, no. 14. Edited by Edwin F. Holmes, p. 7.)

IONA CELTIC ART. (See Alex Ritchie)

JAYS (JAMES CHARLES JAY), London.
Richard Attenborough originally owned the address in Oxford Street, London where he practiced as a large pawnbroker. The property was sold in 1887 to James Jay, a silversmith and pawnbroker of Essex Road, North London. There was some controversy (described in full by Culme, *Gold and Silversmiths*, p. 257). James Jay ran his business from 142/144 Oxford Street, and Robert William Jay from Essex Street. In 1897 James registered his company as a Limited Liability Company in the name of James Jay Ltd.

The firm also registered their mark at Chester under the name of James Charles Jay using the Oxford Street address on 3 April 1897.

Although he had purchased a considerable stock from Richard Attenborough he appears to have patronised the Arts and Crafts movement as the example below shows. On 16 October 1906 the firm was registered again at Chester by James Charles Jay and Jay Richard Attenborough & Co. Ltd., silversmith of the Oxford Street, London address.

A small bowl standing on three scroll legs which rise above the rim to form handles. It carries the Chester marks, the JJ marks of James Jay and the date letter Script E for 1905/06 and incsribed along the side the words, 'Jays 142/144 Oxford St. Silversmiths'.

ALFRED E. JONES, Birmingham. (Illustration 43)
Alfred Edward Jones studied at the Central School of Arts and Crafts, Birmingham under Edward Taylor and later at the Birmingham Guild of

Handicrafts. It was here that he was greatly influenced by the Arts and Crafts Movement and in 1902 began on his own in Windmill Street. After this, he acquired the firm of Jesson and Barkett and with it the trade mark of St Dunstan raising a bowl. This became the trade mark of his work. The shop attracted a large group of artists, Edward Taylor and his son Hawson Taylor the creator of Ruskin pottery, A. J. Gaskin, Bernard Cuzner and others. They followed the strict principles of the movement until it fell victim to the demand for their wares. Ruskin pottery was used for the liners of their wares in silver. Later he was involved in the Bromsgrove Guild and much of his work went to churches and to the Royal Military Academy, Sandhurst.

In the 1920s and 1930s he designed church plate as well as domestic plate. He died in 1954.

He first registered his mark at Birmingham, A E J within an oval frame in December 1902 but it was not until 3 January 1911 that he registered at Chester as 'Art Silversmith, late of Windmill Street, Birmingham and now of 111 Livery Street, Birmingham'. In 1918 he moved to 80 Pembroke Street, Birmingham.

Cheshire is fortunate in having a fine example of his work. In May 1937 the firm of Ollivant and Botsford of Manchester were asked to provide the great mace for the Corporation of Bebington to commemorate the granting of the Charter of Incorporation 28 September 1937. The firm wisely turned to Alfred E. Jones. The mace has since been transferred to the Metropolitan Borough of Wirral due to reorganisation.

THE BEBINGTON MACE. It is 48½ inches in length and has an open Royal Crown above an embossed head with the Arms of Bebington supported by a double knopped shaft and two caryated scroll brackets. The marks are those of Alfred E. Jones and the St Dunstan Works, Birmingham and the date marks of Chester 1937/38. The design was done by Gaskin of the Bromsgrove Guild.

GRAHAME JONES, Chester. (Illustration 45)

Grahame Jones is the grandson of James Lowe, his mother being the daughter of James Lowe the Chester goldsmith.

He completed his apprenticeship at the time of the closure of the Chester Assay Office which had been interrupted by his service in the Royal Navy. After 1962 he was transferred first as a drawer at the London Hall and later assistant foreman of the gold marking floor. He stayed for six years before returning to Chester. He has always played an important part in the Company and was made Alderman of the Company.

He tells his own story on page 159.

He has worked on repairs to silver and gold articles. His mark was lent to Peter Lowe who had no mark but made the silver dish in the Company which bears the inscription

'This silver dish was assayed and hallmarked by Mr G. Jones a member of the Chester Company of Goldsmiths at the Assay Office on the 24th August 1962 which was the day of the closure. The above named person also made this article.'

The four marks also include the mark of Grahame Jones and the date letter M. (1962)

PATRICK LEONARD, Salford.

Patrick Leonard first recorded his mark at Sheffield in 1835 (F. Bradbury, *History of old Sheffield Plate*, p. 486). There is no reference to him in the Chester Plate Duty Books (1784-1840) unless (which seems possible) a single reference to Patrick Landra' in 1835 refers to him and this is supported by the fact that the only record of plate submitted by him 15 May was six tea spoons. The census returns of 1841 show that his youngest child, Henery (sic) was six years old and born in Ireland which suggests that he came from Ireland about the time of the registration in England, along with his wife Mary and his four children. He appears as a working silversmith at Stage Buildings, 7 St Mary's Passage, Manchester but later moved across the river to Salford and lived at 18 Stanley Street, which was off New Bailey Street. His eldest son Thomas was apprenticed to his father.

Patrick Leonard seems to have specialised in simple flat ware, but also commissioned to make medals and badges for the Oddfellows and Masonic Lodges.

Sotheby's sale (London) 25 May 1972 (lot 156) 'An early Victorian Odd-fellow's jewel, the centre applied with a typical embossed plaque within an engraved surround of scrolling leafage below a coronet and feathers, the rear inscribed $4\frac{1}{2}$ inches high by Peter Leonard 1844'. Peter for Patrick is a mistake often made at auctions. This jewel was given to 'The Brothers of the Duke of Devonshire Lodge, Ripley to P. G. Frost as a testimony of his services Febry 17 1845'.

Another jewel for the Oddfellows passed in 1980 to the Salford City Museum (see *The Bulletin of the Friends of the Salford Museum Association*, March 1980). This has a similar design with the coat of arms of the Odd-fellows and has the name of Isaac Simmons who had been responsible for the circular arms. These are five marks on the obverse side including the mark of Patrick Leonard and the date letter Gothic F (1844/45). It was given to George Robinson for past mercies as Noble Grand of the loyal Prince of Wales Lodge No. 3173 M.U. Mitcham District Jany 26 1846.

Flat ware by Patrick Leonard is mainly of fiddle pattern design. His work as a ladle maker is illustrated in a comparatively small punch on a toddy ladle. The bowl is round, diameter $1\frac{3}{4}$ inches and is $\frac{3}{4}$ inch deep. The bowl is attached to a whale bone handle with a silver sleeve and the handle is tipped with a silver ferrule. The length of the ladle is 7 inches. The outside of the bowl has five marks with the maker's mark central; the remaining four months include the date letter Gothic D (1842/43).

THE LATER LOWES, Chester. (Illustration 1, 2, 7, 12, 13, 15, 16, 23-27, 41, 47)

After the death of George Lowe (1) in 1841 the shop and house in Bridge Street, Chester, which at the time of his death was considered rather dilapidated and valued at £900, the sons took over the business and although some registered their own marks the workshop was well supplied with silver-smiths and some of them were practicing silversmiths themselves. Many were engaged at the Assay Office and had little time to produce individual pieces, and some produced nothing.

Under the title Lowe and Sons the firm used JL within a square frame. This mark was registered just before George Lowe died and about the same time John and Thomas Lowe registered their own marks. I&TL within a rectangle, and IL above TL within a square, and possibly TL. The punch J pellet L was registered 16 July 1864 in the time of John Lowe but only a few months before his death and was registered under the application of Lowe and Sons. In 1881 is the slightly different mark J L with a mid way pellet. An unregistered mark JFL within an oval frame is found with the date D for 1884 and could be for John Foulkes Lowe or his brother the Assay Master James Foulkes Lowe. Another brother of John and James Lowe was George Bennett Lowe who registered his mark J L above G L within a square with docked corners who registered his mark 27 October 1896 and 25 October 1906 which appears both with and without pellets. His private address was 48 Liverpool Road, Chester and he shared the property in Bridge Street Row. On 20 February 1912 John Foulkes Lowe's son, John Cecil Lowe (died 1915) and his brother George Frederic Lowe (1871-1934 shared the same mark, C L with F above L below. After the death of John Cecil Lowe, George Frederic Lowe registered his own mark, G F with 5 point stem above and Lo below within the arms of a Maltese Cross, which remained the mark of Lowe and Sons until well after his death when it was taken over by his widow Martha (neé Jones of Towyn), and after her death by her son, John ffoulkes Lowe and his sister Joyce, who registered a new mark J L above J L in a square at the time of the closure of the Assay Office.

Another branch of the family, the descendants of James Foulkes Lowe were also goldsmiths but worked at the Assay Office and had no mark of their own, except Grahame Jones whose mother was the daughter of James Lowe.

FRANCIS MAURICE LOWE, Chester and his son Peter J. Lowe. (Illustration 46, 48)

Reference is made to his activity on page 47 when the Chester Oar bearing the City of Origin mark, it appeared on the oar.

He was only responsible for a limited amount of silver. Among them a small canteen of cutlery which he made for his son Peter and daughter consisting of 6 table forks, six dessert forks, six tea spoons, six dessert spoons, six table spoons and two serving spoons. These were made from blanls which he produced from the Sheffield Smelting Company. They all bear the date letter M (1962) and because he did not have an inidvidual mark himself was allowed by the Assay Master, Mr Ward, to use Vincent Ward's mark A.V.W. (incuse).

Earlier on he had used Mr Ward's mark on other items he had made including a silver hand beaten salt spoon of Britannia metal with the 1953 date mark and a mustard spoon of Britannia standard of the same year. In 1958 date letter H he made a scallop edged dish diameter $5\frac{3}{4}$ inches. In 1953 a jam spoon, and in 1959 a five light candelabra with flat circular base (approx. $8\frac{1}{2}$ inches high. The last piece of silver hallmarked at Chester was made by him and is now in the Ridgway Gallery of the Grosvenor Museum, Chester. These all bear the mark of A.V.W.

His son Peter has been long associated with the retail silver trade and claims to have been responsible for a small hand raised tray diameter $5\frac{7}{8}$ inches assayed in 1962 about which he wrote 'this was my one and only attempt to make a piece of silver . . . Father helped me and I borrowed cousin Grahame's punch'.

JAMES FOULKES LOWE, Chester.

James Foulkes Lowe, the third child and second son of John (1) and Elizabeth (neé Foulkes) was born 17 August 1840. There is a London made cup and a half barrel with later handle with an inscription that states that John Foulkes Lowe gave it to his brother James Foulkes Lowe as a Christmas present on 25 December 1842.

He became a Freeman of the City by indenture to his father 5 February 1862. He went to Trinity College Dublin gaining his B.A. degree. When Thomas Lowe, his uncle, resigned through ill health and blindness on 27 October 1864 he became Assay Master. His recommendation is given in the Minute Book of the Company . . .

> Mr James Foulkes Lowe 'A brother of the Company an able and skilful man experienced in assaying of gold and silver be and is hereby elected and appointed Assay Master of the Company in place of the said Thomas Lowe at the same salary and on the same terms as the said Office was held by the said Thomas Lowe prior to his resignation.

On 17 April 1873 he married Annie the youngest daughter of Moses Roberts of Plas Llangwyfan in Clwyd and lived at Dee Banks, Chester. They had seven children though two died in infancy.

He took a keen interest in rowing and also in the Cheshire Volunteer Rifles. He won the Chester Goldsmith Cup on 29 May 1680 for the best shot of the Volunteer Rifles and had been given a London made cup of 1751/52 by Gurney and Cooke.

He served at Assay Master until his death 27 March 1911, and was buried at Llangwyfan after a service at St Paul's, Boughton. His wife had died in 1909 and he was buried with her.

Five years after his father's death, his son Hugh Cawley Lowe wrote . . .

> he was much loved and respected, kind and forgiving to all who came in contact with him.

Of their children, Herbert Heskett Lowe (1876-1939) served in the Royal Navy and later worked in the Assay Office. James (2) Foulkes Lowe (1882-1946) assisted in the Assay Office but with a break when he served in the Great War where he was seriously wounded, and Hugh Cawley Lowe (1881-1953) who was apprenticed to his father and took up work at the Assay Office until his death.

JOHN LOWE (1), Chester. (Illustration 12, 13, 15, 16, 24-27)

John Lowe was the ninth child and fourth son of George Lowe (1) and Mary Lowe (neé Cawley) and was born 22 September 1804. Baptised at St John's Church, Chester.

He served his apprenticeship under his father and was made a Freeman of the City 1 August 1826 along with his brother Thomas. He married Elizabeth Foulkes the daughter of William Foulkes of Chester at Tilston, 26 September 1833. They first lived at 6 Pepper Street, Chester, rented from Ralph Richardson of Greenfield Hall near Holywell from 24 June 1834 for four years at £18 a year. He then moved to Bridge Street Row after his father had died in 1841. He built a house at 25 Hough Green in 1861.

John and Elizabeth Lowe had eleven children, four of whom were closely linked with the Company and Assay Office namely John Foulkes (2), James Foulkes, George Bennett (3) and William Foulkes. James Foulkes became Assay Master and William Foulkes combined his job with that of public analyst.

John Lowe became Prime Warden of the Company and was a very active member of the Company. He played an important part in the life of the City being Church Warden of St Peter's Church and Sheriff in 1841. It was in his time that the second copper plate was issued. The earlier one had been in use since the 1700 Act.

He was a strong family man and proud of the City's history. The tradition of the Company was fiercely contended by him and he was successful in keeping the Assay Office at Chester. A descendant of John Lowe living in California has a coffee pot with this inscription . . .

Presented to Mr John Lowe, Prime Warden of the Goldsmiths Co by his brother members, for his unswerving exertions on their behalf against the abolition of the Assay Offices Chester Oct. 11. 1855.

The coffee pot is embossed with flowers and leaves and intricate design and appears to be by the London goldsmiths John and Henry Lias.

He died in Chester, 11 September 1864 and was buried in the Chester Cemetery. A memorial to him stands in St Peter's Church, Chester.

The mark (with Thomas) is found on the first copper plate and is likely to have been put there before the second plate was issued. The J pellet L is found before John died, and afterwards, so it would seem that they were used as a Lowe and Sons mark in the post 1840 period. (See note on John and Thomas Lowe below.)

(Sotheby, Belgravia, 21 March 1974. Lot 222) Five John Lowe flask lables of small size shaped oblong engraved with borders of leafage and the titles rose water, two for lavender and two for eau de Cologne. Chester 1848.

Oval magnifying glass in a silver case $1\frac{3}{4}$ inches by 2 inches. Inscribed Thomas Lowe No. 3 Trinity Street, Chester. The marks include those of the maker John Lowe (his brother) and the Gothic T for 1857-58.

Large service fork with five tines $8\frac{3}{4}$ inches in length with fiddle pattern handle engraved with the crest of a griffin above three plumes. There are five marks including the Gothic G 1845-46.

Three small salt shovels of Hanoverian pattern with a set of exceptionally small marks including Gothic I 1847-48.

Plain sugar tongs with fiddle pattern handles $5\frac{1}{2}$ inches in length. The four marks include the Gothic I 1847-48.

[A three piece tea service comprising teapot, sugar basin and cream jug. (Illustration 24, 25, 26) 1881/82.]

JOHN and THOMAS LOWE, Chester (Illustration 15)

(See under JOHN LOWE (1) and THOMAS LOWE. Also Ridgway, *Chester Silver*, p. 112.)

TYPE 1   First Copper Plate compartment 11. Struck three times and on second copper plate compartment L twice. I &T L in a rectangle.

An egg spoon with capital Gothic A (1839/40).

A silver topped horn mull snuff box, overall width $4\frac{1}{2}$ inches, the silver top is hinged diameter $1\frac{5}{8}$ inches. Marked on the inside of the lid with the Chester assay marks and the makers' mark.

127

TYPE 2 First copper plate compartment 13 struck four times. I L above T L in a rectangle with mid way pellets and on second copper plate compartment L without mid way pellets.

A pair of salt spoons 1840/41.

A pair of mustard spoons. OE handles $3\frac{7}{8}$ inches long. Date letter B (1840/41).

A crescent shaped ram's horn converted into a snuff mull with silver topped rim hinged. Diameter of mouth $1\frac{3}{4}$ inches and width of horn $4\frac{3}{4}$ inches. Marked on the lid with date letter B (1840/41).

A silver topped snuff box or mull with a horn body overall width of the curve $4\frac{3}{4}$ inches. The lid is hinged and the marks are on the inside along with the Chester mark B for 1840/41. Diameter of mouth $1\frac{1}{2}$ inches.

THOMAS LOWE, Chester.

Thomas Lowe was the son of George Lowe (1) and brother of George Lowe (2), John Lowe (1) and Robert Lowe (see p. 93). He was born in 1806 and after an apprenticeship with his father was admitted to the Freedom of the City 25 August 1824 and to the Company, 11 December 1826 along with his brother John. They worked together to help his father and in the Chester Plate Duty Books are referred to under the title George Lowe and Sons, when George Lowe (1) was getting old. Shortly before George Lowe died they had a joint mark (see John and Thomas Lowe). There is an otherwise unidentified mark TL within a square frame on the first copper plate (23) and possibly on the second copper frame (L).

Robert Lowe was never married and for a while lived with his brother John in Bridge Street Row. He was Assay Master from 30 December 1841 and remained so for twenty three years, when he tendered his resignation on account of his blindness and other infirmities. He submitted to the Company his claim to a retiring allowance 27 October 1864 and received a gift of £200 and $\frac{2}{3}$ of his former salary.

His growing blindness prompted his brother John to give to him a silver cased magnifying glass, and John who made it in 1857/58 engraved his name and his address upon the folding case 'Thomas Lowe. No. 3. Trinity Street, Chester', which he shared with his widowed sister Sarah Seals.

Although he was not married his earlier years were not without romance. A letter survives written 18 September 1833 to one Ellen explaining . . .

> you will allow me to indulge the delightfully pleasing idea of having you for my help meet through life to be a share of my joys and sorrows and that we may be mutual helps on our journey to the blissful realms of day and then to enjoy an eternity of happiness at God's right hand . . .

But unfortunately it came to nothing. In the same letter he speaks of going to Preston where he helped his brother Robert who there, plied a rather unsuccessful trade.

Thomas was a devout Methodist (his sister Sarah had married a Methodist minister) and belonged to several societies in the City. He died 8 February 1866 and is buried in Chester Cemetery. The present day Company use Thomas Lowe's Bible when they take their oath as members of the Company.

A trivial anecdote was passed on by his great nephew Philip Whitehouse.

When Thomas went to live at 3 Trinity Street he had a favourite cat who used to sit on the arm of his chair and also a monkey named Jacko who was up to all sorts of mischief and who subsequently came to a tragic end.

GEORGE BENNETT LOWE, Chester. (See John Foulkes Lowe)

He shared a mark with John (2) and was the son of John Lowe (1). They traded under Lowe and Sons at 6 Bridge Street Row, Chester using the mark registered on October 27 1896 JL above GL with docked corners and with pellet between, and the JL over GL in a square without pellets found on the second copper plate 5 nos. 541.

WILLIAM FOULKES LOWE, Chester.

William F. Lowe was the seventh child and fourth son of John and Elizabeth Lowe. He was admitted a freeman by indenture 14 April 1871 and Company 8 August 1871, worked as an Assayer at the Assay Office and was also public analyst in the same building. He married Kate Robins of Dublin in St Peter's Church, Dublin 28 October 1878 and lived at 18 Hough Green, Chester.

He is remembered for his gentleness, kindness and for his unpunctuality! One of his sayings being, 'Punctuality is the thief of time'.

William F. Lowe became Assay Master on the death of his brother James, 1 July 1915. He had been deaf for many years and began to learn braille when he also became blind, and was over eighty. His great love was sailing which he continued to do when he was over 50 winning the Dee Sailing Club Challenge Cup in 1927.

He is not known to have made or marked silver and none of his sons were Chester Goldsmiths, though Harold Lowe became Public Analyst.

He died in office as Assay Master in 1931 and was buried in Heswall Churchyard, Wirral.

JOHN (2) FOULKES LOWE, Chester.

John Foulkes Lowe was the son of John Lowe (1) who had the name Foulkes added to his name from his mother, Elizabeth Foulkes. He was born 'at half past 6 o'clock 11 August 1836' at 6 Pepper Street, Chester and christened at St Michael's Church, Chester, 9 September 1836, Mr Thomas being his godfather. After serving seven years as an apprentice to his father he became a Freeman on 25 November 1857, was admitted to the Goldsmiths

Company 25 January 1858, and was by then living in Hough Green. He became auditor to the Company and Prime Warden 27 September 1864 and was appointed Drawer, 31 August 1874 along with Thomas Woolley.

He married Eleanor Roach Sumpcion Carpenter of the City of Bath in 1869, at Melcombe Regis, 9 September, became Sheriff of Chester 1897 and died 13 March 1911. Eleanor died in 1901 and was buried in Overleigh Cemetery.

They had eight children, four of whom died in infancy. Their son, Harry Carpenter Lowe died at the age of eleven when he was drowned in a boating accident at Abergele 27 August 1888, despite a valiant attempt to rescue him by his brother, George Frederic Lowe. Harry was interred in Abergele Churchyard.

He worked with his brother George Bennett Lowe (qv) who also died in 1911.

There is an Alms dish in Abergele Church, diameter 18 inches, the centre depicting the Nativity scene in bass relief. The edge is decorated with eight sets of stones in a circular floral arrangement, 3 sets of garnets, two sets of citrine, 2 sets of amethyst and one of aquamarine. On the underside of the rim is inscribed

> To the Glory of God and in memory of a beloved son Henry Carpenter Lowe who died Aug. 27 1888 aged 11 years. This alms dish was given for the use of the Church of St Michael, Abergele.

The marks include the maker's name JFL, the Chester mark and date letter H. 1891/92.

Examples of his Work:

A block of wood taken (so the inscription relates on a silver plaque attached) from a beam brought from the house where Lady Hamilton lived at Hawarden and 'Bought from Messrs Lowe & Sons Oct. 27 1894'. There are four marks on the silver plaque including the makers' mark and the date letter P (1898/99). The plaque measures $1\frac{7}{8}$ inches by $3\frac{1}{2}$ inches. The mark was registered in Chester on 27 October 1896. A later mark was registered in 1907 (and cancelled with the note 'Partners dead. 11 Bridge Street Row) Feb 20. 1912.' Both George Bennett Lowe and John Foulkes Lowe had died in 1911.

Bowl with the Golden Jubilee medal of Victoria set in the bowl and the inscription 'Presented by the Goldsmiths Company to F. E. Clark June 22 1897'. The marks include JL above GL within a square frame and the date letter N (1896/97).

Communion Cup at St Andrew's Church, Malvern. Priory — dedication of Malvern Priory is to the B.V.M. and St Michael. Height $6\frac{1}{4}$ inches; rim diameter $3\frac{5}{8}$ inches; base diameter $3\frac{3}{8}$ inches (see Peplow, *Plate of the Archdeaconry of Worcester*, 1967).

Also at St Andrew's Church, Malvern Priory is a Communion paten with a plain cover, diameter $3\frac{3}{4}$ inches. These are replica copies of the Communion cup and paten supplied by Nathan and Hayes 1885. Marks include JL above GL.

A name shield on the Chester Regatta Cup base has the JFL mark in an oval and the date letter H (1908/09).

Set of four parcel gilt tureens with boat shaped bowls engraved with bright cut swags and the rim beaded. Each has two loop handles and stands upon an oval pillar foot which rests on a square base where the beading is repeated. Overall height is 3 inches, width of bowl $2\frac{1}{2}$ inches, square base $1\frac{1}{2}$ by $1\frac{1}{2}$. The mark includes the date letter Gothic P (1878/79) and the maker's mark J mid pellet L.

A plain bulbous creamer overall height 2 inches, the bowl $1\frac{1}{2}$ inches, rim diameter $1\frac{3}{8}$ inches, base diameter $1\frac{3}{4}$ inches. Circular ear shaped handle. The marks include J L with mid way pellet.

Circular drum shaped mustard pot with open work sides and blue glass liner. The marks appearing on the interlacing. The lid has a fan shaped thumb with a crest. The handle is ear shaped. Overall height $3\frac{1}{8}$ inches, diameter of lid $2\frac{3}{4}$ inches. Marks include Gothic D (1867/68).

Regatta Shield for the race rowed in 1874. (J. Foulkes Lowe was the cox). Chester date Gothic I (1872/73).

Highly ornate cast spoon, silver gilt $7\frac{1}{2}$ inches in length, the stem elaborately moulded and topped with a group of figures. The bowl is oval with a short rat tail and engraved. The five marks include Gothic S (1881/82).

JOHN CECIL LOWE AND GEORGE FREDERIC LOWE

These were the sons of John Foulkes Lowe and Eleanor Lowe.

John Cecil Lowe was made a freeman of Chester by birth 12 July 1892. He was born in 1870 and was apprenticed to his father being admitted to the Company 1 July 1895. In 1901 he married Beatrice Innes and they lived at 48 Liverpool Road, Chester.

John Cecil and George Frederic registered their mark together on 20 February 1912. He died of sunstroke in 1915.

For George Frederic Lowe (see below).

GEORGE FREDERIC LOWE, Chester. (Illustration 41)

George Frederic Lowe first registered a mark with his brother John Cecil Lowe on 20 February 1912 (qv). His brother died however in 1915.

He had been born in 1871 and educated at the King's School, Chester and was a keen swimmer and footballer playing for the 'Magpies' which became Chester Football Club. He was almost drowned in 1888 when attempting to save his brother, Henry Carpenter Lowe at Abergele.

He had hoped to be a doctor or surgeon but took over the firm when his father died in 1911.

He married Martha Elizabeth Jones of Towyn c. 1909/10 and lived for a while at 29 Dee Banks before moving to Curzon Park, Chester. Martha Lowe rowed him to work and called for him in the evening. He was a keen gardener and an authority on antique silver. He was always fair in his business dealings and whilst many made considerable fortunes at the time when the gold standard shot off the market he insisted on giving his customers the full melting value of gold.

He is remembered as a 'no nonsense' person and quite often could be found working in the shop in his shirt and braces!

He and Martha had four children, Denise, Joyce, George and John ffoulkes Lowe. He died in 1934, aged 63, leaving Martha Lowe to run the business. Later when John was admitted to the Goldsmiths Company on 13 December 1954 she was assisted by him, and his sister Joyce Lowe. From 1936 the mark of George Frederic Lowe was used by his widow after his death.

Examples of his work:

Two handled porringer to be used as a sugar bowl (made by Barnett's of London) but using the mark of Chester and George F. Lowe. Date letter Script L (1911/12). To mark the Coronation of George V and Queen Mary. For the Company, the Assay Master, A. Vincent Ward had a tea pot and creamer made for himself with the same marks and having the Coronation medal in the base.

MARTHA ELIZABETH LOWE and her children JOYCE and JOHN ffOULKES LOWE, Chester. (Illustration 47)

When her husband died in 1934, Martha Lowe took over the running of Lowe and Sons. She was not qualified to become a member of the Goldsmiths' Company as ladies were not admitted but on 13 December 1954, John ffoulkes Lowe, their son, was admitted.

The firm retained the mark of their father until Joyce and John registered their own mark in 1962. The War had stopped the making of silver, and they relied upon London goldsmiths to provide them with silver which they had assayed at Chester.

Examples of Silver from 1934:

Communion cup and paten cover given to the Cathedral of St Boniface, Bunbury, Australia by the parish of St Boniface, Bunbury, Cheshire on the occasion of the visit to Bunbury of the Bishop of Bunbury, Australia 1960. The Communion cup stands $7\frac{1}{4}$ inches high and has a bell shaped bowl. The top and bottom has a diameter of $3\frac{1}{2}$ inches. The paten cover has a wide rim, diameter $5\frac{1}{2}$ inches, rim 1 inch wide. It has a single depression and stands on a foot diameter $2\frac{1}{2}$ inches, total height $1\frac{1}{2}$ inches. The four marks (on each piece) have the letter G (1957/58).

A tall vase with indented rim and an edge of conventional flowers. Total height 10 inches, diameter of rim $2\frac{3}{4}$ inches. Two inches below the rim is a moulded band an inch deep. The vase curves down towards a trumpet shaped foot which is moulded and ends in a shoulder and step. This was presented by the widow of Mr Tom Chadwick to the Ingledene Home for babies at Richmond Hill, Bowdon, run by the Children's Society, for the outstanding nurse of the year from 1964 until the home closed in 1972. It was then returned to the family. There were four marks including the date letter L (1961/62)

A cast copy of a taper stick (modelled upon one made by Richard Richardson (2) in 1735/36) $4\frac{1}{2}$ inches high having the date M (1937/38).

A cased set called the Manners spoon and a two pronged fork, were copied by Lowe and Sons to celebrate the jubilee of George V and Mary 1937.

JOYCE and JOHN (4) ffOULKES LOWE, Chester.

Joyce and John Lowe were the children of George Frederic and Martha Lowe. They served in the shop in Bridge Street Row with their mother after the death of George Lowe in 1934. The mark of George Lowe continued to be used by the family. John Lowe was admitted to the Company 13 December 1954. Ladies were not admitted to the Company but some years after the closure of the Assay Office, Joyce was admitted an Honorary Member of the Goldsmiths' Company, the second person to be admitted and the first lady.

After the death of Martha Lowe, the firm passed to her children. John also became a London Goldsmith. He had served in the War in the RAF, Air Sea Rescue.

John ff. Lowe fought to keep the Assay Office at Chester, but did not have the support of the Company, and it was due to the efforts of the Bishop of Chester in the House of Lords that the Company itself survived the closure.

No silver was made at Lowe's after the war. They used William Comyns & Sons and E. Barnard & Sons of London to supply orders which were sent to Chester for assay until 1962.

John is remembered for his gentle, kind and generous nature and his great interest in silver. Ill health did not prevent him from taking an active interest in all worthwhile activities in the City and his remarkable conversaziones and exhibitions were greatly appreciated throughout the county. He died in 1973, and later Joyce Lowe sold the business. The present day owners, R. Waltons of Chester, already established in the City have a daughter who is a silversmith, retaining the name Lowe and Sons.

When it became certain that the Assay Office would close, John and Joyce Lowe registered a new mark at the Assay Office and in a short time were responsible for a great deal of silver of very high quality, now much sort after by collectors.

The catalogue issued by Lowe and Sons in 1962 contains information of the gold and silver which bore their mark and the date of the last few months of the Assay Office, capital M.

> Delamere jug in four sizes $2\frac{1}{8}$, $2\frac{7}{8}$, $3\frac{1}{2}$ and $5\frac{1}{2}$ inches high varying in price from £8.8.0 to £45.0.0.
> Replica of the Armada dish in four sizes $3\frac{1}{4}$, $4\frac{1}{4}$, $8\frac{1}{4}$, $11\frac{1}{4}$ inches ranging from £2.12.6 to £52.10.0.

Napkin rings, condiment sets, paper knives (reproduction skewers) and tumbler cups. The skewers were sold for £3.7.6 and the tumbler cups from £5.5.0.

Silver waiters of two designs, gadrooned border and chippendale border, in four sizes, 6, 8, 10 and 12 inches with a price range of £12.12.0 to £45.0.0.

Reproduction of Georgian creamers on three hoof feet 3 inches high (£7.0.0.) Sugar basins $3\frac{1}{2}$ inches high (£6.0.0). Trefid spoons $6\frac{1}{2}$ inches in length (£3.17.6). Two pair of candelabra, a copy of one of George I (1723), $10\frac{1}{2}$ inches high (165.0.0.). Sauce boats of two capacities $\frac{1}{3}$ pint and $\frac{1}{2}$ pint at £13.10.0 and £15.15.0 respectively. One pair of hand made candelabra with four branches, a copy of one by Paul Lamerie, 18 inches high was priced at £750.0.0. In keeping with other Assay Offices, sets of six spoons, each having the different hallmark of the existing Assay Offices were £6.7.6. a set and cased.

All this silver was heavy and well made and reflected the quality of the silver which had passed through the firm's hands since 1792.

The brochure did not report on all the silver sold by Lowe's at this time. A number of gold tumbler cups were made of 9.375 ct. gold. Two are known to the author. One rim diameter $2\frac{9}{16}$ inches and $2\frac{1}{4}$ inches deep. There were two sets of Apostle spoons issued by them, and a gold Christus.

After the closure of the Chester Assay Office, Joyce Lowe registered a new mark at London M J L within a triangle. This was never used; but in 1986 she registered another mark combining those of her niece Sarah Lowe JL SL with mid way pellet within a rectangle. This was used on the two magnificent maces which she presented to Chester Cathedral in September 1987 in memory of her brother John ffoulkes Lowe. They were made by John Christopher Webb (qv) and bore his London mark, and those of Joyce and Sarah Lowe, as the sponsors' mark.

JOSEPH MAYER, Liverpool.

Joseph Mayer was born in Newcastle under Lyme in 1803. As a boy, the finding of a hoard of Roman coins lead him to a lifetime interest in collecting and in 1867 he gave his collection to Liverpool Corporation. He was apprenticed to James Wordley, a silversmith in Liverpool, at 56 Lord Street and later entered into partnership with him. This was dissolved in 1844, and he set up by himself at 68/70 Lord Street. He later went into partnership with Thomas Jeremiah Paris which lasted until 1873.

In Culme (*Gold and Silversmiths*) there is a detailed description of the work he handled for many well known Victorian silversmiths and companies such as Wilkinson and Co. of Sheffield, John and George Angell of London, A. G. Piesse, John Edward Terry & Co., London and others. He sold their wares in his Liverpool shop. He himself was a notable goldsmith, and in the Chester Exhibition organised through Sotheby's and the Grosvenor Museum in 1984, a gold snuff box was exhibited by him dated 1850/51. It had been presented to the Rev. Edward Hull for his work as 'the learned Zealous and liberal chaplain of the school for the indigent blind by friends who admire his talents and respect his virtues, Liverpool MDCCCLI'.

This is now in the Merseyside County Museum. The oblong snuff box $3\frac{1}{2}$ inches by $2\frac{3}{8}$ wide and $1\frac{1}{4}$ inches deep has the base showing allegorical figures after Flaxman, the top, a representation of St George's Hall (then unfinished) and on the sides strapwork around circles containing figures.

Culme also lists numerous pieces of silver, usually very elaborate and patriotic which appeared in the Great Exhibition of 1851.

He died 20 January 1886.

Mason's mallet of hard wood with ebony handle and silver mounts. The top engraved with Gothic arcading and inscription

> Presented to Robert Frost, Esqr, Mayor of Chester by George Clarke and Son, Contractors to the Hall, Chester October MDCCCLXV. The sides are applied with plaques showing the Old Exchange, the Town Hall and the Cathedral.

8 inches long. Hall marks for 1865/66. Kept at the Town Hall (Sotheby's Chester Exhibition. 216).

SAMPSON MORDAN & Co., London

The firm was founded in 1815 by Sampson Morden who made his name by inventing the ever pointed and propelling pencil. Under his successors the firm became a Limited Liability Company. Their City Road factory was rebuilt in 1900. They sold their patents for propelling pencils in 1941 when their factory was destroyed by enemy action.

The firm registered in London and Chester. At Chester the registration is 18 February 1899, again in January and November 1904. It is with the second of these marks that an elaborate hat pin stand in the shape of a harp, the pins forming the strings was marked. Dated 1905/06.

a set of four Edwardian menu holders modelled as owls with coloured glass eyes. (cased) 1909.

BERTHOLD MULLER, London.

Franz Carl Berthold Muller was first known at Hatton Garden, but by the time he registered his mark at Chester, 10 March 1898, he had moved to 187 Wardour Street, Soho and traded as B. Muller & Son. The elder Muller died in Heidelberg in 1911. The firm acted as an agent for imported wares especially from the Hanau works at Neresheimer, Germany, who made fine copies of earlier masters of German origin. Muller also imported wares from W. Lobensteyn, Schoonhoven, Holland and also for James Turner of the Colonnade Buxton, which were imported through Chester.

A wager cup given as a wedding present in 1905 having the grapes mark of Nuremberg and the import mark of Chester (acorn) the .925, the script D (for 1900) and the mark of Bernhold Muller.

In an interview with A. Vincent Ward in 1973, the last Assay Master spoke of a great deal of silver being sent by train to Chester from London including a large number of figures and he spoke of a dutch figure of a boy and girl in the form of a pepper pot, each figure with detachable heads by Berthold Muller.

NATHAN AND HAYES, Birmingham. (Illustration 34)

The Company was formed at 285 Icknield Street, Birmingham in 1855 by a partnership of George Nathan and Ridley Hayes. Their London show rooms were in Hatton Garden. They recorded their marks at Birmingham in 1888. At Chester the mark was changed and on 9 May 1894 became GN over RH within an ornate shield.

The firm concentrated upon making antique reproductions in preference to the then fashionable art nouveau designs. Not only did they turn to the finds made by Schliemann in the near east but to European and Assyrian patterns. These were almost always assayed at Chester. There was never any question of them making copies in order to deceive. The copies they made were not always exact reproductions. The firm also registered their mark at Chester 12 March 1912 and at this time were issuing some very attractive pieces of heavy guage, among these was a sweetmeat basket with swing handle, oval in shape, standing on a circular base, copying a late 18th century form. The date letter K 1910/11.

Among earlier pieces are . . .

Copy of a Danish goblet found in a grave at East Seeland, c. 2nd century AD. (see also Sotheby's Catalogue 27 February 1992, lots 219-221).

Copy in silver gilt of a gold ewer found at Mycene, now in the Athens Museum, part of the Schlieman collection. 14th century BC.

Copies in silver gilt of other cups found in the Tholos tomb at Vaphio, Laconia. These were extremely popular and could be bought in boxed sets of four cups. The sides were embossed with scenes of the capture of wild bulls.

Copy of the two handled Nestor Cup from Mycene c. 1400 BC.

Copy of a gold cup with dog's heads on the handles from a grave in the citadel of Mycene.

Copies of a London made font cup of 1521/22. The original is illustrated in Charles Jackson's *History of English Plate*, p. 690, fig. 900. It carries the inscription 'Benedictus Deus imdona suis Ame'. This was copied in Chester and Birmingham (hallmarked in Chester) in 1902 but a similar font cup (without the inscription) was made in 1910 to commemorate the Coronation of King George V and Queen Mary. The original cup is $4\frac{1}{2}$ inches high and the rim diameter is $4\frac{3}{4}$ inches.

A large plate, diameter 12 inches with a narrow moulded rim and a base diameter of 5 inches having a repeat of the rim moulding. Across the surface of the plate, a folded damask napkin with incised decoration. It carries the Chester mark and the date Script G (1907/08). Now in the Victoria and Albert Museum. The design owes much to Russian influence.

A two handled porringer with a gadrooned base of late 18th century design. One has been noted with the Chester date 1899/1900.

Small sided hot water jug with octagonal sides close to the spirit of the Arts and Crafts Movement. Date letter 1897/98.

Church silver was also made by Nathan and Hayes. At St Andrew's, Malvern Priory Church are a Communion cup and paten, dated 1907/08 (being replicas of a cup and paten in the same church which had been made by Lowe and Sons, Chester in 1885.) It is $6\frac{1}{2}$ inches high, bowl diameter $3\frac{5}{8}$ inches and base diameter $3\frac{3}{8}$ inches.

Copies of boat shaped sugar or bon-bon bowl with swivel handle and pedestal, (standing on a square base) being a copy of a late 18th century bowl.

ALEXANDER RITCHIE, IONA CELTIC ART (Illustration 33)

Alexander Ritchie was born at Tobermorey on the island of Mull in 1856. He came with his family to Iona in 1868 when his parents took the lease of the new St Columba Hotel, formerly the free Church Manse, and the adjoining farm. Alexander went to sea becoming a ship's engineer for twenty years. He returned to Iona in 1890 owing to a serious leg injury in the West Indies. For some time he became a guide on Iona and took a great interest in the island's history, where his father took an interest in the Iona Press. Alexander and his wife Euphemia attended classes at the Glasgow School of Art, where they developed their skills as a wood carver and an embroiderer using the ancient carvings at Iona and the decorations on the books of Lindisfarne and Kells as their guide. Returning to Iona in 1900 they were given permission to open a small shop and craft centre near the Nunnery ruins which were patronised by the growing number of visitors to the island. Alexander Ritchie now expanded his work to include silver jewellery and brass ware, submitting the many designs to the firm of Darby in Birmingham. He also registered his mark at Chester on 9 May 1910 as Alex Ritchie. Iona Celtic Art. Iona, the application sent by Sanders and Shepherd of Birmingham. He insisted that his work should be of the highest quality. His brass work was made by Lawson's of Glasgow.

Alexander Ritchie died in 1941 two days after his wife and they are buried in the Reilig Odhrain burial ground on Iona.

Their work was enormous and they used elsewhere the marks of AR at Chester and A&ER and ICA (for Iona Celtic Art) as well as the stamp IONA.

(A record of his life and his work is in *The Celtic Art of Iona* by Iain MacCormick. Published in 1994 for the Iona Heritage Trust by the New Iona Press Ltd., Iona.)

The output and variety of his wares in silver was considerable. Among the decorations used were reproductions of the Viking longboats found on the clan tomb stones at Iona.

PHILLIP'S SALE, LONDON. 2 MAY 1984.
LOT 206. A vesta case chased with a Viking longboat on a frosted background in the Arts and Crafts style marked 'iona'. Hallmarked at Chester 1911 (illustration 33). See *The Finial*, August 1995.

A number of brooches hallmarked at Chester were noted at the Royal Mile Jewellers, 363 High Street, Edinburgh, ranging from 1906 to 1909. The earliest — an early Scottish Luckenbooth brooch design also had the mark CS & FS of Saunders and Shepherd.

GEORGE ROSEATER, Devon.
George Roseater registered his mark at Chester on 23 November 1913. He was working at Teynmouth, Baighton and Newton Abbot.

At Chester he is represnted by a large replica thimble 6 inches high which was worn on the City ambulance during the First World War. It was inscribed

The Thimble, Chester 1916.
and has the Chester mark for 1915.
Exhibited at Sotheby's Chester Exhibition, 1984. p. 177a.

138

FREDERICK JAMES ROSS, Winchester. (Illustration 35)

The second half of the 19th century saw an increase in the number of tourists to our cities. This was often coupled with a growing antiquarian interest. A number of silversmiths took advantage of their presence and produced interesting models and reproductions of historic artefacts of local interest.

Among the silversmiths in the provinces was Frederick J. Ross of Winchester. He registered his mark at London, FJR within a rectangle with clipped corners, 3 December 1904 and in a plain rectangle with slightly rounded corners 12 March 1906, both in two sizes. At Chester he recorded his mark 28 August 1905. He traded as J. Ross & Sons at 43 and 44 High Street, Winchester, his private address being Rona¹dsha' St, Cross Hill, Winchester.

The firm appears to have had some standing. In the trade directory of 1887 he is listed as Jacob and Ross Jewellers and Silversmiths of the same address in High Street. It remained as such until 1895 and in 1902 it became F. J. Ross & Sons. In 1913 it was only at 43 High Street, and ceased to be listed in 1942.

The firm produced a considerable number of souvenir pieces including a number of small silver models of the Winchester bushel kept by the City. The original is illustrated on the cover of *Weights and Measures of the City of Winchester* by Maurice Stevenson, published by Winchester Museums Service. The model is a faithful copy but with a diameter of $2\frac{1}{2}$ inches. It stands on three cloven feet and has two square handles. On the side is an inscription 'Henricus Septimus dei gracie rex danglie et Francie', and has the Tudor badges of a rose, a greyhound, a portcullis and also an anchor. The original bushel was sent in 1497 to thirty county towns and five other cities or ports, was of bronze and with the standard yard became known as 'the Winchester standard'.

Another souvenir for visitors was a spoon showing on the finial a representation of 'the faithful servant'. A picture which hangs in Winchester and shows the numerous articles associated with a good servant.
(See *The Finial*, February 1994.)

CORNELIUS SAUNDERS and FRANCIS SHEPHERD, London.
(Illustration 32, 39)

The firm was founded in 1869 in London, operating from 58-61 Peter Square and 2-3 Bartlett's Passage, both in Holborn Circus. They registered first at Chester with CS and FS each in oval and in 1899 the CS FS with a star between in a long rectangle with clipped corners in three sizes, when it became a Limited Company. After 1904 in a new factory in Fetter Lane their output was considerable including jewellery. (see Culme, *Gold and Silversmiths*, p. 403)

They also took in and made for others especially Alex Ritchie of Iona (see Alex Ritchie, where an A.R. IONA marked Luckenbooth brooch also carries the CS*FS mark as well. Dated 1906).

Among the more unusual pieces are Doulton jug mounts, silver mounted Doulton set and a series of miniatures including

A pepper in the form of a small oval tea pot.

A cylindrical bun top with a scroll handle, 1 inch high.

A coffee pot with a wooden handle fitted into a sleeve.

Milk churn probably a pepper with side handles.

An oval mirror in a stand.

In Glasgow Museum and Art Gallery is a pepper pot in the form of a toy horse on wheels (design 366450 registered 1900), all these are marked at Chester. (Illustration 32)

ISAAC SIMMONS, Manchester. (Illustration 30, 31)

On the jewels of many Masonic Lodges, or those of the Foresters and Odd-fellows appears the name of Isaac Simmons. The mark is incorporated into the cast design of the coat of arms and appears in very small capitals. He sold his designs to leading silversmiths including George Unite of Birmingham who had registered his mark in Birmingham in 1825 and later in London. A silver breast plate resembling a Masonic badge was made by George Unite in 1867 using the Isaac Simmons design. It was made to commemorate the British North American Act of 1867 providing for the Federation of Canada (see A. Crisp, *The Silversmiths of Birmingham*, p. 135. Illustrated).

Isaac Simmons was a Manchester silversmith. Bradbury (*Old Sheffie'd Plate*, p. 487) lists his mark at Sheffield, 21 February 1839 and the IS is found on numerous Masonic and Friendly Society jewels. His address is given as 9 St Ann's Square, Manchester. The IS mark is also found at Chester, struck twice without date but must be after 1841 as it is on the second copper plate. His name is also found on several jewels which also have the IS personal mark together with the Sheffield and Chester marks.

An eight pointed star given, as a long inscription relates to G. M. Wm Wishlade in 1846, has the Sheffie'd mark and date for the previous year. There are several jewels with the coat surrounded by an ornate shield engraved measuring $4\frac{1}{2}$ inches by $3\frac{1}{2}$ inches which are known with the Chester marks and the IS of Simmons and dated 1842/43.

WILLIAM SMITH, Liverpool. (Illustration 8, 9, 10, 11)

William Smith entered his mark at Chester, of incuse type usually associated with the work of Watchcase makers, on 7 November 1871 on the third copper plate giving his address as 40 Mount Pleasant, Liverpool. Jackson claims that there was a WS mark in both, a rectangle and oval without cerifs attributed to William Smith whilst a mark of W.S. with pellet and cerifs is found in 1869 attributed to William Smith of 79 High Street, Belfast in 1869.

The mark of WS incuse is only found on the pieces recorded below and the attribution is confirmed by an added inscribed note which reads (in script).

W. SMITH FECIT

and   W. Smith Sculpt

found on the base of the casket. (see below).

In the few pieces which have been traced the incuse mark is accompanied by a small cross within a lozenge.

His work seems to be a departure from any other style. It appeared first in the Sotheby's Belgravia Catalogue for 26 October 1972 (Lot 168).

> A fine Victorian silver gilt wine ewer with gold inlay in eastern style the matted elongated beluster body overlaid with a network of arabesques in two coloured golds, the curious multilooped handle further applied with interlaced gold strapwork issuing from the tapering neck: hinged over. 10½ inches Maker's name W.S. incuse. Chester. 1879. 25 oz 9 dwt (all in).

Another item in the Sotheby's sale on 25 January 1975 (Lot 172).

> A fine Victorian shaped rectangular silver gilt casket with gold inlay, the matted body and curved cover overlaid with a network of scrolling foliage and arabesques incorporating several caryatids all in two colour gold, the borders further decorated with formal leafage or flower heads, on four bun supports. 7¼ inches, 4¼ inches high, fully hallmarked, maker's mark W.S incuse Chester 1875, the underside signed in freehand script
>
> W. Smith fecit   and   'W. Smith Sculpt'
>
> 35 oz 6dwt.

A third item by W. Smith is a gilt salt cellar in the form of a quarter sphere supported by three trefoil like supports, standing on three narrow scroll feet, the sides decorated with foliage after the manner of the decoration on the casket. The sides are all different. Overall radius of the bowl is 1½ inches, height 1⅝ inches.

There are five marks including Chester, Duty mark, WS incuse and the date letter O for 1877/78. Weight 2 ozs 5 dwt.

A tea set has been reported.

RICHARD JOHN WAKEFIELD, Birmingham.

Richard John Wakefield was a manufacturer of silver jewellery working from 48 Tenby Street North, Birmingham. He does not appear to have registered at Birmingham but did so at Chester on 3 May 1897.

Two very similar oval brooches have been seen, the tops heavily embossed with leaves and flowers with eight petals, the edge indented and containing pellets. They are fully hallmarked including the maker's mark and the date letter R for 1900/01.

(An almost identical brooch though smaller with the same decoration is by a maker T.W but assayed at Birmingham in 1901/02. The brooch is surrounded by beads and 14 larger beads form a surround. The leaves are small pieces of yellow gold and the flowers of red gold.)

WAKELY & WHEELER, London.

The Chester Goldsmiths' Company commissioned Wakely and Wheeler to make a half pint tankard, gilded, in Britannia standard silver to mark the Coronation in 1953. It has the date letter C for 1953. (Illustrated in *Touching Gold and Silver,* p. 108, plate 184.)

A similar silver gilt tankard of Britannia silver of Chester assay 1953 was sold 23 March 1978 by Sotheby's, Belgravia. (Illustrated Antique Collector, March 1978.)

WALKER AND HALL, Sheffield.

What is now a very large commercial firm throughout the country began in humble circumstances when George Walker opened his business in Sheffield in 1845 and because of his connection with John Wright and also with Henry Elkington was deeply involved in the electroplating side of his work. He was later joined by Henry Hall and after 1853 began trading as Walker and Hall. They were joined by Walker's nephew, John E. Bingham and worked at the Electro works in Howard Street. After their retirement, Charles and Albert Bingham took over and in the first years of the 20th century had connections as far away as Melbourne, Sydney and Capetown.

It was at this time that they registered their mark at Chester on 29 September 1906, retaining the Walker and Hall names in their W & H mark; the flag mark was introduced about the same time. Those who entered the mark at Chester were Albert E. Bingham and John Edward Bingham from the Electro Works, Sheffield.

A. V. Ward, the last Assay Master at Chester said their connection with Chester came about through a minor difference of opinion between them and the Sheffield office. They entered the flag mark at London in 1903.

A Chester example is found on two small toast racks on four cushion feet with the W & H flag mark and the date Script G (1907/08).

HUGH WALLACE, Altrincham, Cheshire.

Hugh Wallace was a worker in various metals specialising in blending copper and pewter. He produced some interesting trays and plates in these metals. He registered his mark at Chester.

In silver, a cream jug is reported by him having the same maker's mark as that used on his copper and pewter wares. It was 3 inches high carrying the mark B (1927).

ARTHUR VINCENT WARD, Chester. (Illustration 42, 46)

A. Vincent Ward was the last Chester Assay Master.

He was born January 1885 and was the son of Frederick William Ward, a member of the Company, who had married the eldest daughter of Thomas Woolley, who was Warden of the Company; he in turn had married Elizabeth Duke, the sister of Joseph Duke and was thus descended from the Duke family who were prominent Chester Goldsmiths in the 18th century. Vincent's mother died when her fourth child, Thomas, was born, and he was adopted by Albert Ward and his wife who had no children. Between Vincent and Thomas there were two other children, Theo, a girl, and Hugh. When their parents died, Vincent and Theo went to live with their grandparents, Thomas and Elizabeth Woolley who had no children of their own. The family home was at 16 The Walls, Chester overlooking the Dee and Vincent could remember skating on the River when he was about ten years old. Frederick William Ward had been employed by Thomas Woolley who had a house and shop at 55 Bridge Street Row, Chester and concentrated upon selling jewellery. With the break up of the family his brother Hugh went to live at Brymbo, Wrexham and was later ordained into the priesthood becoming Vicar of West Kirby. Frederick William Ward was admitted to the Company 5 August 1879 and made small silver pieces including spoons. Thomas Wolley, Vincent's grandfather had F. E. Clarke working for him doing repairs and he eventually became Assay Master in 1931 continuing until 1954 when A. V. Ward followed him.

A. Vincent Ward had his mark registered at Chester of a plain AVW incuse form similar to that used by watchcase makers. Although the mark had appeared (by being borrowed) on a number of pieces of silver he actually made only two pieces of silver, which were seen at his home, Highfield, Sea Hill Road, Saughall in January 1973. They were made by him to commemorate the Coronation of Queen Elizabeth II and are of Britannia silver with the five marks including the date letter C. They were both small salt spoons, one 2 inches in length and the other $3\frac{1}{2}$ inches, just large enough to take the marks.

A. Vincent Ward as last Assay Master played an important part in the closure of the Assay Office at Chester in 1962, and retired on a pension. The last piece of silver assayed at Chester was a dish, carrying his mark.

GEORGE WARD, Manchester.

George Ward was principally a medal maker.

There are numerous GW marks registered at Chester but the one which appears to be his is in a rectangle with clipped corners and a pellet between the letters.

A medal with an inscription in a $1\frac{1}{2}$ inch diameter circle with beaded edge and placed within a sixteen point star. The medal is slightly concave with a round attachment at the back. There are five marks on the back including the maker's mark (slipped) and the Chester mark. The inscription reads that it was presented to William MacGowan for his 'disinterested and indefatigable exertions in establishing and conducting Moss Lane Phonetic classes Jany 20th 1849'. There is no date letter.

A medal with the inscription on a plain surrounded by a wide embossed edge in all diameter $2\frac{1}{2}$ inches, the border being $\frac{1}{2}$ inch wide. This is set against a sixteen point star engraved, diameter 4 inches. The inscription shows that it was presented to 'P.C.R. Brother John Irwan by the members of the Court Pride of Hulme 2178 for his past valuable services Augt 8th 1849'. There are five marks on the reverse including the maker's mark but no date letter. On the back is an attachment for a ribbon.

J. F. WATHEW, Chester.

J. F. Wathew married Mary, the sister of George Lowe (2). He is mentioned in the Chester Directory 1840 as a silversmith and lived in Bridge Street Row. He advertised at the back of the Directory under a Royal Arms finely engraved.

J. F. Wathew
Wholesale and Retail
GOLDSMITH & JEWELLER
Bridge Street Row
Chester.

A superior stock of clocks and watches always on hand.
He registered his mark at Chester in several forms with and without the interval pellet on the second copper plate (W) 1843, according to Jackson.

After the death of Richard Richardson (4) in 1835 his business passed to J. F. Wathew which later passed to his son in law, Francis Butt. (qv).

JOHN CHRISTOPHER WEBB, St. Albans. (Illustration 44)

John C. Webb, the son of Christopher Webb of St Albans, a leading stained glass artist. He worked at St Albans before moving to Portway House, Erdington.

He was well known both here and abroad for some remarkable silver work, most of which was assayed at London, but shortly before the closing of the Chester Assay Office he registered at Chester. The two Churchwarden's staves at Bunbury, Cheshire are by him. Mounted on wood shafts the heads are carrying both the crown, the arms of the Diocese and the one with the mitre arms of St Boniface . . . the book pierced with a sword. It was given by the parents of Edward Shore who was Churchwarden at Bunbury. The Wardens' staves are fully marked including the Chester mark, and the date letter L for 1961/62.

Only one other Chester hallmarked piece is known. A small hand raised plate given at the baptism of Simon Whitely with a Latin inscription. Silver made by John Webb may be seen at the following places:

The Borough Mace, Enfield.
Churchwardens' Staves, St Nicholas Church, Harpenden.
Altar Candlesticks, Harpenden.
Altar Candlesticks, St James Church, Bushey.
Processional Cross, Stone Church, Bucks.
Wall Candelabra (Private).
Pastoral Staff, Sheffield.
Processional Cross, Uganda.
Altar Cross and Candlesticks, Norbury Parish Church, Cheshire.
Wafer Box, Pembroke College, Cambridge.

R.J.W.

Two ceremonial trumpets were assayed at Chester and were made for John Lockett, Esquire, High Sheriff of Denbighshire 1939-1940, as the inscription reads. They are in a private collection but were illustrated in Sotheby's Chester catalogue, p. 103 and plate 177. The trumpets are 31 inches in length and are hung with a silken banner with the coat of arms of Denbighshire. They are fully hallmarked with the maker's initials RJW and the Chester date letter for 1938.

ALFRED WILCOX, Birmingham.

Alfred Wilcox is listed at Chester as a Jeweller living at 172 V. Square and Tenby Street, N. Birmingham: registered 2 November 1898. He was also a watchcase maker and his mark appears on a watchcase (series x) N date (1896/7).

THOMAS WOOLLEY, Chester.

(See under A. Vincent Ward.)
There is a stand paten or credence paten at Betws Gwerfil Goch Church having a diameter of 6¾ inches with a moulded rim and deep depression: it stands on a pedestal stem with a narrow step, a bold shoulder and a single moulding. Total height 2¼ inches. There are five marks on the underside of the plate:

    i.   Maker's mark.
   ii.   Duty mark of Victoria.
  iii.   Lion passant guardant.
   iv.   Chester.
    v.   Date letter H (1871/72).

The plate is inscribed:

The Gift of Caroline Sobieski Lynes
Great Grandmother of Robt Wynne
of Garthmeilio 1879

The Assaying of Gold at Chester

(Additional information can now be added to the section on Chester Gold)
(see *Chester Silver*, p. 52f.)

The Gold Plate Standard Act came into force 1 October 1798 which meant that goldsmiths could now use 18 cts in every pound weight Troy. No directions were given about the older standard of 22 cts, and this carried no distinguishing mark until 1844, though in London in a note kept by the Assay Master at Goldsmiths' Hall, it is mentioned that in 1816 the impression of the Sun was to be used on the 22 carat standard from and after 29 May 1816. In 1854 by order of the Council (11 December) the marks for 15 cts, 12 cts and 9 cts were introduced. The 12 cts continued to be used until 1932 when 14 cts gold was introduced in place of 15 and 12 cts.

It was always assumed that the Chester Assay Office controlled the marking of both silver, gold and parcel gilt plate. When the last process was used, the gilt, especially on tumbler cups was of a very pale yellow, almost lemon.

The reappearance of the Chester Plate Duty Books (1784-1840) throws much new light upon the extent of gold being used at Chester.

It was used to make gold medals. Abbott (1813), J. L. Samuel & Co. (1823), Thomas Appleby (1791), Thomas Morrow (1796), George Walker (1798), Robert Bowers (1801) and James France (1786) are examples.

Spectacle frames in gold were made by R. Jones (1814) and at the same time '6 gold salt spoons', though one would have thought that these were parcel gilt though they are not so listed.

Many buckles and clasps were sent to Chester from Liverpool and Manchester before 1784, but only those of silver and gold are listed. Nicholas Cunliffe, a general silversmith made a gold stock buckle in 1803 and Robert Jones a pair of gold knee buckles.

The watchcase makers of Liverpool produced gold watchcases, but after 25 March 1798 they no longer appear in the Plate Duty Books. After that date, duty was removed and any duty which had been paid was returned to them. The record shows that there were few gold watchcases in comparison to the number of silver watchcases. William Tarlton made nine in 1785 compared with 114 the same year in silver. Thomas Helsby produced fifteen in 1797 and 323 in silver.

By far the greater trade was in gold wedding rings and mourning rings at Chester, Liverpool and Manchester. During the period of the Plate Duty Books, James France of Manchester, between 1788 and 1818 made over 35,000 and his work was carried on by Elizabeth (probably his widow) who produced another 5,000 until 1824. In Liverpool, Robert Jones produced 4,518 and when he was joined by his son (from 1813 to 1832) produced another 3,871 rings. Many other Liverpool silversmiths produced small numbers of wedding rings and the appearance of only one in 1833, two in

1835 and a single one in 1836 by other goldsmiths appear to be special orders and may have been made elsewhere, though assayed at Chester. Their chief occupation was in making watchcases.

Chester had several silversmiths who made gold rings a priority. George Lowe (1) and his son George Lowe (2) made 21,627 and John and William Twemlow between 1787 and 1833 made 843. Mary Huntingdon and her partner from 1815 to 1830, 390, and George Walker and his son between 1785 and 1834 made 9,401.

The Manchester silversmith Thomas Newton, one time linked with the Newton and Hyde partnership between 1822 and 1826 submitted 4,176 and when working by himself from 1827 to 1840 a further 3,434. The George Lowe (I) Day Book occasionally refers to the sale of gold rings. One for a Mr Bromfield cost 6/4d.

There was a natural connection between watchcase makers and box makers, for they were skilled in making the hinges necessary for their manufacture. Thomas Helsby of Liverpool in 1797 submitted fifteen boxes and the year later states specifically that one was a gold box. Such expressions can only mean what the record says. A little later the same year comes the expression 'one gold case' which means a watchcase. A large table snuff box is known by IH/TH made of a blend of silver and gold, referred to in the Plate Duty Books but accepted as silver. Thomas Helsby also turned his hand to a large variety of objects, and in 1820 made a gold tooth pick case and in 1822 a gold cane head, and John Helsby in 1834 made a gold watch swivel.

One of the interesting references in the Plate Duty Books is to William Pugh of Birmingham. At Birmingham he is referred to as a 'goldworker' where he registered his mark in 1773. But at Chester his name appears as 'William Pugh of Birmingham' in 1810 when he submitted three gold boxes, three more in 1813 and another three in 1814. It was clearly against the rules for a silversmith from Birmingham to register at Chester, or indeed anywhere other than Birmingham. His mark has not been identified on the Chester copper plates.

In the Eaton Hall Accounts there are some interesting references to the Chester Race Cup which was run in May. These appear to be gold tumbler cups, each cost £50 and were given by the Grosvenor family. From the accounts they seem to have been provided by Chester goldsmiths.

1762	To Joseph Duke for a gold cup run for at Chester . . . £50
1762	To Mr Ald. Richardson for a Gold cup run for at Chester Races and won by Nancy £50
1776	To Joseph Duke for a gold cup run for at Chester, £50 To Jo. Duke for the difference in value of the Gold Cup run for at Chester this meet.g. & that which Short Horse won 1776 £9.10.7

Mr Alderman Richardson mentioned here is Richard Richardson (2) who was responsible for a large number of silver tumbler cups. He died in 1769 and there is no reason to suppose that he could not have made a tumbler cup in gold in 1762 as mentioned in the Eaton accounts. Joseph Duke died in 1810 and Richard Richardson (4) acted as a witness to his will. No tumbler cups have been attributed to Joseph Duke and it is possible that the 1776 cup was made either by Richard Richardson (4) or brought in London as seems to have been the case in later references to gold cups in the Plate Duty Books.

These appear as

	Ounces	dwt	grs
Ap. 28 1785 Richard Richardson. Chester. A gold cup	10	5	– at 8/- p.oz.
May 4 1789 R. Richardson. Chester. One gold cup	9	18	–
Ap. 26 1790 R. Richardson. Chester. 1 gold cup	10	5	12
May 4 1791 George Walker. Chester. 1 gold cup	10	5	–

This Richard Richardson is Richard Richardson (4). The weight of the cups corresponds with the very few cups that have survived. The cups mentioned in the Eaton Accounts, and those mentioned for 1764, 1765, 1769 and 1771 races were won by the Hon. John Smith-Barry of Marbury Hall, who had the four cups made into a gold cup and cover by Parker & Wakelin of London, and it is now in the Manchester City Art Gallery. Those mentioned in the Plate Duty Books have not been traced. However, there are three surviving cups, all tumbler cups. One is for the 1766 and is assayed in London with the assay date of 1765/66 by (it is assumed) Joseph Steward (II). This is now in the Ridgway Gallery of the Grosvenor Museum. The side of the bowl carries a magnificent coat of arms. It weighs 10.14 ounces and is $3\frac{7}{8}$ inches high. The second cup is reported to be 1774 (which may be the assay date or the date when the race was won). The third cup is London made of 1792 (see Michael Clayton, *Dictionary of Silver and Gold,* fig. 705).

A tumbler cup provided by George Lowe and referred to in his Day Book as the retailer for Peter and Ann Bateman and carries their mark (1791/92) was sold at Christie's, London, 16 October 1963. Weight 9 ozs. 11 dwt.

The date letter changed from 1839 (usually 5 July) to August (usually 5 August) and from 1839 to the meeting on 3 August 1889 remained as such, the day being regulated by the occurance of a Sunday. On 3 August 1889 they decided to change for 1890 to 1 July and this continued until the Assay Office closed on 24 August 1962.

Buckle, Clasp and Button Makers

The fashion in clothing dictated the use of buckles, clasps and buttons. As many of them were conspicuous they were made to look beautiful and became expensive.

One of the main centres for buckles was Birmingham in the eighteenth century. The proximity of steel and Sheffield plate helped in their manufacture, and it was only a matter of time before silver and gold were used, steel being retained for the steel chapes.

Matthew Boulton was among these early buckle makers. He moved from Lichfield to Birmingham Snow Hill and established a buckle making industry along with other toy maker's making trinkets, snuff boxes, seals and other articles in gold and silver. The steel workers made such things as cork screws, candle snuffers, watch chains and buckles. The term 'toy maker' was loosely applied to these small articles. It was at Snow Hill Birmingham that Matthew Boulton's son, Matthew, was born in 1728. He took over his father's firm on his death in 1759. He had already shown considerable skill inventing a new form of buckle. At Soho where he built a new works by 1762 and established a centre for the manufactury of silver and steel jewellery, buttons, seals and buckles, and before the establishment of the Birmingham Assay Office sent his goods to Chester. It is quite likely that silver buckles would be sent there though none is known to the author.

How many buckles, clasps and buttons were sent from Liverpool and Manchester to Chester before 1784 we have no way of finding out. From 1784 onwards silver and gold buckles, clasps and buttons are recorded.

Many of the watchcase maker's also turned their hands to their manufacture. John Clarke of Liverpool (1817) made a single pair of buckles though he was a specialist wedding ring maker. Nicholas Cunliffe, a general silversmith of Liverpool, made a gold stock buckle in 1803, John Fisher from 1785 to 1790 sent ten pairs of buckles to Chester and Robert Jones also from Liverpool sent a pair of gold knee buckles, a shoe buckle, a parcel of children's clasps, and 65 pairs of clasps. At Manchester, James France, a ring maker, two pairs of clasps. Chester presents a different picture: Thomas Hill in 1788 submitted 48 buckles, 73 pr knee buckles, a stock buckle, a pair of clasps and 45 pairs of shoe buckles. At Chester, George Lowe from 1792 to 1828 submitted 2 pair of boot buckles, 4 knee buckles, a belt clasp, 5 habit clasps, 39 shoe clasps, 12 clasps, and 3 buckles. Richard Richardson in the six years from 1784 submitted 15 buckles, 3 stock buckles, 13 shoe buckles, 7 shoe clasps, 20 knee buckles, 58 clasps and 2 bridle clasps. It is not clear what is the difference between a clasp and a buckle for the two terms are used separately when referring to shoe fasteners. William Twemlow only submitted 5 pairs of buckles between 1797 and 1818 but George Walker between 1785 and 1800 submitted for duty 7 buckles, 11 knee buckles, 7 clasps, 3 hat buckles, 4 shoe buckles, 2 shoe clasps, always in pairs. John Walker submitted 2 pairs of buckles in 1806 and Mary Huntingdon, a shoe clasp in 1828. In the *Adam's Weekly Courant* (Chester) for 28 April 1767 there is an advertisement which shows that Chester could both sell City made buckles and retail others from elsewhere.

'. . . twenty four pair of shoe buckle rims, made by William Cox silversmith of London mark'd WC'

(William Cox (2) entered three marks as a buckle maker 1776-91). The reference to '1 Bugle' (George Lowe 1809) weighing just over an ounce seems to prove that it referred to a buckle!

Buttons of various types were also made. George Lowe from 1791 made both gold and silver buttons. (1791); 30 breast buttons. (1792); 20 silver coat buttons, 1 pair gold buttons (1793); 24 silver buttons. (1794); 18 pairs of sleeve buttons. James Dixon of Liverpool also made coat buttons (1785), as also did J. Fisher, Walley and Jones (1786) '14 pair gold buttons'. James France (1786) 21 buttons, (1785); 99 coat buttons, 24 breast buttons and a pair of gold buttons. Richard Richardson of Chester also made large numbers of buttons.

Caddy Spoons

The standard and definitive work upon Caddy spoons is John Norie, *Caddy spoons, an illustrated guide,* published by John Murray. In it he remarks (pages 50/51) 'As a class, period Chester caddy spoons remain the most elusive and scarcest of any known to have been assayed at the English offices. In the absence of proof to the contrary, it must be assumed that few caddy spoons were submitted for assay at Chester during the Georgian era and precious few during the Victorian one either.' This observation had been supported by the fact that very few Chester caddy spoons had been reported from collectors. Three examples by the Lowe family are reported, the most important being one which is fully marked by George Lowe 1837 with the duty mark used in the time of William IV; the Victoria head was not introduced until the beginning of series 8 with the date letter A (1839/40). Other examples are known by John Lowe 1847 and 1855, the latter being fully authenticated by having the Chester mark, an interesting shell bowl example with the mark of John Sutter (1835). Another caddy spoon has been reported having the maker's mark J.C and to be 1805. This is far too early for John Coakley and one assumes that the reading of the I date letter has been mistaken for the I of series 7 which would put it as 1827/28. Coakley made forty one caddy spoons according to the Chester Plate Duty Books between 1828 and 1833.

Captain Norie had been slightly mislead by a remark made by Mr Vincent

Ward, when he told him that most of the Chester records had been destroyed, and justified the prophetic remark of Captain Norie that 'in the absence of proof to the contrary' . . . Proof to the contrary is now available and the following list of Chester caddy spoons is gleaned from the three large volumes of Plate Duty Books and give a record of the caddy spoons assayed at Chester from 1784 to 1840, a unique record.

GEORGE LOWE (1) and GEORGE LOWE (2)

1793	(6)	1816	(7)
1796n	(1)	1817	(17)
1801	(5)	1826	(18)
1802	(6)	1827	(12)
1805	(9)	1828	(18)
(1809	'4 silver ladles')*	1830	(8)
(1811	'6 silver ladles')*	1835	(6)
1808	(3)	1837	(8)
1815	(12)		

* these 4 with a 'cup cover' weighed $3\frac{1}{2}$ ozs.
* these 6 with a bottle ticket weighed $3\frac{3}{4}$ ozs.

ROBERT LOWE, Preston.

1830	(1)
1832	(3)

JOHN COAKLEY, Liverpool.

1828	(12)
1829	(6)
1830	(14)
1831	(4)
1832	(2)
1833	(3)

RICHARD RICHARDSON (4), Chester.

1784	(1)

J. FRANCE, Manchester.

1787	(14)
1788	(12)
1791	('7 Cadie ladles')

WILLIAM TWEMLOW (at Nantwich and then Chester).

1790	(1)
1797	(1)

151

GEORGE WALKER, Chester.
1794   (4)
1796   (3)

JOHN WALKER, Chester.
1823   'a cady mount'

R. JONES AND SON, Liverpool.
1822   'a cady handle'

JOSEPH DUKE, Chester.
1840   (1)

JOHN HELSBY, Liverpool.
1832   (3)

JOHN SUTTER, Liverpool.
1835   (14)
1836   (9)
1837   (8)
1838   (12)
1839   (30)

R. ADAMSON, Liverpool.
1833   (1)

John Helsby also made '17 mount for shells' and in 1830 made a 'shell snuff box top'. Caddy spoons were sometimes referred to as shells and these entries are confusing. John Sutter submitted '60 shells' in 1836.

The Lowe Day Book, which George Lowe began in 1792, contains a number of references to the sale of caddy spoons, and shows that 'plated Caddy shells' were sold for 1/-, that silver ones were usually 1/6d, that in 1793 a 'caddy handle' was 5/6 and that 'to plate for a caddy handle' (the same entry) was an extra 1/-. Possibly a more elaborate caddy spoon cost 4/6 and in 1795 '1 tea caddy' 3/- and '2 Caddy Shells' 11/- and a single one was 5/-.

1. George Lowe 1
   (1768-1841)

2. George Lowe 2
   (1793-1876)

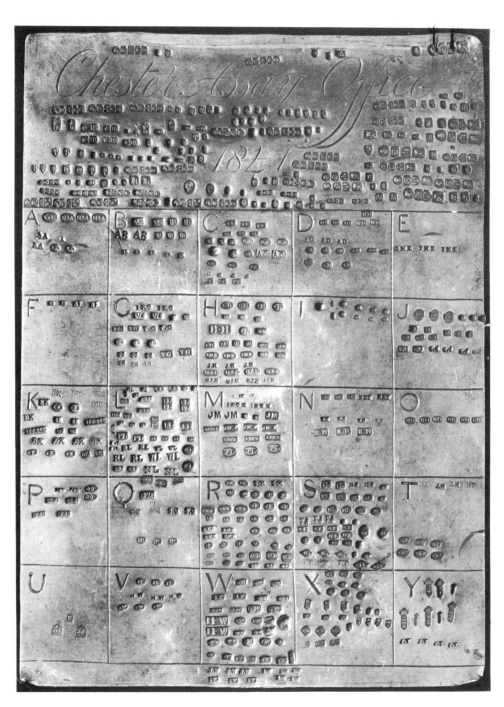

3. The 1841 Copper Plate.

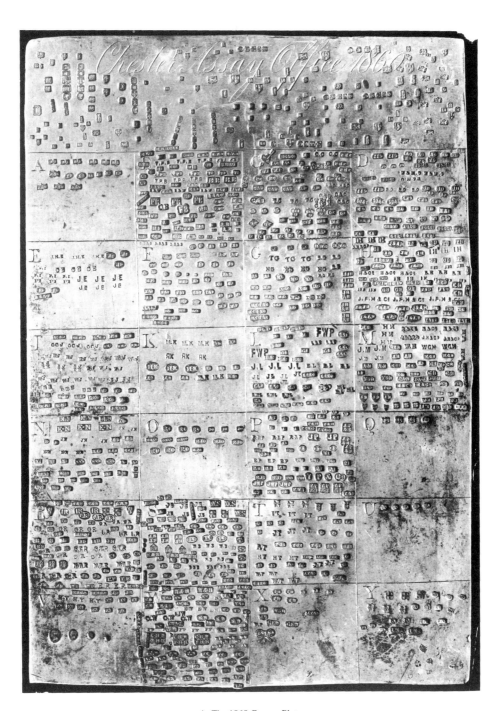

4. The 1860 Copper Plate.

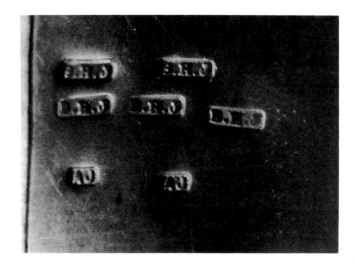

5/6. Examples of marks in the second book of makers' marks.

28 Aug. 1878
  B. H. Joseph & Co.,
  20 Frederick St.,
  Birmingham.

25 March 1879
  Johnson & Co.,
  31 Hill Street,
  Coventry.

18 August 1880
  William Crowson,
  10 Augusta Street,
  Birmingham.

17 November 1880
  Conway & Co.,
  21 Chester House Street,
  Holborn Circus, London.

1 January 1881
  J. A. Chalk,
  Percival Street,
  Clerkenwell, London.

25 February 1881
  W. E. Cooper,
  30 Edgebaston Street,
  Birmingham.

26 April 1881
  Andrew Conway,
  21 Chesterhouse Street,
  Holborn Circus, London.

20 May 1881
  Henry H. Clarke & Co.,
  25 Northampton Street,
  Birmingham.

10 October 1881
  William Henry Christie
  5 Bull Ring, Coventry.

  J. W. Crowthe,
  60 Shudehill, Manchester.

7. Water Jug by George Lowe 2, 1830-31.

8. Ornate wine ewer by Wiliam Smith, Liverpool, 1879-80.

9. Casket by William Smith,
   Liverpool, 1875-76.

10. Salt by William Smith,
    Liverpool, 1877-78.

11. Marks on No. 10.

12. Mustard Pot by John Lowe, 1842-43.

13. Four boat shaped salts by John Lowe, 1878-79.

14. Mark of John Sutter
    on a teaspoon, 1837-38.

15. Mark of John Lowe
    and Thomas Lowe on a
    mustard spoon, 1840-41.

16. Mark of John Lowe
    on a teaspoon, 1855-56.

17. Mark of Henry Tarleton on a watchcase, 1855-56.

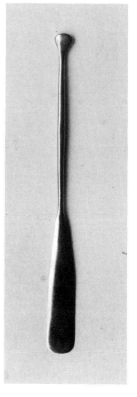

18. Grapefruit spoon by D.F., 1948-49.

19. Box by J. Millward Banks, Birmingham, 1911-12.

20. Blade by J. Millward Banks, Birmingham, 1911-12.

21. Toast rack by
Walker and Hall, Sheffield,
1907-08.

22. Mug by John Miller. Newcastle on Tyne, 1825-26.

23. Three graded jugs by Lowe & Sons, 1947-48.

24. Tea pot by J. Lowe, 1881-82.

25. Sugarbasin by J. Lowe, 1881-82.

26. Creamer by J. Lowe, 1881-82.

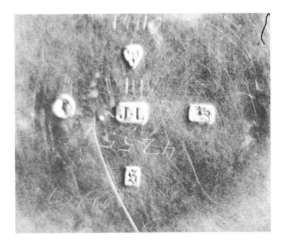

27. The marks on 24, 25, 26.

28. Mershom pipe by John Helsby, Liverpool, 1843-44.

29. Cylindrical toilet box by John & Thomas Helsby, 1843-44.

30. Marks of Isaac Simmons, Manchester with Chester assay marks, 1842-43.

31. Mark of Isaac Simmons, Manchester with Sheffield assay marks 1846-47.

32. Pepper by Saunders & Shepperd, London, 1903-04.

33. Vesta Case by Alex Ritchie, Iona, 1911-12.

35. Spoon finial by F. J. Ross, Winchester, 1933-34.

34. Antique mug by Nathan & Hayes, Birmingham, 1906-07.

36. The gold marks of
    18ct., Chester.

37. String box by James Deakin & Sons Ltd., Sheffield, 1900-01.

38. Marks of James Deakin on 37, 1900-01.

39. Three miniatures by (l to r) Saunders & Shepherd, J. M. Banks and
    Saunders & Shepherd.

40. Bowl by Iverna Cubbin, Chester, 1922-23.

41. Mark of George F. Lowe, Chester, 1871-1934.

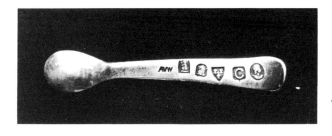

42. Mark of A. Vincent Ward
on a small salt spoon,
1955/56.

43. Bebington Borough Mace,
   by A. Edward Jones
   (Dunstan Works), 1937-38.

44. Churchwarden's stave, Bunbury Parish Church, Cheshire,
   by John C. Webb, St. Albans, 1961-62.

45. Grahame Jones at the Chester Assay Office, 1962.

46. Francis M. Lowe and A. Vincent Ward
     marking the last piece of silver assayed
     at Chester, 24 August 1962.

47. Marks used in the last few months of the
     Chester Assay Office including those of
     Margaret Joyce Lowe and her brother
     John ffoulkes Lowe.

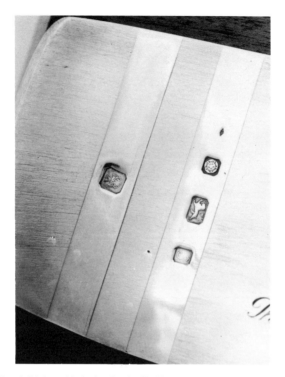

48. The Francis M. Lowe blade showing the Sheffield marks for 1992 and the Chester City of origin mark and those of the maker Greg Mora, Chester.

49. The four punches used for the City of Origin mark.

Coffin Plates

Michael Clayton in his *Collector's Dictionary of the silver and gold of Great Britain and North America,* p. 74, drew attention to the rare appearance of silver coffin plates, this was to be expected for most of them still lie buried. It is therefore of considerable interest that the Chester Plate Duty Books list the makers of coffin plates.

The Plate Duty Books record the following silversmiths from Chester and Liverpool who submitted coffin plates for duty, along with the date and number of plates made.

GEORGE LOWE (1) and GEORGE LOWE (2), Chester.

1795	(2)	1818	(2)	1829	(4)
1796	(1)	1819	(6)	1830	(6)
1798	(1)	1820	(3)	1831	(7)
1801	(1)	1821	(7)	1832	(4)
1806	(1)	1822	(1)	1833	(2)
1809	(2)	1823	(8)	1834	(4)
1813	(2)	1824	(9)	1835	(8)
1814	(8)	1825	(8)	1836	(6)
1815	(2)	1826	(2)	1837	(9)
1816	(8)	1827	(5)	1839	(1)
1817	(4)	1828	(7)	1840n	(2)

RICHARD RICHARDSON (4), Chester.

1785	(1)	1789	(4)
1786	(2)	1790	(4)
1787	(3)		

GEORGE WALKER (I), Chester.

1791	(1)	1796	(3)	1801	(2)
1792	(5)	1797	(4)	1802	(3)
1793	(3)	1799	(3)	1804	(3)
1795	(2)	1800	(3)	1804	(1)

ROBERT BOWERS, Chester.

1799	(1)	1805	(1)	1811	(2)
(1801	2 silver plates)	1806	(3)	1812	(1)
1803	(2)	1808	(2)	1813	(2)
1804	(8)	1809	(2)	1814	(1)

WILLIAM TWEMLOW, Chester.

1810	(1)	1816	(1)
1811	(3)	1818	'One plate'
1814	(2)	1820	(1)
1815	(5)		

MARY HUNTINGDON, Chester.
1821 (3)
1822 (4)

H. M. and S. HUNTINGDON, Chester.
1825 (2)
1829 (2)
1830 (2)

THOMAS WALKER, Chester.
1830 (1)

JOHN WALKER, Chester.

1806	(3)	1811	(2)	1820	(1)
1807	(1)	1815	(1)	1822	(1)
1808	(4)	1815	(1)	1823	(1)
1809	(2)	1817	(4)	1824	(2)
1810	(1)	1818	(1)	1826	(1)

JOHN HELSBY, Liverpool.
1831 (1)

WILLIAM JONES, Liverpool.
1809 (1)

ABBOTT and JONES, Liverpool.
1808 (1)

Six coffin plates have been found at Mold Parish Church, North Wales which have considerable interest as five are fully hallmarked with the Chester Assay marks. the sixth may have been of sub standard silver. The five are all by Chester based goldsmiths. George Walker (three), John Walker (one) and Richard Richardson (4) (one). The date letters on the George Walker plates are 1790/1, 1794/95, and 1798/99, those by John Walker 1823/24, and that of Richard Richardson 1785/86.

The dates of the deceased and the date mark seems to show that the plates were held in stock already assayed and waiting for customers.

These coffin plates seem to be the only specimens recorded but the 253 plates recorded in the Plate Duty Books seem to show that most still lie buried.

The Lowe Day Book kept by George Lowe records the coffin plate which was paid for by 'Colonel St George 25 November 1795 by 6', unfortunately the cost is on a disfigured page. It was apparently the first one he had made, but one in 1795 is recorded as 'To a coffin plate 5 oz 4 and cost 1. 19. 2d.'

154

Flat Ware

The Plate Duty Books introduce one to a number of flat ware makers at Chester, Liverpool and Manchester who might otherwise remain unknown as their wares were so limited that if they still exist they might go unrecognised. In some cases only one tea spoon was submitted for assay, which makes one believe that it was made by somebody else although it would bear the initials of the silversmith submitting the article. This is still a disputed topic, and perhaps the gold cups submitted by Richard Richardson might settle the question. Unfortunately they have not been traced. The same would apply to flat ware.

At Chester between 1784/5 and 1840 there was Robert Bowers, who from 1803 to 1814 sent 404 tea spoons, 75 table spoons and 39 dessert spoons. George Walker began working in 1791 to produce 21 tea spoons, 6 toy spoons, 7 dessert spoons and from 1792 to 1797, 54 tea spoons and 19 dessert spoons. In 1803, 6 dessert spoons, a tea spoon in 1804 and a child's spoon the same year. John Walker (his son) over a period of twenty four years from 1807 produced 93 tea spoons (the best year being 1811 with 51), 33 dessert spoons, 36 table spoons. He also made 25 table forks and 4 dessert forks. George Lowe was responsible for 41 tea spoons and 2 table spoons.

Richard Richardson from 1785 to 1788 submitted 111 tea spoons, 26 table spoons and 27 dessert spoons. Thomas Walker in 1830, 32 tea spoons, and 18 dessert spoons and in the following year 72 tea spoons, 12 dessert forks and 24 table forks. William Twemlow made 247 tea spoons and his son, John Twemlow, 188 tea spoons, and '30 forks' between 1814 and 1830. Contemporary with these silversmiths were James Dixon, '4 spoons', Joseph Duke, 6 tea spoons and John Falconer, 4 tea spoons which hardly qualifies them as spoon makers. Thomas Hill, 38 tea spoons, 7 table spoons, a dessert spoon and a fork.

At Manchester there was James France who was a ring maker but turned his hand to flat ware for two years from 1787. In this short period he made 642 tea spoons, 12 table spoons in 1787 and in the second year 216 tea spoons and 12 dessert spoons. He then returned to ring making.

Liverpool however became an important flat ware centre due to the work of two men, John Coakley followed by John Sutter. Before their time there were a few who added flat ware to their output. Robert Jones produced 10 fish knives in 1827 and 18 dessert forks and Walley and Jones in about 1787 made 216 dessert spoons. John Gilbert in 1791 submitted 6 silver forks, and R. Adamson in 1833, 24 tea spoons and 6 table spoons, though this was the only year he came to Chester; the other Adamsons were watchcase makers. The Helsby family under John Helsby in 1832 produced flat ware.

359 tea spoons, 22 table spoons, a variety of spoons for salt and caddy and 17 other listed as spoons.

The advent of John Coakley in 1828 seemed to dominate the market. From then until 1833 he produced 6,791 tea spoons, 297 dessert spoons, 634 table spoons and in addition 12 table forks, 52 dessert forks and 64 listed as forks. There were also 4 fish forks (1830). Shortly after 1833 John Sutter arrived from Newcastle on Tyne and we no longer hear of John Coakley, perhaps they joined forces or John Sutter replaced Coakley. He began in 1834 and was producing a large variety of silver goods in 1840 when the Duty Books record ends. Between 1833 and 1840 he produced over 5,000 tea spoons, 1,600 table and dessert spoons and over 1,000 table and dessert forks, these were all in addition to a variety of ladles, salt spoons, egg spoons and ladles which were common to most silversmiths.

Thimbles

In the Chester Plate Duty Books there is only one reference to a thimble. Nicholas Cunliffe of Liverpool submitted one in 1806. If however an article did not reach a certain weight (5 dwts) it was not liable either for duty or assay, though many did have them assayed. There are a few references to thimbles in the George Lowe Day Book. In 1792 he provided a thimble for Mr Bowers 1/3, and on another occasion in 1794 he paid 8p for two 'old thimbles' but managed to sell '2 silver thimbles' for 3/-. There is no indication that he had made them.

(In the City there is kept a very large thimble. See George Roseater p. 138)

Edwin F. Holmes, editor of the *Thimble Notes and Queries,* No. 14, Spring 1993, has recorded the results of examining over 300 Chester thimbles. It would seem that Charles Horner of Halifax, who first registered his mark at Chester (CH) in 1903 became one of the leading thimble makers in the country. There were however many other silversmiths who registered their marks at Chester and who put their own marks on the thimbles they sold, but who had purchased their thimbles from Charles Horner. Among these were Eustace George Parker of Hale, Altrincham who registered his mark at Chester, 18 January 1899. Also Henry Wilkinson Ltd. of Birmingham, Isaac Silverston & Co., Birmingham, 9 November 1898, John Thompson and Sons, London, Robert Pringle, London, Smith Brothers, Birmingham, Turner Brothers, Birmingham. Hutchinson and Co., London, Saunders and Shepherd, Birmingham, William Harrison Walter, London, Samuel Foskett, London and Woolf Myrstone, Manchester.

Other silversmiths who registered at Chester and may have made thimbles independent of Charles Horner or Henry Griffiths were Hilliard & Thomson,

Birmingham (registered 20 January 1898), James Swan, Birmingham, Marion & Co. London, (14 July 1900), Olney Amsden & Sons, London (23 April 1900), Salmon & Gluckstein, London (7 March 1896). Other thimble dealers who used their own marks at Chester were George Green, London (12 February 1896), Henry James Cooper, London (30 May 1899), Siegfried Steinhart, Birmingham (30 June 1900) and Samuel Greenhough & Sons, Bolton (9 April 1895).

It will be noted that nearly all these thimbles were made after 1886.

The Watchcase Makers

The 'watchmakers' were connected with the Chester Goldsmiths Company from the end of the 17th century, but at this period were much fewer than the goldsmiths. When by the Act of 1701 the old order was changed to incorporate a new form of Assay Office any qualified goldsmith and watch-case maker could register at Chester, and these included a large number of watchcase makers who came from Prescott, Liverpool, Coventry and Birmingham. Their marks were recorded on the first copper plate begun in 1701 and were recorded in great numbers until a new copper plate was provided in 1841. After 1773 the Birmingham silversmiths shared the restrictions of the newly founded Assay Office until 1854 when the restriction was lifted.

No record survives of the amount of gold and silver watchcases sent to Chester apart from the information contained in the three large Plate Duty Books. In 1784 duty registered by the introduction of a sovereign's head on all assayed silver. This also applied to watchcases, but in 1798 when after pressure the law covering watchcase makers was repealed, duty was no longer paid by them and any money paid by them after 25 March 1798 was returned. Chester therefore has only figures from 1784 to 1798. For the number and quality of watchcases before and after these dates one is forced to rely upon surviving specimens.

It seems clear that not only did the watchcase makers supply cases in gold and silver, but also when occasion arose, snuff boxes, tobacco boxes and patch boxes. This was understandable as the technique of making hinges for them was part of their trade. These boxes were still subject to duty and appear from time to time after 1798 along with the maker's name.

There were watchcase maker's in the Liverpool area before 1700, but neither they nor the silversmiths there could register at Chester as they did not qualify for membership of the Company. Among them was William Luthwait (Lithwhite) who was fined by the Goldsmiths of London in 1698/9. Much later when the 1701 Act admitted them to register at Chester we are

157

introduced to many more who continued to use the copper plate and helped to smother it with marks, for the first copper plate lasted until 1841. The names of these watchcase makers and their corresponding marks have had to be worked out from directories and other records. In 1784 however the Chester Plate Duty preserves their names until 1798 and after that date only from occasional references to other forms of their work which still required a duty mark.

The watchcase makers which appear in the Plate Duty Books are John Adamson, John Adamson and Son, James Barton and Co., David Beyendorfe, Richard Boulger, John Clifton, John Ellison, Thomas Harison, Thomas Helsby, William Hull, Nicholson Lee, Edward Maddock, Thomas Pierrepoint, James Richards, Henry Rigby, William Tarlton, Thomas Green.

The records showing the maker's name, address and mark started in 1863, but the worker's trade (e.g. watchcase maker) was introduced for the first time in the 1894 register of marks. Jackson may have had access to the register covering the period 1886 to 1894 but the book is now missing. For the later period from 1870 to 1920 the volume of registrations of watchcase makers from the various centres can be summarised as follows.

Coventry 104. Liverpool 56 (3 more from Prescot and 1 from Bootle). London 33 (and 12 from Clerkenwell and 1 from Islington). Birmingham 23. Manchester 7. Middlesbrough 2. One from each of the following, Birkenhead, Bradford, Eastham (Wirral), Leeds, West Bromwich, Sheffield, Worcester, Skipton, Glasgow, Belfast and Switzerland. These have for the most part been recognised along with their marks, but over the same period there are reasonable attributions to the following: Liverpool 105. Coventry 22. London 3 (Clerkenwell 2). Manchester 2. Birmingham 2, Chester 1.

(Information in this summary is gratefully acknowledged to Philip Priestley and his definitive work (*Watchase Makers of England 1720-1920*. NAWCC Bulletin Supplement 20. Spring 1994.)

Memoir of Alderman Grahame Jones on the Last Days of the Chester Assay Office

Alderman GRAHAME JONES

It was many years ago, as a little boy, I had my first glimpse of the world of the assayer and hallmarker. My grandfather, Mr James Foulkes Lowe, took me into the Assay Office with him one day. I gazed in wonderment, as any little boy would, at the trays of gold and silver wares glittering as the rays of the sun bounced off them. In 1954 I left school and was interviewed for two apprenticeships, one being trained as a forester on the Grosvenor Estate. The second apprenticeship I was offered was a goldsmith and assayer, which I decided to take.

On the 27th August 1954 I arrived at the front door of the Chester Assay Office at 13/15 Goss Street and was met by Mr Alf Arundale, an elderly gentleman in his sixties. Alf had been employed by the Chester Goldsmiths Company fom the early part of the century and apart from the period of the Second World War and the latter part of the forties when he was working for the Ministry of Defence, had spent most of his working life at the Chester Assay Office, and when trade started to improve after the war, returned to the Assay Office to help out with the sampling and marking.

On my first day I watched Alf unpack the hamper containing the gold and silver packets. This hamper was sent daily from our agent in Birmingham. His name was Mr J. Heavan but traded under the name of S. E. Cooke, and was a manufacturing jeweller in his own right Every working day, he would call at the premises of the manufacturing jewellers in the Birmingham jewellery quarter and collect any work that required assaying and hallmarking. The hamper containing the packets would be despatched from the now closed Birmingham Snow Hill Station and arrive at Chester General Station at 7 a.m. The hamper would be brought up to the Assay Office on the British Rail fish lorry delivering the fresh fish to the old fish market which was only 20 yards away from the front door of the Assay Office. I often could smell the fish as I unpacked the hamper. Work would also arrive by post from many parts of the county. I was requested to work for a probationary period of three months before I signed my indentures and in this period started to acquire the skills of the sampler, assayer and hallmarker. I would help to weigh the gold and silver in. It was important that this operation was carried out correctly as many of the packets weighed hundreds of ounces and an incorrect weight recorded could result in too much or too little 'makeweight' being sent back to the customer at the end of the working day.

At Chester the three sided cutting tool which was used for taking metal off the wares, was called a scraper. I was given my own set of scrapers and it was my responsibility to keep these cutting tools sharp and in tip top condition. The scraping or drawing of the metal from the article had to rank as one of the more skilful operations carried out at an Assay Office. A slither of gold or silver would be taken off each item and this task had to be carried out without damaging the article.

I would hold the article I was scraping against a steel peg $1\frac{1}{2}''$ in diameter and $6''$ high which was inserted through a central hole in a concave steel tray $14''$ in diameter and into a square hole in the bench. The scraped metal would fall into the tray. Slightly more in weight than what was required would be scraped off, and the gold scrapings were transferred to a watchglass, together with a small docket with the description of the items, the standard declared and the customer recorded on it.

It was in these early days that I started to learn how to use a touchstone. At times a low standard or base metal piece of jewellery would be mixed up in a high standard packet, and if there was a doubt at the sampling stage and the rogue piece could be detected it could save the assay 'going down' and this is when the touchstone or Lydian stone if used with skill, could prove helpful. The touchstone would be used in conjunction with standard touchsticks and acids. A streak would be made on the surface of the touchstone, using the doubtful article to make the streak and using the process of elimination by streaking various touchsticks. The nearest standard to the doubtful article would be arrived at. To help me obtain the most accurate results, certain made up standard acids would be used in conjunction with the touchstone and touchsticks.

The reason why a small quantity of metal was kept from each sample was because it was common practice for all the British Assay Offices to send samples of all the items that had gone through the assay in the previous twelve months to the Master of the Royal Mint and after the samples had been assayed, the results would be sent through to each Assay Office.

At the end of each working day the left over part of each assay for that day would be transferred from the individual watchglasses to the separate standard boxes, i.e. Sterling Silver and Britannia Silver. This left over gold and silver is called 'diet' and the operation of transferring the diet to the diet boxes each day was carried out in the presence of the Deputy Warden and Warden of the Worshipful Company of Goldsmiths.

The scraping and sampling was carried out on the second floor of the

Assay Office, which was also the gold and silver hallmarking floor. The 'L' shaped room was Victorian in appearance. At the end of the room by the entrance door were heavy benches, and on the benches were an assortment of silver hand marking bases. One of my regular jobs as an apprentice was to keep the working surface of these tools in good condition as they were used quite regularly for hand marking the Sterling Silver and Britannia plate. On a bench next to the entrance door were the heavy duty scales and troy weights used for weighing in the bulk silver. In the centre of the room were some heavy presses for gold and silver plate marking and round the corner of the 'L' shaped room was another set of scales and weights which were used for the 'weighing in' of the bulk gold, and a number of marking presses. A rope lift was situated in the centre of the room, which was used daily for lifting the heavy box of gold and silver hallmarking punches, which when not in use were kept in the large safe on the first floor. The gold and silver scraping and sampling were carried out in different parts of the workroom for obvious reasons.

Mr Francis Lowe who I was indentured to, was in charge of the hallmarking operation. Other than himself, Mr Arundale helped with the hallmarking as soon as the drawing and sampling had been carried out. Mr Cyril Clarke who was the son of Mr Frank Clarke the Assay Master was in charge of accounts and wages and would also help out with the silver sampling and marking later in the afternoon. Mrs Mary Lowe would also give us a hand with the hallmarking for so many hours a day. She was a first class marker, very quick and was a great asset to the Goldsmiths Company. Mrs Lowe was also the Assay Office typist.

As I was the apprentice, I had to spread myself around a bit. As soon as the scraping and cutting samples were in the watchglasses, I would take them downstairs to the balance room wihch was on the first floor, for them to be made up into assays. Mr Vincent Ward was in charge of the balance room work and assay operation and was very shortly to become Assay Master on the death of Cr Clarke and Mr Tom Ward, his brother, would become Prime Warden of the Goldsmiths' Company.

Three of my many duties as an apprentice were, to make up the lead cornets which held the assays, cut up the fine parting silver so that each piece was the same size for a full assay, three quarter assay, half assay and quarter assay, which were kept in separate tins. I also made the cupels which held the assays during the operation of cupellation. For making the lead cornets, pure lead foil was purchased by the Assay Office in 4" x 2" rectangular shaped pieces. They were kept in a drawer in the balance room and it was my responsibility to make sure there were adequate quantities of these pieces of foil made up into cornets. The fine parting silver was cut into a uniform size on the hallmarking floor. I used a special cutting tool to cut the silvers for each gold standard and as Mr Ward, Mr Arthur Godwin and myself were making up assays I had to make sure there was an adequate supply for the three assay balances. Mrs Lowe would also give a hand when we were extremely busy in the balance room and would use the fourth assay balance to make up the assays.

The cupel making was carried out in the cupel room which was situated on the ground floor next to the furnace room. I used an Indian clay called Mabor to make up the cupels. The Mabor would come in to the Assay Office as a white powder in large drums. The Mabor was made into a damp condition by adding 8 parts distilled water to 1 part beer. When I required more beer I would take an empty jug and knock on the back door of the Dublin Packet, which was a Public House approximately thirty yards from the Assay Office. The licensee would fill the jug up for me. His name was William Ralph Dean, better known to the football world as Dixie Dean, late of Everton and England. I would mix the powder with the beer and water until the mixture was the right composition. The stainless steel cupels would be filled up with this damp powder and I would press the cupels out, using a large hand press. The cupels would take weeks to dry out properly so there always had to be a large stock of cupels on the shelves.

In my second year Mr Vincent Ward let me make up the assays myself. I had my own assay balance which I looked after. I had to test the balance on a daily basis. For the first few months I made up the gold assays. The assay samples after weighing would be put into a lead cornet together with the parting silver. The lead cornet would then be folded up with the sample inside. When all the gold assays had been 'made up' they would be transferred to a 60 or 30 partition tray. Depending on the number of assays on the day, a number of trial assays would be placed at certain positions amongst the assays. The 'trial' gold and silver used for making up the assays was specially bought in and the assay weights used for making up the assays were checked on a regular basis by the National Physics Laboratory and were used only for this operation. I would then take the assay samples to the furnace room for the operation of cupellation to start. First of all I would squeeze each 'lead' into a ball. The assays would then be transferred to the 'Mabor' cupels which had been placed in the gas furnace at least two hours previously. When the assays 'flashed' and turned into a silver coloured globule, I would prepare to take them out of the furnace as the cupellation part of the process had finished. During the cupellation, the lead foil which held the assay sample had melted and parted from the gold sample and sunk into the cupel together with other impurities. What one had left was the fine gold in the original alloy plus the parting silver, plus the original silver in the alloy plus any slight impurities that had not parted from the assay button at the cupellation stage. The gold 'assay buttons' would then be flattened with a hammer and then put through a rolling mill when they would come out as a silver fillet. The fillets would then be annealed and rolled up into a cornet. I would then place the cornets into a tray of platinum cups which was lowered into a boiling solution of two parts distilled water and one part nitric acid and after thoroughly washing in a distilled water bath was placed into a boiling solution of two parts nitric acid to one part distilled water, which would be a much longer boil. After this boil the fine gold assay cornets were again washed in distilled water and then gently dried by heat.

The 'gold coloured' assay cornets would be now ready for 'weighing back' and I would take them to the balance room. Mr Vincent Ward, after recording the loss through oxidation of the trial assays would weigh back the assay cornets. If any of the work was found to be 'In Doubt' fresh assays would be made up the following day and they would be 'tried' a second time. If the assay result was still below standard a third 'trial' would be carried out and if found to be still below standard the items that the assays had come off would be broken up. Mr Arthur Godwin, the Deputy Warden of the Goldsmiths Company, carried out all the furnace room work when I was first apprenticed and went out of his way to teach me all he knew. Mr Vincent Ward, the Assay Master, gave me a good grounding in balance room work and within 18 months I was competent in the whole process of assaying. Mr Ward would let me carry out the melts of gold and silver to produce 'makeweight' to give back to the customer. I would normally melt 20 ounces troy of 9 carat gold at a time. I would first work out the amount of fine gold alloy required. For the fine gold I used the assay cornets and for the fine silver I used the silver assay buttons. We would buy in the pure copper if I was making up a gold/silver/copper alloy. When everything was ready I would take the alloy down to the furnace room and place it in a large melting pot together with carbon rods. The melting pot would be placed into a coke fire. When the alloy was molten and well stirred I would pour the molten gold from a height of at least five feet into a large earthenware pot, full of water which had been stirred round before the 'pour'. The secret of a good pour was a fine steady flow into the stirred water. The 9 carat gold when coming in contact with the stirred water would break up into small granules. I often tidied up the inside of the very large safe which was situated on the first floor, which amongst other things held all the hall-marking punches when not in use. I was always fascinated by a very large 9 carat gold decimal hallmarking punch and when I mentioned it to Mr Ward he told me the story connected with the punch.

The 2nd Duke of Westminster who was nicknamed 'Bendor' was blessed with a son, Edward George Hugh, who was born in 1904. The baby was christened in the Chapel at Eaton Hall near Chester and a christening cup wrought 9 carat gold was made for the occasion. The cup was assayed and hallmarked at the Chester Assay Office and a special mark was designed and ordered for the cup. The 9.375 mark was slightly concave to follow the curve of the bowl and was $1\frac{1}{2}''$ in length and $\frac{1}{2}''$ wide. There was also a town mark punch of the three wheatsheafs and sword erect in a shield which was also 1.2″ square. The Earl Grosvenor was never a very strong child and sadly died aged 5 in 1909, and the 2nd Duke of Westminster never did have another son and heir.

In the summer of 1955 there was a rail strike and we were forced to travel down to Birmingham to pick up work from our customers. Mr Francis Lowe and myself left Chester at eight o'clock in the morning and arrived in Birmingham before lunch. We visited our main customers in the Warstone Lane and Vyse Street areas of the Birmingham jewellery quarter and proceeded to fill the boot of the car up with gold and silver wares. Because we had made an effort to pick up the work, our customers also let us have large quantities of gold and silver wares that would normally have gone to the Birmingham and London Assay Offices and by the time we had driven to Tatchbrook Road, Leamington Spa to collect work from Henry Griffiths, the 'fidelity' wedding ring manufacturer, the inside of the car and car boot were full up to the brim with gold and silver wares. In fact J. Harrison the signet ring manufacturer gave us so many signet rings that we half filled a plastic bucket which we had in the boot. This emergency operation carried on for a fortnight and so on alternate days, one of us would travel down to Birmingham to take hallmarked and assayed work back to our customers and pick up fresh work to take back to the Assay Office.

By 1955 I was quite efficient in all the different facets of the work. The Goldsmiths Company were at this time receiving a large amount in troy weight of Sterling and Britannia Silver. Dimmers, Lowes, and Butts would send plate over to us on quite a regular basis. At this time these three retail jewellers were still very much family businesses and were selling quite a fair amount of Chester Assayed and Hallmarked silver plate. Also Charles Horner the silver bangle and bracelet manufacturer from Halifax was sending a regular parcel of silverware each week. F. A. Welch from Hood Street, Liverpool was also sending large quantities of Wedgewood cameo sterling silver mounts to us at least twice a week and coupled with our regular gold and silver work from Birmingham, the Assay Office had become fairly busy. By the latter part of 1955 Mr Godwin was pretty well leaving me to it, as far as the furnace room work was concerned and I was carrying out the whole assay operation for both gold and silver. The gold and silver were assayed by the cupellation method at Chester, but Mr Ward was planning to change the method of assaying silver. When we had any spare time, he would take me into the Assay Office laboratory and would show me the other methods of assaying silver, such as the Volhard method and the Gay Lussac method. In 1956 I received my National Service call up papers, to serve two years in the Royal Navy. I had asked Mr Vincent Ward if it

164

was possible for me to finish my National Service and carry on my apprenticeship when I came out, which he was quite agreeable to.

When I returned to the Assay Office in April 1958 the threat of closure was hanging over us all. The Assay Office had become extremely busy while I had been away and many of our regular customers were sending very large quantities of gold and silver wares every day of the week. My young cousin, Peter Lowe, would come in when required to help us out with the hallmarking and like his mother was an asset to the Assay Office due to the speed and quality of his marking. 'Accurist Watches' started to send large quantities of 9 carat and 18 carat gold watchcases and bracelets, and we had to have special 'spot mark' punches made to mark the cases which were of 'foreign origin' and they continued to send to us until the day we closed down.

From the time I returned to the Assay Office after my Royal Navy service to the closure of the Assay Office my normal working day would be to help Mr Arundale to weigh in the gold and silver wares. I would then spend as much time as was necessary to scrape and sample all the gold wares. I would then join Mr Arthur Godwin and Mr Vincent Ward in the balance room and help out with making up the assays. When the gold and silver assays had been 'made up' I would then take the assays down to the furnace room and carry out the complete assay operation. When the samples had been assayed I would take the fine gold cornets to Mr Vincent Ward and after they had been 'weighed back' I would return to the hallmarking floor to help out with the hallmarking. After the marking had been carried out I would assist Mr Francis Lowe and Alf Arundale in weighing back the gold and silver wares and giving the customer the correct amount of 'makeweight' gold or silver. Being the apprentice, I would then parcel up the postal packets. My last act at the end of a working day was to take the post parcels to the local post office for despatch.

In 1959 greater quantities of work continued to flood into the Assay Office. Bracelet charms were in fashion and we received large packets each day from several of our customers in Birmingham. The amount of assays each day had doubled on average to the numbers of two years previously. Mrs Mary Lowe would quite often give a helping hand with the assays and was 'worth her weight in gold' to us due to her versatility around the Assay Office. It was during this period that Michael Urmston was taken on to serve an apprenticeship, and was a great help to us due to the large amounts of wares that had to be marked each day. Mike initially helped out with the sampling and marking and was a welcome addition to our small group of workers.

During the first half of 1960 it was becoming increasingly apparent that the Assay Office was going to close down by Act of Parliament. Oddly enough we did not have enough time to think about it too much as so much work had started to flood into the Assay Office. To get the work through, the staff worked late on many occasions. Lowe and Sons were sending over large amounts of Sterling and Britannia plate to us. I would walk over to Lowe and Sons with a large wooden tray and John Lowe would have the tray filled to the brim with salvers, candlesticks, tumblers, mustards, spoon sets, serviette rings and many other items that delight the eye and I would then struggle back to the Assay Office with the silver wares clanking in the wooden tray. I very often used to stop on the way back for a breather and sit on the steps of Watergate Street Row with the tray of silver plate resting on my knees.

Butts, the Eastgate Street jewellers had started to send large quantities of Armada dish sets and Dimmers would send spoon sets.

On the 26th February 1960, much to my delight I finished my apprentice-ship and after being made Freeman of the City of Chester by Indenture at a Pentice Court held at the Town Hall, then returned to the Assay Office and was made a Member of the Worshipful Company of Goldsmiths of Chester.

The amount of gold and silver wares continued to increase during 1960 and 1961 and besides the British made wares the Assay Office was flooded with foreign made wares. Beside the vast amount of foreign gold that was assayed and hallmarked during this last sad period, we also dealt with quite a large number of silver foreign wares and we used the beautiful foreign wares Chester silver mark, the acorn and leaves, many times during 1961 and 1962.

It was now quite apparent that the Assay Office could not be saved from closure and the date that was decided that the closure would take place was 24th August 1962. So as we came out of the winter of 1961 the Assay Office was in a situation that was extremely hard to accept. So much work was coming into the Assay Office that even at this late stage I thought there could be a reprieve at the last minute, but it never happened.

When the date letter was changed on 1 July 1962 from 'L' to 'M' an even greater quantity of work started to arrive each day. So many people wanted a piece of Chester hallmarked silver with the last date letter on it that we all did well to cope in those last few months. Looking back thirty years on, this last period before the closure was so busy that the actual closure looming up on us was like a bad dream.

On the last day of the Assay Office's existence, the Birmingham hamper was extremely large and quite a fair number of our regular customers sent work in on that final day. W. H. Collins, W. G. Pellow, T. J. Skelton, J. Harrison, J. Smith & Sons, Smith Ewan & Stylic, Smith & Pepper and Irwin Bros., were just a few of our Birmingham customers that sent that day and also a large quantity of postal customers also sent wares for the last time. Henry Griffiths from Leamington sent a large amount of 9, 18 and 22 carat wedding rings.

I spent most of the day in the balance room and furnace room as there was a large number of assays to get through. Vincent Ward, Mr Godwin and myself made the assays up, and when there were enough gold assays made up for the first 'fire' I then concentrated on the furnace room work while Vincent and Arthur carried on with the Balance room work. The Assays were finally weighed back at 6 p.m. and, fortunately none of the wares were 'in doubt'. I then went to the hallmarking floor and helped my uncle Francis Lowe hand mark a large quantity of silver plate.

When all the gold and silver wares had been hallmarked, the final act was to begin. All the hallmarking punches were 'ground off' in the presence of the Assay Master, Prime Warden, Wardens and myself and with this last duty taking place the Assay Office had closed down.

I was asked by Mr Ward to stay on for another fortnight and help him to sort out a large amount of paperwork and equipment. This to me was the saddest two weeks of my life.

Looking back I am sure that if we had received the right support from our many friends in the trade and if we had all as a Company really wanted the Assay Office to remain open we would have been in existence today, we had a lot going for us. Although our methods were rather antiquated we carried out the work correctly and had the ability to deal with extremely large amounts of gold and silver wares on a daily basis. The Chester Assay Office was respected in the trade and our beautiful Assay Office mark of three wheatsheaves and a sword erect was much sought after, especially on silver.

Towards the end of the 19th century, Chester Assay Office had opened a forwarding agency in Birmingham in order to attract custom and many Birmingham manufacturers took advantage of this. The fact that the Chester Assay Office was open on Saturdays when Birmingham was not, was a particular attraction. At a time when there was plenty of work and Birmingham Assay Office was working at full capacity this situation was tolerated, but when the workload fell off after the First World War, there was bitter hostility between the rival Assay Offices and an unsuccessful attempt was made to close the forwarding agency.

A departmental Committee on Hallmarking under the chairmanship of Sir Leonard Stone was set up and when the report was published in March 1959 the closure of the Chester Assay Office was recommended which was finally effected on 24 August 1962. Other recommendations were not implemented.

There was not one single reason but many for the closure of the Assay Office. As a young apprentice I could not help noticing the complete lack of interest by the senior members of the Goldsmiths Company in what was going to happen, and their unwillingness to fight the threatened closure and only Mr Francis Lowe and Mr John Lowe really fought for the Assay Office to remain open. Birmingham Office had been gunning for us for years as we had been a thorn in the flesh for a long time due to the existence of our forwarding agency and obviously other Assay Offices would benefit from the closure. The Bishop of Chester, the Rt. Reverend Gerald Ellison tried to drum up support in the right quarters but it was of no avail. He did however plead for the retention of the Chester Goldsmiths Company and this was granted.

In July 1964 I was offered a position at the London Assay Office and I started work at the Hall in September 1964. I spent five happy years in London starting off as a gold drawer and marker. In 1967 I was promoted to assistant foreman of the gold marking floor and held that position until September 1969 when my family and I returned to Chester.

Let us all hope that the new Chester Goldsmiths Company mark of origin which has been administered since 1988 and which started off as an idea of Canon Maurice Ridgway will grow from strength to strength and sometime in the future will act as a stepping stone from the old Assay Office which closed in 1962 to a new modern Assay Office once again operating in the City of Chester.

GRAHAME JONES,
*Alderman of the Worshipful Company
of Goldsmiths.*

MARKS ON CHESTER GOLD WARES PRIOR TO 1932

Examples for 1907

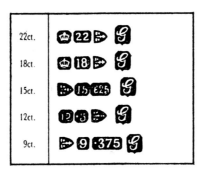

IMPORT MARKS (Post 1904)

From 1904 to the closure of the Assay Office in 1962 an 'acorn and two leaves' replaced the 'letter F' and the 'town mark' for both gold (canted square punch) and silver (oval punch).

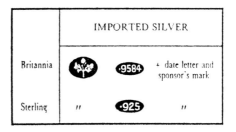

1932-62

The alteration in gold standards in 1932 led to the following changes to the gold import marks.

IMPORTED GOLD		
22ct.	🔲 916	+ date letter and sponsor's mark
18ct.	750	"
14ct.	585	"
9ct.	◇375	"

CHESTER

22 CARAT GOLD	🛡️22	🛡️	🛡️ •916 G		
18	"	"	•750 G		
14	"	"	•585 G		
9	"	"	◇•375 G		
STANDARD SILVER	•925 G				
BRITANNIA SILVER	•9584 G				

The notification sent out to the Trade in 1957/8 to confirm the Assay Marks used that year.

VI

	LION PASSANT	LEOPARD'S HEAD	CITY ARMS	DATE LETTER	DUTY MARK
[20 July 1797-1798]	(mark)	(mark)	(mark)	A	(mark)
[20 July 1798-20 July 1799]	"	"	"	B	"
[20 July 1799-20 July 1800]	(mark)	(mark)	"	C	"
[20 July 1800-20 July 1801]	"	"	"	D	"
[20 July 1801-20 July 1802]	"	"	"	E	"
1802-1803	"	"	"	F	"
1803-1804	"	"	"	G	"
1804-1805	"	"	"	H	"
1805-1806	"	"	"	I	"
1806-1807	(mark)	(mark)	(mark)	K	"
1807-5 July 1808	"	"	"	L	"
5 July 1808-5 July 1809	"	"	"	M	"
5 July 1809-1810	"	(mark)	(mark)	N	"
1810-5 July 1811	"	"	"	O	"
5 July 1811-1812	"	"	"	P	"
1812-5 July 1813	"	"	"	Q	"
5 July 1813-5 July 1814	"	"	"	R	"
5 July 1814-1815	"	"	"	S	"
1815-1816	"	"	"	T	"
1816-5 July 1817	"	"	"	U	"
5 July 1817-5 July 1818	"	"	"	V	"

VII

	LION PASSANT	LEOPARD'S HEAD	CITY ARMS	DATE LETTER	DUTY MARK
5 July 1818-7 Sept. 1819	(mark)	(mark)	(mark)	A	(mark)
7 Sept. 1819-10 May 1820	(mark)	(mark)	"	B	"
10 May 1820-8 Nov. 1821	"	"	"	C	"
8 Nov. 1821-5 July 1823	"	(mark)	"	D	"
5 July 1823-5 July 1824	"	"	(mark)	E	"
5 July 1824-5 July 1825	"	(mark)	"	F	"
5 July 1825-5 July 1826	"	"	"	G	"
5 July 1826-5 July 1827	"	"	"	H	"
5 July 1827-5 July 1828	"	"	"	I	"
5 July 1828-5 July 1829	"	"	"	K	"
5 July 1829-5 July 1830	(mark)	"	"	L	"
5 July 1830-5 July 1831	"	"	"	M	"
5 July 1831-5 July 1832	"	"	"	N	"
5 July 1832-5 July 1833	"	"	"	O	"
5 July 1833-5 July 1834	"	"	(mark)	P	"
5 July 1834-5 July 1835	(mark)	"	"	Q	"
5 July 1835-5 July 1836	"	"	"	R	"
5 July 1836-5 July 1837	"	"	"	S	"
5 July 1837-5 July 1838	"	"	(mark)	T	(mark)
5 July 1838-5 July 1839	"	"	"	U	"

		VIII		
	LION PASSANT	TOWN MARK	DATE LETTER	DUTY MARK
1839-40	🦁	🏰	A	👤
1840-41	"	"	B	"
1841-42	"	"	C	"
1842-43	"	"	D	"
1843-44	"	"	E	"
1844-45	"	"	F	"
1845-46	"	"	G	"
1846-47	"	"	H	"
1847-48	"	"	J	"
1848-49	"	"	K	"
1849-50	"	"	L	"
1850-51	"	"	M	"
1851-52	"	"	N	"
1852-53	"	"	O	"
1853-54	"	"	P	"
1854-55	"	"	Q	"
1855-56	"	"	R	"
1856-57	"	"	S	"
1857-58	"	"	T	"
1858-59	"	"	U	"
1859-60	"	"	V	"
1860-61	"	"	W	"
1861-62	"	"	X	"
1862-63	"	"	Y	"
1863-64	"	"	Z	"

		IX		
	LION PASSANT	TOWN MARK	DATE LETTER	DUTY MARK
1864-65	🦁	🏰	a	👤
1865-66	"	"	b	"
1866-67*	"	"	c	"
1867-68	"	"	d	"
1868-69	"	"	e	"
1869-70	"	"	f	"
1870-71	"	"	g	"
1871-72	"	"	h	"
1872-73	"	"	i	"
1873-74	"	"	k	"
1874-75	"	"	l	"
1875-76	"	"	m	"
1876-77	"	"	n	"
1877-78	"	"	o	"
1878-79	"	"	p	"
1879-80	"	"	q	"
1880-81	"	"	r	"
1881-82	"	"	s	"
1882-83	"	"	t	"
1883-84	"	"	u	"

🅕 Struck in addition to the above on imported wares 1867-1904.

X

	LION PASSANT	TOWN MARK	DATE LETTER	DUTY MARK
1884-85	🦁	shield	A	head
1885-86	"	"	B	"
1886-87	"	"	C	"
1887-88	"	"	D	"
1888-89	"	"	E	"
1889-1 May 1890	"	"	F	"
2 May 1890 5 July 1890	"	"	"	
1890-91	"	"	G	
1891-92	"	"	H	
1892-93	"	"	I	
1893-94	"	"	K	
1894-95	"	"	L	
1895-96	"	"	M	
1896-97	"	"	N	
1897-98	"	"	O	
1898-99	"	"	P	
1899-1900	"	"	Q	
1900-1	"	"	R	

XI

	LION PASSANT GUARDANT	TOWN MARK	DATE LETTER
EDW.VII 1901-2	🦁	shield	A
1902-3	"	"	B
1903-4	"	"	C
1904-5	"	"	D
1905-6	"	"	E
1906-7	"	"	F
1907-8	"	"	G
1908-9	"	"	H
1909-10	"	"	I
GEO.V 1910-11	"	"	K
1911-12	"	"	L
1912-13	"	"	M
1913-14	"	"	N
1914-15	"	"	O
1915-16	"	"	P
1916-17	"	"	Q
1917-18	"	"	R
1918-19	"	"	S
1919-20	"	"	T
1920-21	"	"	U
1921-22	"	"	V
1922-23	"	"	W
1923-24	"	"	X
1924-25	"	"	Y
1925-26	"	"	Z

XII

	LION PASSANT GUARDANT	TOWN MARK	DATE LETTER
1926-27			a
1927-28	"	"	k
1928-29	"	"	c
1929-30	"	"	d
1930-31	"	"	e
1931-32	"	"	ff
1932-33	"	"	g
1933-34	"	"	h
1934-35*	"	"	I
1935-36*	"	"	k
EDW.VIII 1936-37	"		l
GEO.VI 1937-38	"	"	m
1938-39	"	"	n
1939-40	"	"	o
1940-41	"	"	p
1941-42	"	"	q
1942-43	"	"	r
1943-44	"	"	s
1944-45	"	"	t
1945-46	"	"	u
1946-47	"	"	v
1947-48	"	"	w
1948-49	"	"	x
1949-50	"	"	y
1950-51	"	"	z

XIII

	LION PASSANT GUARDANT	TOWN MARK	DATE LETTER
1951-52			A
ELIZ.II 1952-53	"	"	B
1953-54	"	"	C
1954-55	"	"	D
1955-56	"	"	E
1956-57	"	"	F
1957-58	"	"	G
1958-59	"	"	H
1959-60	"	"	J
1960-61	"	"	K
1961-62	"	"	L
1 July- 24 Aug. 1962	"	"	M

Index of Persons and Firms

Abbott & Jones, 72, **75**, 154.
Abbot, J., 72, 146.
Adamson, Hugh, 72, **75**.
Adamson, John, 66, **75**, 153.
Adamson & Son, **75**, 158.
Adamson, R., 72, **75**, 104, 152, 155.
Aitken, William, 114, **116**.
Amsden & Son, 157.
Angell, J. & G., 135.
Appleby, Thomas, 72, **75**, 146.
Armitt, Thomas, 72, **75**.
Armstrong, John, 56, 72, **75**.
Armstrong, Joseph, 56, 72, **75**.
Atker, J, 72, **75**.

Bagg, Sarah, 100.
Ball, William, 72, **76**.
Banks, John Millward, 58, 114, **116**.
　(Illustration 19, 20, 39)
Barker, Edward, Frank & Frederick,
　114, **116**.
Barnard, E. & Sons, 133.
Barnett & Scott, 114, **117**.
Barton & Co., James, 72, **76**, 158.
Bateman Family, 18, 55, 148.
Bateman, Ann, 55, 148.
Bateman, Peter, 55, 148.
Bateman, William, 55.
Bebington, Charles, 57.
Bexwick, Gyles, 56.
Bexwick, Ralph, 56.
Beyendorfe, David, 72, **77**, 158.
Bingham, C. & A., 142.
Bingham, John E., 142.
Blackensee, S., 114, **117**.
Boulger, Richard, 72, **77**, 158.
Boulton, Matthew Snr., 149.
Boulton, Matthew & Fothergill, James,
　21, 53, 54, 149.
Bowen, T. M., 72, **77**.
Bowers, Robert, 55, 67, 72, **77**, 104, 152,
　155.
Bromfield, Mr., 147.
Brooks, John, 72, **78**.
Bryans, Samuel, 72, **78**.
Bullen, Nathaniel, 41.
Burgess, William, 54.
Burrell & Co., 72, **78**.
Butt, Alfred, 114, **117**, 142.
Butt, Francis, 114, **118**, 144.

Careless, C., 72, **78**.
Carpenter, Elizabeth, 130.
Chalk, J. A. (Illustration, 6)

Christian, Edward, 72, **78**.
Christie, W. H. ((Illustration 6)
Clark, Frank Cyril, 31, 32.
Clark, Frank Ernest, 31, 37, 130, 143.
Clarke, Frank E., **35**, 37, **60**.
Clarke, G. & Sons, 135.
Clarke & Co. (Illustration 6)
Clarke, John, 72, **78**.
Clifton, John, 72, **79**, 158.
Close, Henry, 72, **79**, 104.
Close, Samuel, 72, **78**.
Coakley, John, 55, 66, 67, 72, **79**, 150,
　151, 155, 156.
Comyns & Sons, 133.
Conway & Co. (Illustration 6)
Conway, Andrew (Illustration 6)
Cooper, Henry, 157.
Cooper, W. E. (Illustration 6)
Coulthard, Walter, 114, **118**.
Cox, William, 150.
Crane, Walter, 57.
Crompton & Parry, 72, **79**, 105.
Crossley, Fred H., 57.
Crowson, William. (Illustration 6)
Crowther, J. W. (Illustration 6)
Crumpsty, William, 72, **79**.
Cubbin, Iverna, 57, 59, **79**, 114.
　(Illustration cover 40)
Cubbin, Thomas, 72, **80**, **118**.
Cundlyfe, Martin, 56.
Cunliffe, Edward, 56.
Cunliffe, Nicholas, 52, 67, 72, **80**, 104,
　146, 149, 156
Cunliffe, Robert, 51.
Cuzner, Bernard, 57, 122.

D.F (Illustration 18)
Davidson, Simon, 67.
Davies, Daniel, 26, **35**.
Day, Lewis F., 57.
Deakin & Sons, Ltd., James, 114, **119**.
　(Illustration 37, 38)
Dixon, James, 54, 72, **80**, 150, 155.
Duke, Elizabeth, 143.
Duke, James, 72, **80**, 143.
　(Illustration 56, 57)
Duke, Joseph, 17, 18, 22, 72, **80**, 147,
　152, 155.
Dutton, Joseph. 72, **80**.

Eccles, David, 33.
Edward VII, 58.
Edwardes, Peter I., 49.
Edwards, Mrs., 64.

175

Elizabeth II, 143.
Elkington, 54, 142
Ellison & Co., 72, **80**.
Ellison, Rt. Rev. Gerald, 33, 50.
Ellison, John, 72, **81**, 158.
Ellison, W., 72, **81**.
Evans, James, 18, 19, **34**, 36, 37.
D.F. (Illustration 18)

Falconer, Joseph, 55, 72, **81**, 155.
Fisher, John, 72, **81**, 105, 149, 150.
Fisher, Richard, 73, **81**.
Fishwick, Henry, 73, **81**.
Flaxman, 54, 135.
Foskett, S., 150.
Fothergill, James (see Boulton).
Foulkes, Elizabeth, 126, 129.
Fowler, J., 73, **81**.
Foxhall, E., 73, 82.
Foxhall, Thomas, 73, **82**.
France, Elizabeth, 73, **82**, 146.
France, James, 66, 73, **82**, 146, 149, 150, 151, 155.
Frost, P. G., 123.
Frost, Robert, 135.
Fry, Roger, 57.

Garner, John, 23, **35**, 38, 64.
Gaskin, A. J., 122.
George I, 134.
George V and Queen Mary, 30, 58, 59, 133, 137.
Gilbert, John, 73, **83**, 155.
Glover, James, 73, **83**.
Godwin, Andrew Nixon, 28, 31, **35**.
Godwin, Thomas, 32
Godwin, William N., 28, **35**, 37.
Green, George, 157.
Green, Joseph, 22, 26, 64.
Green, Robert, 73, **83**, 103.
Green, Thomas, 73, **83**, 158.
Greenhough & Sons, 187.
Griffin, J. & R., 114, **119**.
Griffiths, Henry, 156.
Grosvenor, Robert, 24.

Hack, John, 73, **83**.
Hadwin, Isaac, 73, **84**.
Hall, Richard, **35**, 36.
Hardman, John, 54.
Harper, Richard, 73, **84**.
Harrison, Thomas, 73, **84**, 158.
Harvey, Mrs., 51.
Haseler Brothers, 114, **119**.
Helsby & Son, Thomas, 84.
Helsby & Sons, John, 73, **85**.
Helsby, John, 73, **85**, 147, 152, 154, 155. (Illustration 28, 29)
Helsby, Thomas, 52, 73, **84**, 147, 158. (Illustration 29)
Helsby, William, 73, **85**.
Hemming, James, 73, **85**.
Hemming, William, 73, **85**.
Hemmingway & Glover, 73, **85**.
Hemmingway, James, 73.
Hemmingway, John, 73, **85**.
Henderson & Thomson, 120.

Henry IV, 49.
Henry VII, 139.
Hewett, Joseph, 73, **86**.
Hodel, J., 118.
Hill, Thomas, 73, **86**, 149, 155.
Hilliard & Thomson, 115, **120**, 156.
Hilton, Robert, 58, 115, 120.
Holme, Edward, 56.
Holme, Randle, 44.
Horner, Charles, 59, 115, **120**, 156.
Hort, N., 75, **86**.
Horton, Henry Riley, **35**.
Horton, Joseph, 31.
Hull, Edward, 135.
Hull, William, 73, **86**, 158.
Hunt, Jane, 18.
Huntingdon, H. M. & S., 73, **86**, 147, 150, 152.
Huntingdon, Mary, 53, 55, 73, **86**, 147, 150, 152.
Hutchinson & Co., 156.
Huxley, Thomas, 65.
Hyatt, William, 18, 19, **34**, 36.
Hyde, Samuel, 95.

Imago, Selwyn, 57.
Innes, Beatrice, 95.
Irwan, John, 144.

Jackson, Sir Charles, 55, 62, 65.
Jay, James Charles, 115, **121**.
Johnson, Margaret, 95.
Johnson & Co. (Illustration 5)
Jones & Abbott, W., 72, 73, **87**, 89.
Jones & Reeves, 73, **87**, 89.
Jones & Son, R., 73, 87, **88**, 152.
Jones & Walley, 73, **87**.
Jones, Alfred E., 53, 115, **121**, 123. (Illustration 43)
Jones, C., **88**.
Jones & Co., C., 73, **88**.
Jones, Edward, 18, 19, 23, 27, **34**, 64.
Jones, Grahame, 34, **36**, 42, 45, 47, 115, **122**, 123. (Illustration 45)
Jones, Hugh, 33.
Jones, Robert, 52, 54, 73, **87**, 104, 146, 149, 155.
Jones, William, 73, 87, **89**, 154.
Jordan, Mrs., 51.
Joseph, B. H. (Illustration 5)
Kelvey of Gainsborough, 25.
Kilshaw, Richard, 73, **89**.
Kind, John, 73, **89**.
King, Jessie, 57.
Kirkman, E., 73, **89**.
Knox, Archibald, 57.

Lamerie, Paul, 134.
Landra, Patrick, 56, 73, **89**.
Langton, Thomas, 43.
Lawson of Glasgow, 138.
Lee, Nicholson, 67, 73, **89**, 158.
Leonard, Patrick, 55, 115, **123**.
Lewis, Edward, 56.
Lias, John and Henry. 129.
Liberty, Arthur Lazenby, 57.
Lithwaite, William, 158.

50. a. & b. Spoon by John Lingley, c. 1580.

51. Castor by Benjamin Brancker, Liverpool, c. 1735.

52. a. & b. Covered bowl with the mark of John Bingley.

53. a. & b. Chocolate stand by William Richardson, 1721-22.

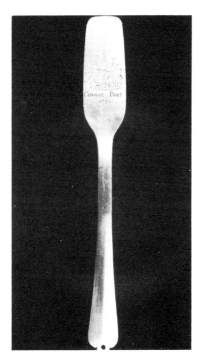

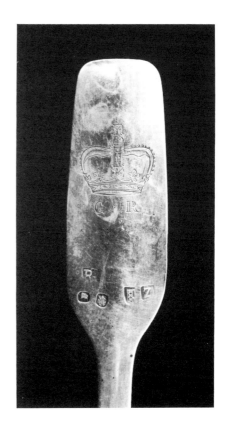

54. a. & b. The Conway Bailiff's oar by
     Richard Richardson 1, 1725-26.

55. The maker's mark of John Scasebrick on a Portuguese moidor weight, 1772.

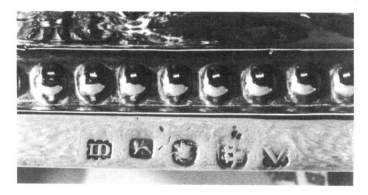

56. 57. Pair of Candlesticks by James Duke, Chester, 1771-72.

58. Tea caddy by Richard Richardson 2, 1764-65.

59. Pair of cylindrical beakers by Richard Richardson 2.

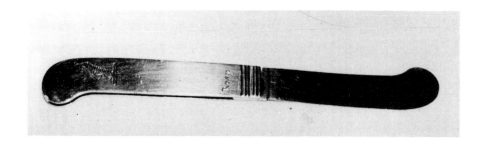

60. 61. Fruit knife by Richard Richardson 2 or 4.

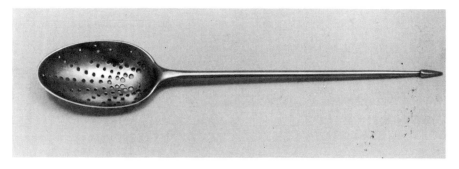

62. Mote spoon by Richard Richardson 2 or 4 (?).

Lloyd George, David, 29, 30, 45.
Lloyd, David, 74, **90**.
Lockett, John, 145.
Lowe Family, 17, 18, 42, 45, 48, 55, 58, 59, 74, **90, 124**.
Lowe & Sons (Illustration 23)
Lowe, Andrew J. F., 45.
Lowe, Anthony J. F., 45.
Lowe, Denise, 122.
Lowe, Francis Maurice, 30, 31, 34, 47, 115, **184**. (Illustration 48)
Lowe, George I, 18, 19, 22, **34**, 36, 55, **60**, 66, 74, **90**, 103, 104, 105, 124, 147, 148, 149, 150, 151, 152, 153, 155, 156. (Illustration 1)
Lowe, George II, 18, 20, **34**, 74, **90**, 147, 153. (Illustration 2, 7)
Lowe, George III, **35**.
Lowe, George Bennett, 27, 28, **35**, 45, 126, 130.
Lowe, George Frederic, **36**, 37, 115, 130, **131**, 133. (Illustration 41).
Lowe, George F., 45, 132.
Lowe, Harold, 129.
Lowe, Henry C., 130.
Lowe, Herbert Hesketh, 126.
Lowe, Hugh Foulkes, 31.
Lowe, Hugh Cawley, 31, **35**, 37, 126.
Lowe, Hugh W., 48.
Lowe, James Foulkes, 27, 28, 30, 31, **35**, 37, 44, **60**, 115, 122, **125**, 126.
Lowe, John I, 18, 19, 23, 24, 26, 27, 33, 36, 37, 42, 45, 64, 90, 115, **126, 127**.
Lowe, John Foulkes II, 27, 28, 37, 47, 115, 126, **129**.
Lowe, John Cecil, **35**, 115, **131**.
Lowe, John ffoulkes III, 33, **34**, 115, **133**. (Illustration 47)
Lowe, Joseph, 18.
Lowe, Martha Elizabeth, 115, **132**, 133.
Lowe, Margaret Joyce, 33, 45, 115, 132, **133**, 134. (Illustration 47)
Lowe, Mary, 18, 126.
Lowe, Peter James, 34, **36**, 45, 115, 122, **124**.
Lowe, Robert, 18, 74, 90, **93**, 151.
Lowe, Roger, 45.
Lowe, Thomas, 18, 19, 22, 23, 24, 27, **34**, 36, **60**, 62, 90, 115, **127, 128**, 129.
Lowe, William Foulkes, 28, **35**, **60**, 115, 126.
Lucas Richard, 74, **93**.
Lutschaurig, Alfred, 26.
Luthwait, William (Lithwaite), 158.
Lutyens, Edwyn, 57.

MacCormick, Iain, 138.
Mackmurdo, Arthur H., 57.
Maddock, Edmund, 74, **93**, 158.
Marion & Co., 157.
Mayer, Joseph, 115, **135**.
Miller, John, 74, **94**, 104. (Illustration 22)
Miller, William, 94.
Molyneux, Peter, 74, **94**.
Mora, Greg, 47.
Mordan & Co., Sampson, 115, **135**.

Morris, William, 56, 57.
Morrow, Richard, 74, **94**, 146.
Morrow, Thomas, 74, **94**.
Morton, Joseph, 74, **94**.
Muller, Berthold, 115, **135**.
Myrstone, W., 156.

Nathan & Hayes, 56, 115, 131, **135**.
Newton & Hyde, 74, **94**, 147.
Newton, Thomas, 56, 74, **95**, 104, 147.
Newton, Frances & Eleanor, 95.
Newton, Frederick, 95.
Nightingale, Edward, 74, **95**.

Ollivant & Botsford, 122.

Pachachi, 48.
Page, Mr., 64.
Paris, T. J, 135.
Parsonage, John, 74, **95**.
Parker, Eustace G., 154.
Pemberton, Benjamin, 41.
Pierce, R., 65.
Piesse, A. G., 135.
Pierrepoint, Thomas, 74, **95**, 158.
Pigot, Piercy (Percy), 44.
Powell, John H., 54.
Preston, Robert, 74, **95**.
Price, Joseph, 65.
Priestley, Phillip, 60, 65, 158.
Prince of Wales, H.R.H., 48.
Pringle, Robert, 156.
Pugh, William, 54, 55, 74, **95**, 147.
Pugin, A. W. N., 54.

Rawnsley, Canon, 58.
Reeves & Jones, 74, 87, 96.
Richards, James, 74, **96**, 158.
Richardson Family, 17, 44, 55.
Richardson, R. Geoffrey, 45.
Richardson, Ralph, 126.
Richardson, Richard I, 17, 41, 44. (Illustration)
Richardson, Richard II, 42, 44, 100, 133, 147, 148. (Illustration 58, 59, 60, 61, 62).
Richardson, Richard IV, 17, 42, 54, 74, **96**, 103, 104, 105, 106, 144, 148, 149, 150, 151, 153, 154, 155. (Illustration 60, 61, 62).
Richardson, Richard (Zimbabwe), 44.
Richardson, William I, 41.
Richardson, William II, 30.
Ridgway, Maurice H., 45, 46.
Rigby, Henry, 74, **97**, 158.
Ritchie, Alexander, 58, 115, **137**, 138, 140. (Illustration 33)
Ritchie, Euphemia, 138.
Robinson, George, 123.
Robinson, Thomas, 41.
Roseater, George, 105, **138**, 156.
Ross, Frederick James, 58, 115, **139**. (Illustration 37)
Rowcliffe, Henry, 27.
Rundell, Bridge & Rundell, 53.
Ruskin, John, 56.
Rutland, Duke of, 58.

Salmon & Glukstein, 157.
Samuel, Joseph Lewis, 74, **97**, 146.
Samuel, Ralph, 22, 23, 24, 25, 26.
Sanderson, William, 100.
Saunders & Shepherd, 53, 59, 115, 138, **139**, 140, 156. (Illustration 32, 39)
Scasebrick, John, 50, 51, **59**. (Illustration 55)
Schlieman, 58, 136.
Scott, Mrs., 64.
Seals, Sarah, 128, 129.
Shields, Robert, 52, 56.
Shore, Edward, 144.
Sobieski Lynes, Caroline, 145.
Silver, Rex, 57.
Silverston & Co., 156.
Simmons, Isaac, 56, 115, 123, **140**. (Illustration 30, 31)
Smets, Harold S., 29.
Smith-Barry, John, 148.
Smith, William, 56, 115, **140**. (Illustration 8, 9, 10, 11)
Solomon, M., 74, **97**.
Steinhart, Siegfried, 157.
Stone, Sir Leonard, 32, 50.
Storr, Paul, 54, 55.
Street, George E., 54.
Stuart, John, 23.
Sutter(s), John, 56, 74, **97**, 103, 104, 150, 152, 155. (Illustration 14).
Swan, James, 157.

Tarlton, Henry. (Illustration 17)
Tarlton, William, 74, **98**, 146, 158.
Tatler, Richard Edward, 27, 28, **35**, 37, **60**.
Taylor, Edward, 122.
Taylor, Howson, 122.
Taylor, J., 74, **98**.
Terry, J. E., 135.
Thomas, John, 51.
Thomas, William, 65.
Thomson & Sons, 156.
Turner Bros., 156.
Twemlow Family, 55.
Twemlow, John, 74, **98**, 147, 154.
Twemlow, William, 74, **98**, 104, 147, 149, 151, 152, 155.

Ullman, Fred E., 48.
Unite, George, 140.

Vale & Co., 74, **100**.
Victoria, 27, 130, 150.

Wakefield, R. J., 115, **141**.
Wakely & Wheeler, 115, **142**.
Walker & Hall, 54, 59, 115, 142. (Illustration 20)
Walker Family, 17, 20, 42, 55, 74, **100**.
Walker, Arthur D., 18, 19, 20, 34.
Walker, Charles Burton, 18, 20, **34**, 74, 100, **101**.

Walker, George I, 17, **34**, 36, 42, 44, **59**, 67, 74, 100, **101**, 104, 105, 146, 147, 148, 149, 152, 153, 154, 155.
Walker, George, (Wine Merchant) 100.
Walker, George II (also Wine Merchant) 17, 100, 147.
Walker, Henry, 20, **34**.
Walker, John I, 17, 20, 22, 50, **60**, 74, 100, **102**, 104, 150, 152, 154, 155.
Walker, John II, 20.
Walker, Thomas, 74, 100, **103**, 154, 155.
Wallace, Hugh, 115, 142.
Walley & Jones, 74, 87, **103**, 105, 150, 155.
Walley, Joseph, 52, 87.
Walley, Ralph, 49.
Walter, W. N., 156.
Walton, Edward, 48.
Walton, Rachel, 48.
Ward, A. Vincent, 31, 32, 34, 37, **60**, 105, 115, 125, 135, **143**. (Illustration 42).
Ward, Arnold G., 45.
Ward, Frederick William, **35**, 143.
Ward, George, 115, **143**.
Ward, George, (Manchester) 25.
Ward, Hugh, 143.
Ward, J. E. V., 30.
Ward, Theo, 143.
Ward, Thomas William, 30, 31, 32, 37, 143.
Wathew, J. F., 115, **144**.
Watson, Thomas, 94.
Wayte, Richard, 56.
Webb, Christopher, 144.
Webb, John Christopher, 59, 115, 134, **144**. (Illustration 44)
Welshman, Robert, 56.
Wemlow (see Twemlow), 74, **103**.
Wesley, Rev. John, 42.
Whitehead, George Lowe, 27, 28, **35**.
Whiteley, Simon, 145.
Wilcox, Alfred, 115, **145**.
Wilkinson & Co., 125, 156.
William III, 21, 27, 49.
William IV, 17, 150.
Williams, G., 28, **35**, 37, 38.
Williams, Jeremy P., 45.
Williams, Sefton Richard, 29.
Wilson, James, 24.
Wilson, Ronald, 109.
Wishlade, W., 140.
Withers, Paul and Bente, 50, 51.
Woolfield, Thomas, 74, **103**, 105, 115, 130.
Woolley, Mrs. John, 28, 29.
Woolley, Frederick Duke, **35**.
Woolley, John, 28, **35**.
Woolley, Thomas, 26, 27, 28, **35**, 37, 143, **145**.
Wordley, James, 135.
Wright, John, 142.
Wynne, Robert, 145.

Appendix 1

Chester Goldsmiths from early times to 1726

Maurice H. Ridgway

ADDENDA

EDWARD CARD of Manchester (p. 32)

29 viii 1572. Edward Cuntlif alias Carver of Manchester Goldsmith asks the Wardens for a search in that County (Lancashire) declaring that there has been none there 16 years or more.

(London Minute Book. L. p. 119)

p. 34   It has been suggested that PC might be for Pott Chapel.
Liverpool Town Books 1550-1571 vol. 1, J. A. Twemlow. 1918.
12 November 1557 mentions Peter Conway aurif. standing surety along with the name of Thomas Feyreclyffe.

J. LINGLEY (p. 42)

London Goldsmiths Book 22. vi. 1543.
William Langley (goldsmith) . . . Hartop presented silver he had taken from Langley, but no note of a fine or swearing.

p 51   17.   *Chester Silver*, p. 220. Sefton Parish Church, Lancashire.
A small plain paten 3½ inches diameter with single mark of John Lingley.
18.   Seal top spoon. Phillips Sale 10 May 1991. Private Collection 1996.
A seal top spoon 6¼ inches in length with a wide bowl and marked with the maker's initials. The top of the spoon pricked with R L above I. (Illustration 50 a. & b.)

WILLIAM MUTTON (p. 51)

p. 51   *Liverpool Town Books 1550-1571* volume 1, J. A. Twemlow. 1918.
November 1557. Richard ap Meredith and William Mutton bound over. Martinmas Fair.
London Goldsmiths' Minute Book, p. 158.
Autumn 1573
William Mutton, Laurence Smythe and John Lyngley fined.

p. 64   26.   Seal Top spoon Phillips Catalogue, 27 June 1980, lot 108 (illustrated). Bought by the Grosvenor Museum, Cheshire, now in the Ridgway Gallery.
The Catalogue reading records . . .
'A seal top spoon of good guage, the tapering hexagonal bowl surmounted by an elongated finely chased gilt fluted terminal, the surface plain, the bowl pear shaped and deeply curved, engraved with a later coat of arms. Length 6¼ inches.'

p. 114   Chelford   Paten or alms dish by James Chadwick, London. 1700 London, and a paten or alms dish by John Gibbon 1709 London. Both pieces have been inscribed with the date 1765.

179

p. 116 Wybunbury   A tankard of 1677 London (sold in 1976).

An altar spoon, maker RW struck three times c. 1725 and a stand paten London 1702.

Worthenbury   The Communion cup and paten are by P. Pemberton, Chester 1704/05 (see below No. 137).

p. 121   The Warrington Parish Registers record the baptisms of three children of Thomas Penn, goldsmith from 1654 and the burial of Thomas Penn the goldsmith 13 May 1655.

JOHN BINGLEY (p. 122)

3. Silver gilt two handled bowl or porringer with cover, height 9 inches, weight 38 ounces. It stands upon a short decorated stem the foot moulded and the rim a series of pellets. The sides of the bowl and the cover are flat chased. It is clearly Provincial. The bowl itself carries two identical marks and the cover is terminated with an elaborate acanthus knop. The appearance of such a bowl by Bingley is startling and is as far as is known unique. The two elaborate cast handles resemble the form of caryatids on London porringers. Since the form of the mark places it shortly after 1701, Bingley may well have been a retailer for other men's work. (Illustration 52 a. & b.)

. . . BRADSHAW (p. 123)

Court Book 10. p. 189a.
Wednesday 1 Feb. 1698/9 Assay F. 11, 4, 1698.
At the Court Mr Bradshaw appeared and was fined 10/- and had to pay 32/- the goods cost for selling sub standard wares.

The reference to sword hilts, seems to show that he was using on them sterling silver and not Britannia standard.

BENJAMIN BRANCKER (p. 123)

Type 1. BB within an oval frame.

1.2 Two alms plates. Huyton Parish Church .Diameter 8¼ inches with a sloping rim 1 7/10ths inches wide and a marked depression. Three punches of Type 1, and inscription beneath a crest. The Gift of Dorothy Case.

3. Hanoverian spoon 8¼ inches long with a rat tail and a drop and having four marks on the stem, two of Type 1 and two of Sterling in two lines. The handle inscribed with C above I I.

4. Tea spoon 3¼ inches long with rounded end and two marks of Type 1 on the stem.

5. Dessert spoon 8¼ inches long with rat tail, and crest on handle above the initials D above G M. Rounded handle. On the stem two marks of Type 1 on either side the Sterling mark.

6. Basting spoon 13½ inches long having a rounded handle on which are the initials N above I A. There are two marks of Type 1 on the stem.

7. Tea pot with plain oval rim foot and pear shaped. Scroll handle and crowned octagonal spout. Mitre-like finial on high dromed lid hinged to the sleeve of the wooden handle. Engraved with the crest of (?) Browne of Liverpool, 6½ inches high. Weight 19.05 ounces. On the under base Type 1 struck twice and the sterling mark in two lines.

Type 2. BB and Liver Bird.

1. Brandy saucepan. Height to the rim 1¼ inches. Diameter 2¼ inches. Length of handle, with silver sleeve 3¾ inches. Weight 2 ounces 2 dwt.

2. A large flagon 16 inches high at St Nicholas Parish Church, Liverpool, given by Mrs Ann Molyneux in 1729 and after being on loan to St Thomas's Church, Park Lane was returned in 1914. It has a high double domed lid and the sides are decorated with appliqué leaves. The handle is of broken scroll type and the base is splayed with additional decorations. There are two strikes of Type 2 on the base and two of the Sterling mark,

four on the top of the flagon side and four on the bezel of the lid. (see *Historic Society of Lancashire and Cheshire N.S.* 31, 37, 1916, p. 10f and *The Cheshire Sheaf,* no. 10, 909.)

3. Tankard in the Liverpool Museum. Overall height 5½ inches. Broken scroll handle rising slightly above the rim 2¼ inches diameter. It has a moulded rim, base diameter 4¼ inches. The weight is inscribed beneath 18 .12, and n6 which probably means there were probably at least five other tankards. Marks Type 2 with sterling.

4. Marrow scoop 9¼ inches in length with two marks of Type 2 and possibly the sterling mark between (rubbed).

5. Coffee Pot with domed lid and finial. Height 9¾ inches and base diameter 4¼ inches. Liverpool Museum. Engraved with coat of arms. (see *Connoisseur,* March 1963. Illustrated).

6. Castor. Baluster shaped with baluster finial. The top has six panels of circular round holes with two engraved lines diagonally between the holes. Height 6¼ inches. Weight 3 ounces 17 dwt. Two marks of Type 2 on the under base and once on the castor top. The sterling mark is struck once on the underbase. (Illustration 51)

7. Brandy Saucepan with wooden handle fitting into a sleeve. The lip has two drops. Height to the rim 1¾ inches, diameter 2 3/16ths inches. Length of handle, 4 inches. Weight 2 ounces 15 dwt. Marks set evenly in a circle, two of Type 2 and two of Sterling.

NATHANIEL BULLEN (p. 124)
Llanarmon yn Iâl, Clwyd
Type 1 and Type 2.

4–5. Communion cup and paten kept in a case. The two marks are found together but are indistinct. The cup is 6¼ inches high, rim diameter 4 inches. The sides of the beaker shaped bowl are almost vertical with a slightly everted rim. The bottom of the bowl is angled to a trumpet shaped stem and foot diameter 4⅛ inches. There are three marks on the side of the bowl Type 1 and Type 2, the third mark is not clear. An inscription on the side of the bowl . .

The guift of Mrs Mary Lloyd
of Gelligynam to the Church
of Llanarmon Sept 29th
1677

The paten which accompanies this cup is 5¾ inches diameter and stands 1¾ inches high.

6. Spoon. Private Collection. 1982.
A ribbed rat tail spoon with trefid handle having the initials W above I E. Bottom marked with maker's mark and Bulls head. Length 7¼ inches.

7. St George Parish Church, nr. Abergele.
The Communion cup given 1677 (with no marks) is almost certainly the work of Nathaniel Bullen. It is 6 1/5th inches high, rim diameter 3 9/10ths inches and closely resembles No. 4. The paten is by Thomas Robinson.

NATHANIEL BULLEN. Type 4
(See *Chester Silver,* p. 220)

Three casters. Height 7 inches and foot diameter 3 inches and the two smaller casters each 5¾ inches and 2½ inches. The maker's mark very rubbed but the rest clear. Date letter C (1703/04).
(NOTE. At the Chester Exhibition by Sotheby, these were illustrated but attributed to Nathaniel Bullen Type 4. A careful examination by Dr Campbell reveals the mark to be that of Peter Pemberton Type 4).

7. Dog nose spoon with plain rat tail. Length 8 inches, the handle scratched with the initials E.P. There are five marks including the maker's mark (Type 4) and the date letter C (1703/04).

PETER PEMBERTON (p. 157 and xvi)

16. Private collection. Rat tail dessert spoon with rounded end and with slight resemblance to a dog nose 7½ inches in length. The bowl rather small 2½ inches by 1 2/5th inches. On the handle are inscribed a coat of arms and crest attributed to Prestwick, Lancashire, and MP also engraved. On the stem are five marks, (i) Maker's mark; (ii) Chester City coat; (iii) Britannia; (iv) Lion's head erased; (v) Date letter almost obliterated but had left hand vertical of Roman capital letter. The bowl may have been reduced.

17. Private collection. Rat tail spoon with dog nose and plain handle. (i) Maker's mark; (ii) Chester City coat; (iii) Britannia; (iv) Lion's head erased; (v) Date letter E (1705/06).

18. Tankard. Private Collection, Chester Exhibition 1973. Description as in 5 and 11. Height 6¾ inches. Thumb moulded and rather wide and joins the body of the tankard with pierced four leaf clover. Rim diameter 5½ inches, base 5 2/5ths inches. There are five marks on the side of the tankard (i) Maker's mark; (ii) Chester City coat; (iii) Britannia; (iv) Lion's head erased; (v) Date letter D (1704/05). These are repeated on the lid but with the date letter beneath the lion's head erased.

19. Stand paten. Cerrigydrudion Parish Church. Diameter 7⅝ inches with pronounced depression. On the rim (½ inch wide) and edged with two scribed lines are five marks. (i) Maker's mark; (ii) Cheser City coat; (iii) Britannia; (iv) Lion's head erased; (v) Date letter C (1703/04). The date letter and the Lion's head erased, marks are repeated on the base (diameter 3⅝ inches). On the surface of the plate is a series of concentric hatchings. The stand is splayed with a moulded foot.

20/21 A pair of dog nose spoons with rat tail. The handles having the letters DL above AEM on each. There are five marks (i) Britannia; (ii) Chester City coat; (iii) Maker's mark; (iv) Date letter B (1702/03). When these were sold at Uthwaite and Litherland, Liverpool 26 November 1975, lot 323, the catalogue recorded the date letter as P (incorrectly) length of each spoon 8 inches.

22. Dog nose spoon and rat tail with rounded drop. Date letter rubbed but probably for 1701/02. Scratched on handle H above H I.

23/24/25 (See note under Nathaniel Bullen (*Chester Goldsmiths*) p. 124. Casters.) These are now listed as by Peter Pemberton. Type 4.

BENJAMIN CRITCHLEY (p. 132)

Guildhall Library, Apprenticeship Index.
Ref. 46/37. 1718 Trafford Hale, son of John apprenticed to Benjamin Critchley of Chester, Goldsmith, 20.
Benjamin Critchley was Warden of the Company 1733/1735/1755 and his son Joseph Critchley 'engraver' was admitted a freeman of Chester, 29 November 1755, listed as son of Benjamin Critchley, goldsmith.

PETER EDWARDES (1) (p. 133)

The Chirk Castle Accounts supply the following information.
1678 Nov. 1. Payd Mr Peter Edwardes of Chester goldsmith for mending the head of a silver kane of my Masters in August last 10/-.
1678/9 Feb. 15. Payd Mr Edwards, the goldsmith for boylinge and washinge the scones 12/6.
1681/2 May 17. Payd Peter Edwards of Chester gouldsmith the 3 Jan 1681 for 2 cups for the child and for a gould hart and locketts and mending other things 1/19/6.

PETER EDWARDES (II) (p. 135)

London Court Books 10, p. 191a.
8 Feb 1698 Mr Peter Edwards of Chester appeared by Mr Cole & submitted for putting to sale substandard gold and silver wares was ordered to pay £2-14-8 the goods cost and £5-8-10 charges.

3. Punch bowl. This is now in the National Museum of Wales.

4. The Tobacco Box is at present (1996) for sale in London. The London mark is that of Edward Cornock (Grimwade 390a) post 1707.

PETER EDWARDES (II) (see *Chester Silver*, p. 220) (p. 137)
5. Lincoln Civic Plate.
Deposited by the Royal North Lincolnshire Militia to whom it was given (as inscribed) by 'Major Edward Snow Mason, Royal North Lincolnshire Militia to his brother Officers 1878'. The badge of the Militia is also engraved.
A plain cylindrical flat lidded tankard tapering towards the rim 6¾ inches in height with a reeded base. Overall width 10 inches, diameter of cover 6 inches. Scroll handle and corkscrew thumb piece. Fully marked on the side of the tankard and also on the lid. (i) Maker's mark (ii) Chester City coat (iii) Chester City crest (iv) Date letter A first series (1687-1690). Weight 34 ounces. (Information from the Revd. Peter Hawker. (1977).

SAMUEL EDWARDES (p. 137 and plate 56)
The spoon is now attributed to a west country goldsmith, Ellen Dare of Taunton. (See T. Kent *'West Country Silver Spoons 1550-1570*)

p. 140   The Gi mark on the first copper plate is now confirmed as Gittens of Shrewsbury.

p. 141   SH mark. This is almost certainly the mark of Robert Shields of Liverpool.

p. 142   Ie mark. This is certainly the mark of Henry Jenckes of Shrewsbury.
In the Shrewsbury Guild book disbursements for 1688/90 give a widow Jenckes goldsmith in receipt of a small sum and an earlier list in 1688 Henery Jenckes, son of Anne Jenckes of Ludlow co. Salop widow made freeman as apprentice with John Whittakers goldsmith deceased and Katherine his relict for £5. At St Chad's, Shrewsbury 19 December 1685 Elizabeth daughter of Mr Henry Jenckes, and a burial August 2 1706 Henry Jenckes, Goldsmith.
The Manchester Collegiate Church (now the Cathedral) Registers record the baptism (listed as Births) of three children of 'Mr Richard Wythe, goldsmith' between 1654 and 1661.

EDWARD LEWIS (p. 143)
Picton (Liverpool) Libraries. MS. 11. 53270.
'Edward Lewis one of the first to settle in Liverpool as a silversmith and jeweller in Water Street 1672-78. When James ii granted a new charter to Liverpool (1685) Edward Lewis appears as a member of the Common Council of 1684. He died in 1691 and his widow continued the business. His assistant Robert Shields married the widow August 1692 and continued the business'.

THOMAS MADDOCK (p. 143). Mark Type 2
Tripod ring having three marks, none other, on each. The ring is rectangular in section. The legs of curved handle form rest upon cushion ball feet each having a large hole, as though incomplete.

BENJAMIN PEMBERTON (p. 146) (Type 1)
Marrow scoop. etc. See *Chester Silver*, p. 122.
Marrow scoop 8⅜ inches long, the wider blade ¾ inch wide with a crest of a wolf's head emerging from a crown. There are five marks including the maker's mark and the date letter X (1723/24).

BENJAMIN PEMBERTON (p. 148)
6   Private collection. 1970.
Plain marrow scoop. Length 8¼ inches. Five marks including the date letter Y (1724/25).
7.   Marrow scoop. Very similar to No. 6 but marks arranged in different order.

PETER PEMBERTON (p. 149) Type 1

Also Nos. 4 and 5 (p. 151). Mark 1. Sotheby's, 19 November 1970, lot 161.
Two trefid spoons each having four marks including the PP crowned date letter B (1690/92), Chester City coat and Chester City crest. Initials A above SA. Rat tail composed of beads (four on one and two on the other).

6. Trefid spoon. Private Collection, Bournemouth, 1974.
Trefid spoon with reeded rat tail and drop. Overall length 8 inches. Worn bowl handle inscribed SL above CF and four marks on the stem (i) Date letter E (1694/95) (ii) STERLING (iii) repeat Sterling (iv) Maker's mark Type 1.

p. 148   6.   Tumbler cup. 2 inches high, 2 oz. 7 dwt. with initials E above R.I. c. 1690. Type of mark not given. (Sotheby's Catalogue, 14 April 1977, lot 174.)

THOMAS PENN

Although nothing is known of his work he is recorded here as a goldsmith in the Chester locality. His name is associated with the Warrington Parish Church registers at the time of the Commonwealth.
Thomas Penn, Goldsmith. John christened 27 August 1648.
Thomas Penn, Goldsmith. Ann daughter Christened 13 August 1654.
Elizabeth Penn, daughter of Thomas Penn the goldsmith christened 30 September 1651.
Thomas Penn the goldsmith died 13 May 1655.

PIERCY PIGOT (p. 158)

Richardson Papers, No. 8, 30 Nov. 1692 (Chester Town Hall).
Apprenticeship indenture binding Percy Pigott, son of Hugh Pigott of Hodnett co. Salop gent to Alexander Pulford of Chester Goldsmith. Goldsmith for seven years to learn his master's trade.

p. 158   *The family of Proby in Chester and Ireland*, G. P. Crawford (*Chester Archaeological Journal*, vol. xxviii. Pt. 1. p. 97f.)
The family had a Welsh origin (ap Robin) and later branches are found in Ireland. William Proby the goldsmith was probably the son of John Probye of the City of Chester, vintner. An inventory of John's goods (16 April 1662) was appraised (with three others) by one John Lingley. William Proby of the City of Chester goldsmith had licence 7 July 1681 to marry Elizabeth Hulme of Cheser spinster at St. Mary's, Chester or St Bridget's, Chester.

p. 159   L. Chaffer's *Handbook to Hallmarks*, Ed. G. A. Markham, 1897, p. 30 gives the mark on this spoon and adds that it had a 'rat tail bowl'. The plume marks have never been established.

ALEXANDER PULFORD. (p. 158) Type 2

(See *Chester Silver*, p. 220).
1. Mug. Private collection. Edinburgh. 1973. Exhibited Lowe's Festival Exhibition, Chester, 1973.
A small mug with reeded handle, gadrooned on lower portion below the junction of handle with the body. It has a rim foot and plain top. The interesting feature of this mug is that it carried the only known (second) mark of Alexander Pulford now Type 2. The conjoined AP within a shaped shield. (See also *Chester Silver*, appendix 2, p. 220).

p. 159   Court Book. London Goldsmiths. 10, p. 191.
        8 February 1698/9.
        Mr Pulford of Chester appeared & submitted for selling substandard wares. Ordered to pay £4-4-9 on goods cost & £3-10-9 charges.

p. 158/9   (See note on Percy Pigot)

RICHARD RICHARDSON (I) (p. 161). Type 3.

The Chirk Castle Accounts.

1708 Ap. 23 . . . for 12 Silver spoons & six tea, 7 spoons gilt and case £4/6ʃ .

The appearance of tea spoons at this date is interesting, but there is no evidence that Richard Richardson was responsible for making them. He was employed by the Middleton family. Compare the same accounts . . .

1726 June 10 Pd Mr Richardson of Chester, Goldsmith for repairing ye little silver tankard and engraving ye crest upon 't . . . 4/-.

(See also the marrow scoop with the arms of Middleton. Richard Richardson (I) Type 4) 14.

p. 169

28. Paten or arms dish. St John's Church, Chester.
 Ref. *Church Plate of the City of Chester*. Ball, p. 44.
 Saucer shaped with a small moulded edge, diameter 8½ inches.

29. Marrow scoop. Private collection. 1974.
 Ref. Sotheby's Catalogue, 23 October 1969, lot 38.
 There are five marks including the date letter S (1718/19).

30, 31 Two spoons similar to 23/24 seen in 1974 having the crest of a sphinx and the date letter N (1713-14).

32. Water Bailiff's Oar.
 Ref. Phillip's Sale, Chester, 2 October 1983, lot 180.
 Country Life, 23 February 1984. Illustrated article by Frank Davis.
 Chester Silver, Ridgway, p. 221.
 A water bailiff's oar, made for Conway, 9¼ inches in length and evidently made from a table fork blank. The blade engraved on both sides. On one side a three masted ship with the inscription beneath 'CONWAY PORT 1725' and on the other, the Royal Crown with GR. The handle is ribbed and has a trefid end pierced with a small hole. Sold to a private collector. (Illustration 54 a. & b.)

33. Basting Spoon.
 Ref. Phillip's Sale, Chester 25 November 1992, lot 139.
 Hanoverian pattern basting spoon. Stem half ridged joined to the bowl by a rat tail. 14½ inches in length. Bowl 4 3/16ths inches by 2¾ inches and 1 inch deep. There are five marks including the maker's mark and the date letter Script B (1727/28).

34. Mug. Private Collection.
 With crest of a bird holding a branch and five marks on the base including the date letter V (1721/22).

35. Beaker. Private Collection. 1970.
 A very plain beaker with very slightly curved sides. Diameter 3¼ inches and 3⅞ inches high. The base is 2¼ inches. On the side, the crest of a leopard's head crowned, and on the opposite side in script

Richᵈ Reeves
The Gift of
J.W.Dod Esqʳᵉ
1846

 (Note the donor was John Whitehall Dod of the Dods of Cloverly Co. Shropshire.)
 There are five marks on the base, (i) Maker's Mark (Type 3) (ii) Lion's head erased (iii) Chester City coat (iv) Date letter P (1715/16) (v) Britannia and the letters E B.

36. The Beaumaris Oar.
 Ref. *The Corporation Plate and Insignia of the Cities and Corporate Towns of England and Wales.* Llewellyn Jewitt and W. H. St John Hope, p. 2.

Silver oar, thirteen inches in length and was formerly worn by the water bailiff but is now used by the Harbour Master representing the Council as Harbour authority. On one side, the ship and castle of the Borough arms and the inscription

Wm Brynker Esqr Mayor 1726

and on the other

Caddr Williams Ellis Owen Bayliffs 1726

The oar bears the following hallmarks:
(i)   Ri in a shield for Ralph (sic ?) Richardson.
(ii) Leopard's head crowned.
(iii) Lion passant gardant.
(iv) Date letter Z (Chester 1725/26).

37. Flagon. Llanfair Dyffryn Clwyd, N. Wales.
The Parish Church has a flagon 14 inches high with domed and stepped lid diameter of rim 4½ inches with a cast thumb piece hinged to the top of the S shaped scroll handle. The body of the flagon has almost vertical sides and is separated from the base by a reeded girdle. Below the rim is a plain band and double scribed line. The foot is shouldered with a reeded rim to the base. The side is inscribed with the sacred emblems surrounded by a ray and an inscription saying that it was given by Eleanor Lloyd in 1713. The five marks include the maker's mark (Type 3) and the date letter M (1712/13).

RICHARD RICHARDSON (I). Type 4. (p. 170)

An additional mark known as 4b is now listed. This is a Ri without a pellet in a square frame with clipped corners. The only piece known is listed below and as it is dated well within the life time of Richard Richardson (I) almost certainly belongs to him. (see 4b).

8. (p. 186) Brandy Warmer in the Manchester City Art Gallery. (Type 4)

9. Tumbler cup (see *Chester Silver*, Ridgway, p. xvi). (Type 4).

10. Brandy warmer. With lip, a baluster bowl, rim diameter 2¼ inches and 1½ inches deep. The lip ends with a bead. The wooden handle fits into a sleeve, overall length 4¼ inches. Five marks on base including date letter V (1721/22).

11. Stand or Credence Paten, St Michael's Church, Chester (redundant) (see No. 12).
Stand paten 6¼ inches diameter with narrow moulded rim and sloping depression inscribed on the plate

Ex Dono Robti Pigot Arm Tempore Majoratus Anno Dom 1723

It rests upon a stand having a moulded foot of a step, shoulder and narrow flange. Total height 2¼ inches. Diameter of base 2⅞ inches.
There are five marks, (i) Maker's mark (Type 4); (ii) Lion passant guardant; (iii) Leopard's head crowned; (iv) Chester City coat; (v) Date letter X (1723/24) (seen at Lloyd's Bank, Chester, 1972).

12. Communion cup, St. Michael's Church, Chester. (redundant)
A Communion cup with a bell shaped bowl having a moulded rim, 7 inches high, diameter of rim 3⅜ inches. A simple moulding divides the bowl from the stem which is hour glass shaped with a knop having a collar on both sides and a flat moulding to divide it. The foot is moulded with a narrow flange, diameter 3⅝ inches.
There is an inscription on the side of the bowl

Ex Dono Robti Pigot Arm Tempore Majoratus Anno Dom 1723

The marks are the same as on the paten (no. 11) (Type 4).

13. Spoon. Private Collection, Knutsford. 1969.
A rat tail spoon 7¾ inches long, bowl 2¾ inches by 1⅝ inches with a rounded end but no ridge upon the handle which is engraved with the initials M C. There are five marks, (i) Maker's mark (Type 4); (ii) Chester City arms; (iii) Britannia; (iv) Lion's head erased; (v) Date letter I (1709/10).

14. Marrow scoop. The spoon handle is of old English form having the arms of Middleton. The end is formed into a marrow scoop. Total length 8¼ inches, width of scoop 5/16th inch. The date letter is imperfect but appears to be Q (1716/17).

15. Communion cup (see 16). Holt Parish Church, N. Wales.
   A Communion cup, height 6½ inches, diameter of rim 3¾ inches with a bell shaped bowl standing on a pool shaped stem divided by a very narrow knop with narrow collars above and below the knop. The foot is double stepped and has a shoulder mould and a flange, base diameter 3½ inches. There are five marks including the maker's mark and date letter T (series 2) 1720.

16. Stand Paten. Holt Parish Church, N. Wales. (see no. 15).
   Stand paten, diameter 6¾ inches having a narrow moulded rim ¾ inch wide, forming a single shallow depression. It stands upon a spool shaped stem ending in a step and shoulder and a flange. Overall it stands 2¼ inches high. The diameter of the foot is 3 inches. Marks as on the Holt Communion cup (15).

17. Communion cup. Capel Garmon Parish Church, N. Wales (closed).
   Communion cup, 6½ inches high with bell shaped bowl, diameter 3½ inches. The stem is plain having a centre knop which is little more than a band of mouldings ¼ inch wide. Below this the stem sweeps down to a moulded foot with a step and shoulder and narrow flange. There are five marks including the date letter X (1723/24). There is an inscription on the side of the bowl saying that it was the gift of Thomas Wynne in 1723 (in Latin).

18. Marrow scoop.
   Plain heavy double ended marrow scoop, 9 inches in length, weight 1 oz. 15 dwt. There are five marks including the maker's mark (Type 4) and the date letter S (1718/19).

19. Tumbler cup.
   Plain and parcel gilt, height 1¾ inches. There are five marks including the date letter X (1723/24).

RICHARD RICHARDSON (I) Type 4a. (p. 171)

6/7. Two spoons. Private Collection. 1965, purchase from Lowe and Sons, Chester for £25 each. Identical spoons, Hanoverian handle, overall length 8⅛ inches. Rat tail, bowls 2¼ inches by 1⅝ inches. Engraved TB. Five marks in excellent condition. (i) Maker's mark; (ii) Britannia; (iii) Lion's head erased; (iv) Chester City coat; (v) Date letter R (1717/18).

8. Spoon. Private Collection. Suffolk. Seen 1969. Rat tail spoon, overall length 8¼ inches. Weight 2 ozs. 3 dwts. Engraved BH in contemporary Script letters. Five marks, (i) Maker's mark (Type 4a); (ii) Britannia; (iii) Lion's head erased; (iv) Chester City coat; (v) Date letter Q (1716/17).

9/10 Two gownsmen's badges kept at the Grosvenor Museum, Chester. An oval and curved badge to be worn on the shoulder 4¼ inches by 3 3/10ths inches engraved with the representation of a skull on an orle placed above a scroll with the motto in capitals 'Richd King'. The whole within a border of wreathed leaves. On the back of each are four ring attachments and the single mark of Richard Richardson (I). (Type 4a).

11–20. Ten gownsmen's badges similar to 9/10, kept in the Grosvenor Museum, Chester. Similar to 9/10 but having a human skull beneath a crest of a stag passant, on an orle.

21. Miniature porringer. Private Collection. A small porringer, diameter 2 inches and 1⅛ inches high with slightly bulbous bowl. The bottom half gadrooned with small decorations resembling acorns above each lobe. Two S shaped handles on either side. Beneath the foot, four marks of the maker Type 4a and no other mark.

22. Nutmeg grater. Ref. Bourdon Smith Catalogue 26. Spring Number 1983 and illustrated No. 12. The cylindrical 3½ inches long and diameter and 1 inch diameter. The sides are inscribed in panels of leaf like angular scales. The top has a rose design and the mark is found on the bottom and on the inside of the cover, and

the base has also an inscribed L. Although the Ri appears to be very similar to other Ri (within a square) there is a small pellet after the i. The inside of the cylinder has a cylindrical grater. (See No. 23)

(A similar grater. Ref. Nutmeg graters, Judith Banister. *Antique Dealers and Collector's Guide*, October 1965. *Dictionary of Gold and Silver*, Michael Clayton. Illustration 385.) Similar but with scratched design. One of them was by Richard Richardson (I) and had a scratched design of a rose, thistle and a tulip (c. 1710).

37. Plain Pap boat 4⅛ inches long and 2¼ inches wide, 1 inch deep with an almost circular bowl. Private Collection. 1973. On the base is an inscription . . .

Jane Jones
(a rose)
March ye 1st
1726.7

There are four marks, (i) Maker's mark (Type 4); (ii) Lion passant gardant; (iii) Leopard's head crowned; (iv) Chester City coat. There is no date letter, and the marks are punched on the inside of the bowl.

38. Punch ladle. Private Collection. 1964. (Information from Michael Clayton).
Punch ladle with long silver handle and half way down a strap hook to catch on the lip of the punch bowl. The bowl is baluster shaped with an out turning rim. It is inscribed with the arms of Chester and the words . . .

Robert Pigot Esqr Mayor 1724.

The marks include the maker's mark Type 4a and the Chester date letter for 1723/24.

39. Communion cup. Llangernyw Parish Church, N. Wales.
6 inches high with a bell shaped bowl, rim diameter 3¼ inches. Spool shaped stem and very worn and narrow band. The foot has a curved step and shoulder and a very narrow flange. Diameter of foot 3½ inches. On the bowl . . .

Llangernew 1721

There are four marks including the maker's mark (Type 4) but no date letter (but before the death of Richard Richardson in 1729/30).

RICHARD RICHARDSON (I) Type 4b. (p. 171)

This is a newly recorded mark and presumably of Richard Richardson (I).
1. Tumbler cup. Private Collection. Mold. 1973. Engraved on the base H.1 along with the five marks including Type 4b and the date letter P (1715/16).

2. Basting spoon.
Hanoverian basting spoon 13¼ inches in length with a ribbed handle and a rat tail spoon, the bowl 4¼ inches by 2¼ inches. Weight 5 ounces. There are five marks on the handle bottom marked. (i) Date letter P (1715/16); (ii) Chester City coat; (iii) Lion's head erased; (iv) Britannia; (v) Maker's mark (Type 4b).
The handle is enrgaved C above C S.

RICHARD RICHARDSON (I). Type 6. (p. 172)

1. The Communion cup at Kendal is for 'sick communicants' and has the inscription 'Given for the sick Communicants in the Parish of Kendale 1728'.
It is 5¾ inches high, has a bell shaped bowl with a knop between the hour glass stem and the base ends with a step shoulder moulding and a narrow moulding. There are five marks including the Script C and maker's mark, Type 6.

2. The Communion cup at Lancaster is also for sick communicants and is reported in *Lancashire and Cheshire Antiquarian Society Transactions*, vol. xxxi. 95 (illustrated). The paten cover is missing but it is 5¾ inches high, diameter at tip and base 2¼ inches and has the same inscription as no. 1 but with Lancaster in place of Kendal. The marks and date are the same as Kendal.

3 Llansannan Parish Church, N. Wales.
   Communion cup, 7 inches high with a bell shaped bowl and spool shaped stem divided by a knop. Diameter of rim 3¼ inches. Foot diameter 3¾ inches. There are five marks including the date letter Script A (1726/27) and the maker's mark, Type 6.

4. Tumbler cup.
   Plain and parcel gilt tumbler cup, height 1¾ inches. There are five marks on the base including the date letter Script C (1728/29).

RICHARD RICHARDSON (I). Type 6
The mark appears on the ewer at Coddington, Cheshire. The date Script B was misplaced under the same mark used by Richard Richardson (II) (see *Chester Silver*, Ridgway, p. 136) with the date mark for 1727/28 which seems to be the earlier piece and made in Richard Richardson's lifetime.
   The Communion cup and accompanying paten at Wybunbury (date 1728/29) are listed in *Chester Silver* under Richard Richardson (I) (nos. 1 and 2, p. 135) but were made in his lifetime and should be in *Chester Goldsmiths* under Type 6.

RICHARD RICHARDSON (I). Type 7. (p. 172)
1. Tumbler cup. Sotheby's Sale, 14 January 1971, lot 182. Private Collection.
   Tumbler cup base engraved with contemporary initials, parcel gilt. Diameter 2¼ inches. Fully hallmarked with date letter Script B (1727/28).

2. Penley Parish Church, N. Wales.
   Communion cup 8⅞ inches high with a bell shaped bowl diameter 4 1/5th inches. Stem divided by a knop. The base mouldings are stepped and shoulder and a flange. The foot diameter 4⅜ inches. There are five marks on the side of the bowl including the maker's mark, Type 7 and the date letter Script B (indistinct) (1727/28). Inscribed on the side
                          For use of Penley Chapple 1727

RICHARD RICHARDSON (I). Type 7
7. (See *Chester Goldsmiths*, xvi) Punch ladle.
   The punch bowl referred to was exhibited at the Festival Exhibition in 1951 and also illustrated along with a punch ladle, Plate xvii. The description of the punch bowl by Timothy Lee, London 1722, is correct but the punch ladle which accompanies it is by Richard Richardson (I) and is engraved with the name of 'Robt Pigot Esqr Mayor 1724'. The handle is of silver not wood, and the identification of the ladle to William Richardson seems to be an error. (Information from Michael Clayton)

WILLIAM RICHARDSON (I)
   (See *Chester Silver*, p. 221)
   This interesting frame has now been identified as a Chocolate or Coffee pot stand. When described in 1984 the saucer was missing and the asking price was £1,000. Seen again in a private collection in 1995 it had a Chinese blue and white saucer Kang Hsi pattern of 1710-20, replacing the previous damaged saucer. It is fully hallmarked with five marks including the date letter V and maker's mark, Type 1. Diameter 4⅞ inches. It stands on three cushion feet, total height 1 inch. (Illustration 53)

10. Coconut cup. Private collection. 1973. (*Chester Silver*, p. 221)
    A coconut cup, bound with deckled rim and standing on a trumpet shaped stem linked with four bands of silver to the rim. Under the foot are four identical marks of William Richardson (Type 1).

11. Spoon.
    Rat tail Hanoverian spoon length 7⅞ inches. The initials H.T.M. engraved on the handle. Weight 1 ounce 9 dwts. Five marks including maker's mark, Type 1 and date letter T (1719/20).

189

12. Basting spoon. Private collection. Phillip's Sale, 27 April 1984, lot 134. (not RR as catalogued)
A large basting spoon 14¼ inches long with Hanoverian handle and ridged having the crest of a stag trippant on an orle. The bowl measures 4¾ inches by 2⅞ inches and has a drop and rat tail. There are five marks including the date letter Z (1725/26) and the maker's mark, Type 1.

THOMAS ROBINSON. Type 1. (p. 175)
7. Mug. Private Collection. Edinburgh. 1983.
Mug. Very similar to Mug 6 but in place of the fluted bottom half of the bowl there is an ornate decoration repoussé of acanthus leaves and on the top half of the bowl the inscribed intials A+W. It has a strap handle which is reeded. On the base are four marks, (i) Maker's mark (Type 1); (ii) Chester City coat; (iii) Chester crest; (iv) Date letter B (1690-1692). Also a weight mark scratched 3-17-0.

8. Two candlesticks. (see *Chester Silver,* Ridgway, p. 221)

THOMAS ROBINSON. Type 2. (p. 180)
18. Tumbler cup. Ref. Sotheby's Sale Catalogue, 30 May 1968, lot 100.
'A George 1 Chester Tumbler cup quite plain apart from the engraved initials I.S.A. on the base, gilt interior. 2¼ inches diameter by Thomas Robinson 1721. Weight 1 oz. 17 dwts'.

19–23. Five spoons. Ref. Sotheby's Catalogue, 15 January 1970, lot 67.
Hanoverian tablespoons with rat tail bowl, the terminals engraved with initials 1711. They were sold with a sixth spoon, London 1726.
The stem of each carries the marks, (i) Maker's mark Ro; (ii) Chester City arms; (iii) Britannia; (iv) Lion's head erased; (v) Date letter L (1711/12).

24. Tumbler cup. Diameter 2¾ inches. Height 2⅜ inches. Plain except for a crest of a stag's head and five marks including Date letter I (1709/10).

25. Tumbler cup. Private collection. 1970. Diameter 2½ inches. Height 2 inches. (marks as on 24) and also the crest.

26. Basting spoon. Chester exhibition. 1973. Basting spoon 14¼ inches long, bowl 4⅛ inches by 2½ inches, rat tail bowl. Marks include date letter Q (1716/17).

27. Marrow spoon. Private collection. 1973.
Fully hallmarked including the maker's mark Ro and the date letter G (1707/08). Length 7⅞ inches. Rat tail.

28–37. Ten tablespoons (formerly in the Grosvenor Collection). Private collection. Edinburgh. 1970. Date believed to be 1713.

38–39. Two dog nose tablespoons with rat tails 7¾ inches in length from the Guest-Williams Collection. Sold 31 Jan. 1974 Sotheby's Sale, 31 January 1974. Lot 140. Each with initials L above I E. On one spoon the five marks ill struck, date letter G (1707/08) on the other only three marks, (i) Maker's mark; (ii) Chester City coat; (iii) Britannia.

40. Spoon. Private Collection.
Rat tail tablespoon, identical to 4/5 with same intertwined initials. Date letter Q (1716/17).

41. Basting spoon. 15 inches long with rat tail. Bowl measures 4¼ inches by 2¾ inches. The handle is ribbed. Now in the Grosvenor Museum, Ridgway Gallery, Chester. Crest of talbot's head on handle.

42. Spoon. Rat tail Hanoverian spoon with contemporary initials on the handle. Initials I above I I. Length 8⅛ inches. Date letter Q (1716/17).

43. Spoon. Table spoon 8¼ inches in length having a rat tail and initials engraved on the handle H above RS. Bottom marked with five marks including date letter G (1707/08).

44–45. Two Tumbler cups. Diameter 2¾ inches with stag's head cabossed on the base along with five marks including the date letter I (1709/10).

46.   Tumbler cup diameter. Private Collection. An exact copy of 44/45 complete with crest and same measurements.

JOHN SCASEBRICK (p. 191)

The marks of John Scasebrick on a Portuguese Moidor Weight. (Illustration 55)

RALPH WALLEY (p. 180)

9.   Tankard. Ref. Sotheby Parke Bernet, New York, 18 June 1974, lot 323.
'Plain tapered cylindrical form with moulded borders & S scroll handle. The cover with flat top & lobate scroll thumb piece. Fully marked 37 ozs. Height 8⅝ ins.' (not illustrated).
(Additional information: Height 7⅝ inches to lid. Overall height 8¾ inches. Diameter of base 6 inches. Diameter of rim 4½ inches. Weight 37 ozs.)

RW (p. 184)

This mark has not been associated with Ralph Walley. It is very much smaller and is found on a trefid spoon with four marks including the Chester City arms and the Chester crest with the date letter A (1687-90).

Appendix 2

CHESTER SILVER 1727-1837, Maurice H. Ridgway

ADDENDA

MATTHEW BOULTON and JAMES FOTHERGILL (p. 63)
8–11. Four identical Candlesticks. (Private Collector, USA).
   Ref. A.D.C. Heritage. Catalogue 1989, p. 16 (illustrated).
   These are in addition to the two candlesticks 3/4 (which are now in the United
   States) and are identical with them except that the 'nozils' are plain whereas the 3/4
   have gadrooned edges.
       They are 13 inches high. The Boulton and Fothergill pattern book shows them
   with gadrooned edges (p. 41). Date letter for 1768/69.

NICHOLAS CUNLIFFE (p. 74)
A conche shell having a half hinged lid of silver of oval form 3½ inches by 2¾ inches with
an inscribed coat of arms crest and motto 'Renew my age' on the lid. There are six marks
on the side of the cover including the Duty mark, date letter D (1821/22).

JAMES DIXON (p. 75)
Marrow spoon. Private collection. 1992.
Marrow spoon 8¼ inches long with a drop to the bowl and a narrow marrow spoon, the
groove 2¾ inches long. Marked with five marks including the mark of James Dixon and
the date letter W (1772/73).

Table Candlesticks. Purchased from Kaye, Chester. Grosvenor Museum, Ridgway Gallery,
1995.
Two table candlesticks. Height with nozzle 12 2/5ths inches, without nozzle 12 3/10ths inches
and 12 2/5ths and 12 1/5th respectively. Five marks on sides of bases including maker's
mark, Ridgway, Type 1. Lion passant only on nozzles and date letter V (1771/72).
(Description by Peter Boughton, Grosvenor Museum.)
       'The square upwardly curving bases have diestamped ornament in the form of beaded
   borders with beriboned oval medallions between leafy festoons. One medallion on
   each base is engraved with the crest of a lion sejeant erect, whilst the other medallions
   are oval paterae. The nine sided cluster column stems taper upwards, with two pairs
   of horizontal rings, and single rings before the columns outwards at either end. The
   capitals act as sconces, each formed from two tiers of nine stylalised palm leaves and
   terminating in a nine sided gadrooned rim. The detachable nozzles have wide nine sided
   drip pans with gadrooned edges. The bases are loaded with wood, each having a turned
   circular moulding and a central silver button. On both candlesticks the engraving is
   worn, and there are small areas of repair to the stems and capitals.'
The design has strong connection with candlesticks made in Sheffield and it is possible that
these were made in Sheffield and submitted by James Dixon. (Illustration 56, 57)

JOSEPH DUKE
Wine funnel. Ref. Schredds. 1981.
A wine funnel or cup having no strainer. The cap is attached by a chain to the side of the
funnel sits snugly over the end and converts the item into a cup. It is decorated with an

Adam style form. There are two marks on the side of the cup, Lion guardant and the maker's mark (Ridgway, *Chester Silver*, p. 77).

GEORGE LOWE (I) (p. 104)

A third mark has been noted. Type 3. This is GL in a rectangle with clipped corners on the right hand top corner very considerably clipped. The mark is found on the following . . Type 3.

1–6 Six 'toy spoons' and a (7) toy pair of tongs with fiddle pattern handles (1816/17). (see p. 91, vol. 3. (1815).

TM (p. 117)

This is the mark of THOMAS MILLER who lived at Newcastle on Tyne. It appears along with the duty mark, lion passant guardant, leopard's head and the date letter G (1825/26) on a plain mug (see vol. 3, p. 94). The Chester Plate Duty Books record the making of several mugs by him that year.

JOHN FISHER (p. 81)

It seems clear from the evidence of the Chester Plate Duty Books that the mark of IF refers to John Fisher.

NICHOLAS LEE (Nicholson Lee, Liverpool). Watchcase maker. (p. 95)

An examination of the mark shows that either that the second initial was deliberately removed leaving the first N. The second letter had a vertical stroke the rest is missing.

It has been suggested that the mark could be that of Newton and Hyde but in the time between 1822 and 1826 (Duty Books) they only submitted gold rings.

p. 85   At a sale in 1992, two pieces were aquired together . . . a cover paten on a stand diameter 3½ inches, height 1 1/10th inches which has three marks, (i) Maker's mark, Richard Richardson (II) (Type 2); (ii) Lion passant guardant; (iii) Leopard's head crowned and no other mark but the date 1735 under the foot. It was made as a companion to the second piece which was made for administering to sick Communicants. This is a mug (without any handle), shaped like Type c on page 161, *Chester Silver*. It is 3¾ inches high and the rim diameter 2½ inches. There is an engraved inscription on the side of the cup. The maker's mark appears three times on the side of the cup.

Poculum Eucharistias (this in Greek characters)
in usum Infirmorium et Aegrotorum
L·H·S
1732

The fact that these pieces have been together for some time and belong to the same period may indicate Peter Hopwood of Preston.
(See article and illustration *Silver Society*, No. 13, p. 2)

RICHARD RICHARDSON (II). Type 1

19. Communion cup. Llanynys Parish Church, N. Wales.
    8¾ inches high having a bell shaped bowl rim, diameter 4¼ inches. Spool shaped stem with moulded foot, base diameter 4¼ inches. An inscription on the side of the bowl . . .
    The Communion cup of Llanynys. David Pierce Edwd Jones
    Church Wardens, 1735
    There are five marks including the maker's mark (Type 1) and the date letter Script K (1735/36).

20. Stand paten. Ysceifiog Parish Church, N. Wales.
    A stand paten, diameter 7½ inches with a narrow edge forming a single depression. On the surface of the plate an inscription saying it was given by Samuel Mostyn Esq. of Caulcott in 1736. There are five marks including the maker's mark (Type 1) and the date letter Script K (1735/36).

21. Communion cup. Llanynys Parish Church, N. Wales.
Communion cup. 8¾ inches high having a bell shaped bowl, rim diameter 4½ inches. The stem spool shaped with moulded foot, base diameter 4¾ inches. An inscription on the side with the names of the wardens and the date 1735. There are five marks including the maker's mark (Type 1) and the date letter Script K (1735/36).

RICHARD RICHARDSON (II). Type 2

23/24.   Communion cup. Llannefydd Parish Church, N. Wales.
The Communion cup and the stand paten were drastically altered by Richardson (II) (Type 2). The cup of presumably the same date as the paten 1575 (dated). Only the maker's mark has been added.

25.   Stand or Credence paten. Whitford, N. Wales.
Credence paten diameter 8¼ inches with a narrow moulded rim and a single depression. It stands upon a trumpet shaped stem with narrow knop with a foot having a step and shoulder and a narrow flange, diameter 3¾ inches and stands 2½ inches overall. There is an inscription saying it was the gift of the Reverend Edward Davies in 1773. There are five marks on the side of the bowl including the date letter Script H (1733/34).

26.   Llangynhafal Parish Church, N. Wales.
Stand paten 7 inch diameter and 1⅞ inches deep having a narrow border and a single depression. The stand is moulded and has a shoulder and flange. Diameter of base 2¾ inches. Given in 1733. Date letter Script G (1732/33).

27.   Communion cup. St Asaph Cathedral, N. Wales.
Communion cup, 6½ inches high with bell shaped bowl and moulded rim, diameter 3 1/5th inches high. The sides are curved to a moulding which has a single knop wih collars. The foot has a step and shoulder ending in a narrow flange. Base diameter 3 4/5ths inches. There are five marks including the maker's mark (Type 2) and the date letter Script E (1730/31).

28.   Paten cover. Private collection 1996.
A plain paten cover with the date 1735 inscribed on the foot. There are three marks on the surface of the paten, Maker's mark (Type 2), Lion passant guardant and Leopard's head crowned. Diameter 3⅜ inches, weight 1 ounce 19 dwts.
This paten was bought with a chalice used for the sick of baluster form with three marks struck on the side of the bowl below the rim of conjoined PH (possibly Peter Hopwood of Preston). The side is engraved with a mixture of Greek and Latin which can be translated 'The cup for the Eucharist for the use of the sick and diseased 1732'.

RICHARD RICHARDSON (II). Type 4 (p. 149)

Asparagus tray.
A shallow tray with sloping sides to a small lip, measuring 9½ inches by 6¼ inches. It has a heavy side handle and engraved thumb piece which bears a crest of an eagle. Weight, 17 ounces. The marks are struck on the base including the date letter a (1751/52). The handle has two marks, the maker's mark and the lion passant guardant.

p. 149   (see also p. 152, Type 5)
The Beer Jug (No. 1) was sold again in 1996 and it was now possible to describe it 'of baluster form and on circular spreading foot, with wicker covered double scroll handle. Egg shaped collar at top and disc collar at base of handle. Short curved spout pierced — below rim — Engraved with coat of Arms (Wynn of Gwydir). Height 7¼ inches. Diameter 4 inches. Weight 29 oz. 19 dwt. There are four marks on the base, (i) Richard Richardson (II) Mark Type 4. (It was imagined though not stated that it was Mark Type 5); (ii) Chester City coat; (iii) Lion passant guardant; (iv) Date letter a (1751/52). There is no Leopard mark.

RICHARD RICHARDSON (II). Type 5 (p. 158)

17. Whitford Parish Church, N. Wales.
Communion cup. (See no. 6. Type 6)
A gilt Communion cup with a bell shaped bowl $7\frac{1}{4}$ inches high and rim diameter $4\frac{3}{8}$ inches. The bowl stands upon a spool shaped stem divided by a slender moulded band and leading to a step and shoulder and a flange, base diameter, $4\frac{1}{4}$ inches. On the side of the bowl there is an inscription saying that it was a gift of Henry Lloyd of Trellewelyn in 1775. There were five marks including the date letter f (1756/57).

18. Meliden Parish Church, N. Wales.
Communion cup $6\frac{1}{4}$ inches high with a bell shaped bowl and slightly everted and moulded lip diameter 3 1/10th inches. There is an inscription on the bowl . . .

Plwufolion Gallt Melyd 1757

(Translation: The Parishioners of Meliden)
There are five marks including the date letter h (1758/59).

19. Llanrwst Parish Church, N. Wales.
Communion cup evidently made for the use with the sick, $5\frac{3}{8}$ inches high having a bell shaped bowl, diameter $2\frac{1}{4}$ inches with slightly everted lip. It stands upon a spool shaped stem divided by a knop. The base has a shoulder moulding with a flange, diameter $2\frac{3}{4}$ inches. It is inscribed

Llanrwst Parish 1758

The five marks include the date letter i (1759/60).

20. Iscoed Parish Church, near Holt, N. Wales.
Communion cup of domestic origin.
Iscoed was deemed a parish on the 19th century. Its cup is a porringer. In the church records it is stated that in 1757

'A silver cup for ye sacrament was purchased'

and that 13s. was paid for it. The cup remains in the church and bears the inscription

Iscoed Chapel 1758

It is a small two handled cup of porringer form. Rim diameter $3\frac{1}{4}$ inches, height $3\frac{1}{4}$ inches. There are two reeded strap handles making an overall width of $5\frac{1}{4}$ inches. There are five marks underneath including the maker's mark 5D, and the date letter e (1755/56).

RICHARD RICHARDSON (II). Type 5A
Cylindrical Beakers.
1.2 Ref. Sotheby's Sale, New York, 28 October 1992, lot 143. Private Collection.
A pair of cylindrical drinking beakers with straight sides each engraved on the side with the initials G.W., 2 inches high and diameter $2\frac{1}{8}$ inches. The bases are engraved with

Brawdgarwch yn Llannerchymedd 1761

(Translation: Brotherhood at Llannerchymedd 1761). (Illustration 59)

Folding Fruit Knife.
The shaped blade of the fruit knife folds into a pistol grip handle with a crest and the words ROSE. There is a silver spring in the handle. Length overall $6\frac{3}{8}$ inches. The blade is 3 inches long and $5\frac{3}{8}$ inches wide. The style of knife is about 1750. It has only the maker's mark. (Illustration 60, 61) (Type 2 or 4)

RICHARD RICHARDSON (II). Type 5B
Tea Caddy.
A drum shaped tea caddy with beaded decoration and a flower mounted on the lid. The lid has a flush hinge. Height $3\frac{1}{2}$ inches to the finial, diameter $3\frac{1}{2}$ inches. The side is engraved with a coat of arms of St Aubyn of Clowance near Camborne, Cornwall. Weight 9 ounces 1 dwt.
There are five marks in a circle on the base.
    (i) Maker's mark (Type 5B)
    (ii) Lion passant guardant.

(iii) Leopard's head crowned.
(iv) Chester City coat.
(v) Date letter O (1764/65 (Illustration 58)

RICHARD RICHARDSON (II). Type 5D
A set of twelve plain convex sleeve buttons. Diameter $\frac{3}{4}$ inch. With the maker's mark.
p. 164   Sotheby's Sale, London. 30 May 1996.

> 'Silver seal of office engraved with the Arms of the Diocese of Chester impaling Peploe within a scroll and floral cartouche, also with the Seal of S. Peploe LLD Chancellor of the Diocese of Chester 1763 within a gadroon band at the rim, part fitted case. 5 oz. 13 dwt. Length 3 inches.'

> It is oval shaped with semi circular handle at right angles to back of seal. It carries only the mark of Richard Richardson II, Type 5D.

Scent funnel.
Plain conical funnel with small ring under the upper funnel edge on the outer surface, with a straight cylindrical spout. Overall 2 5/12ths, length of spout $1\frac{1}{4}$ inches, diameter of mouth 2 inches. Single mark of Richard Richardson (II), Type 5D.

RICHARD RICHARDSON (II). Type 6 (p. 169)
Church plate.
8. Whitford Parish Church, N. Wales.
    (See Richard Richardson (II) Type 5. No. 18).
    A gilt Communion cup, height 6 inches. It has a bell shaped bowl with slightly everted lip, diameter 3 inches. It stands upon a spool shaped stem having a narrow band with upper and lower collars. The foot is marked with a slight step and shoulder and a flange. Base diameter $3\frac{1}{8}$ inches. On the underside of the flange are the names of the two Wardens and on the side of the bowl
    WHITFORD PARISH
1771
    There are five marks including that of the maker (Type 6) and the date letter T (1769/70).
9. Llangwm Dinmael Parish Church, N. Wales (abandoned).
    A Communioin cup, the base and sides have been badly compressed but its present height is 9 inches. It has a bell shaped bowl with everted lip, diameter $4\frac{1}{4}$ inches. The stem is divided by a narrow knop with collars and the base is moulded, diameter $4\frac{1}{4}$ inches. There is an inscription . . .
    Llangwm Sacrament Cup
    The four marks are indistinct but appear to be Richard Richardson (II), Type 6, there is no date letter visible but it would seem to be 1766 or 1769. Weight 13 ozs.

RICHARD RICHARDSON (II). Type 7 (p. 177)
Asparagus tray.
Ref. Phillips, Chester. 25 November 1992, lot 138.
An asparagus tray of shallow rectangular form $8\frac{3}{4}$ by $5\frac{3}{4}$ inches. There is a coat of arms and a motto in Welsh above. Maker's mark include that of Richard Richardson (II) (Type 7) and the date letter R (1767/68). Weight 11 ounces.

RICHARD RICHARDSON (III). Type 1 (p. 173)
Church plate.
4. Communion cup. Treuddyn, N. Wales. (see no. 5)
    Communion cup $5\frac{1}{8}$ inches high with a goblet shaped bowl and a very slightly everted lip. Rim diameter $2\frac{5}{8}$ inches and the bowl $2\frac{1}{4}$ inches deep. It rests upon a plain stem with a very narrow moulded band 3/16th inch deep leading to a rounded moulding and a flange. Base diameter $2\frac{5}{8}$ inches. An inscription on the side says that it was given by E.H. There are five marks which include the maker's mark (Type 1) and the date letter a (1776/77).
5. Paten cover. (see no. 4)
    A paten cover to accompany Communion cup (4). Diameter $3\frac{1}{8}$ inches having a solid knop, diameter 1 inch with solid top. The flat plate has an angled depression to fit over the mouth of the cup. Total depth $1\frac{1}{4}$ inch.
    There are no marks but its close association with cup (4) establishes the maker and date.

RICHARD RICHARDSON (IV). Type 1a

Mote Spoon.

A mote spoon, the only one ever recorded as being Chester with the mark of Richard Richardson (IV) (Type 2) (though it could be 4). It is almost certainly not the mark of Richard Rugg as the down stroke of the second R is much longer than that of the first R. The spoon is 5¾ inches long with a single drop to the bowl. The handle tapers to a pear shaped terminal. The bowl is pierced with numerous round holes and lines are inscribed between the rows of holes. It carries only the mark, and doubts have been raised as to whether Richard Richardson made it. (Illustration 62)

RICHARD RICHARDSON (IV). Type 2 (p. 179)

Church Plate.

1. Llansannan, N. Wales. Type 2.
   Communion cup 5½ inches high with a bell shaped bowl having a moulded rim, diameter 3 inches. The bowl rests upon a spool shaped stem divided by a ¼ inch band of three mouldings. The foot has a step and shoulder moulding followed by a flange. Base diameter 2⅞ inches. On the side of the bowl is a sacred symbol of IHS with rays and beneath this

Llansannan
1785

   There are six marks including the maker's mark and the date letter k (1785/86).

2. Llansannan, N. Wales.
   Paten cover made to fit over no. 1 but which have no marks. Diameter 3⅜ inches. It has a narrow border and a depression to take the mouth of the Communion cup. The stand is a plain cavetto and is blocked, 1¼ inches diameter. The overall height ⅞ inch. Contemporary with the Communion cup (1785/86).

p. 182   Ladle. Type 2.
5. Private Collection.
   A double lipped punch ladle. One on either end, measuring 5 inches by 2½ inches. The lips are raised as on many pap boats. There is a turned wood handle 10½ inches long which is socketed into a silver sleeve 3¾ inches long. This is attached to the bowl at an angle and is joined to the side of the bowl with a heart shaped collar. There are six marks on the bottom of the bowl including the maker's mark and the date letter n (1788/89).
   (Compare *Chester Silver*, George Walker, p. 200)

WILLIAM RICHARDSON (II) and RICHARD RICHARDSON (II). Type 1 (p. 188)

CHURCH PLATE.

6. Communion cup (see no. 7). Llanycil Parish Church, N. Wales.
   Communion cup 8¾ inches high with a bell shaped bowl and everted lip. Diameter of rim 4½ inches. The stem is divided by a narrow knop with a centre mounding with an ogee moulding above and below ⅜ inch wide in all. The foot consists of an ogee moulding followed by a shoulder and a narrow flange. Diameter of base 4⅜ inches. On the side of the bowl a representation of the sacred symbols IHS with cross and nails surrounded by rays. Inscription on the side saying that it was the gift of Robert Jones the Rector in 1742.
   There are five marks on the side of the bowl including the maker's mark (Type 1) and the date letter Script Q (1741/42).

7. Stand paten (see no. 6). Llanycil Parish Church, N. Wales.
   A stand paten diameter 9¾ inches with a narrow ⅜ inch moulded rim creating a single depression. It stands upon a stem with overall height of 3 inches. The stem is concave ending with a moulded foot, a concave moulding followed by a shoulder and a wide flange. The sacred symbols are engraved on the centre of the plate and the inscription is engraved on the underside which are the same as found on the Communion cup (no. 6) as are the marks.

197

8. Communion cup. Nercwys Parish Church, N. Wales.
Communion cup 8¼ inches high having a bell shaped bowl, rim diameter 4¼ inches. The stem is divided by a very narrow band knop, diameter 1 7/16ths inches. The foot is moulded and has a flange, base diameter 4 inches. It is inscribed on the underside
Nerquis Chapel

There are five marks including the maker's mark and the date letter Script T (1744/45).